The Reformation of the Bible

The Bible *of the Reformation*

Das wort sie sollen lassen stan

The Reformation of the Bible

JAROSLAV PELIKAN

The Bible of the Reformation

Catalog of the Exhibition by

Valerie R. Hotchkiss & David Price

Yale University Press

New Haven & London

Bridwell Library

Southern Methodist University

Dallas

Published with assistance from the Louis Stern
Memorial Fund.

Designed by Richard Hendel
Set in Monotype Garamond type by
The Composing Room of Michigan, Inc.
Printed in the United States of America by
Worzalla, Stevens Point, Wisconsin.

Library of Congress Cataloging-in-Publication Data
Pelikan, Jaroslav Jan, 1923–
The reformation of the Bible : the Bible of the
Reformation / Jaroslav Pelikan ; catalog of the
exhibition by Valerie R. Hotchkiss and David Price.
p.   cm.
ISBN 0-300-06667-8 (alk. paper). — ISBN 0-941881-18-0
(pbk. : alk. paper)
1. Bible—History—16th century—Exhibitions.
2. Reformation—Exhibitions.   3. Bible—Versions—
Exhibitions.   4. Bible—Bibliography—Exhibitions.
5. Bible—Criticism, interpretation, etc.—History—
16th century—Exhibitions.   6. Bible—Illustrations—
Exhibitions.   7. Bible—In literature—Exhibitions.
I. Hotchkiss, Valerie R., 1960–   . II. Price, David,
1957–   . III. Title.
BS447.P45   1996
220.4′074′7642812—dc20   95-38683
                                                  CIP

A catalog record for this book is available
from the British Library.

The paper in this book meets the guidelines for
permanence and durability of the Committee on
Production Guidelines for Book Longevity of the
Council on Library Resources.

10   9   8   7   6   5   4   3   2   1

TO DECHERD TURNER

Scholar among Librarians

Librarian among Scholars

Bridwell Library
Perkins School of Theology
Southern Methodist University
Dallas, Texas
March–September 1996

The Rare Book and Manuscript Library
Columbia University
and Burke Library
Union Theological Seminary
New York, New York
November 1996–February 1997

The Houghton Library
and the Widener Library
Harvard University
Cambridge, Massachusetts
January 1997

Yale Center for British Art
Yale University
New Haven, Connecticut
February–April 1996

CONTENTS

Preface, ix

Acknowledgments, xi

List of Abbreviations, xiv

Introduction, 1

1 Sacred Philology, 3

2 Exegesis and Hermeneutics, 23

3 Bibles for the People, 41

4 The Bible and the Arts, 63

Catalog of the Exhibition, 79

Bibliography, 179

Index of Biblical Passages, 191

Index of Names, 193

It was a touching personal tribute, but also a unique scholarly opportunity, when my friend and student Valerie Hotchkiss, librarian of the Bridwell Library at Southern Methodist University in Dallas, invited me, in observance of my impending retirement in June 1996 after fifty years of teaching, to serve as guest curator for the exhibition "The Reformation of the Bible / The Bible of the Reformation," and to compose these four essays, which are intended to round out the Catalog of the exhibition but also to stand on their own as a small monograph about this large subject.

In deference to the celebratory nature of the occasion, I have been persuaded to indulge in the occupational hazard of the veteran scholar, the habit of self-citation. For the sake of truth in packaging, nevertheless, I should stipulate at the outset that despite a quite thorough grounding and a strong continuing interest in the Hebrew and Greek of the Bible, I am not by training or vocation a biblical scholar: my lifelong scholarly preoccupation has been not with what the Bible *means* but with what it *has been taken to mean,* during, among other periods, the age of the Reformation. As reviewers of my lifework, *The Christian Tradition: A History of the Development of Doctrine,* have repeatedly noted, one of its distinctive features, by contrast with its predecessors, has been its attention, throughout the five volumes, to the history of doctrinal exegesis through the centuries; that attention has stood me in good stead for the writing of Chapter 2. In writing these essays I have also benefited from having edited the exegetical volumes for the American Edition of *Luther's Works,* as well as from having written the companion volume to them, *Luther the Expositor,* in 1959. In addition, I did write my B.D. thesis at Concordia Seminary, Saint Louis, in 1946 on the Bible of Kralice, the principal Czech translation of the Scriptures. For the fourteenth edition of *Encyclopaedia Britannica* I contributed the major article on BIBLE. And at the invitation of the Book-of-the-Month Club in 1992 I compiled six volumes of *Sacred Writings* of the major world religions, including of course the Tanakh, the Biblical Apocrypha, and the New Testament, accompanying the set with a small guide entitled *On Searching the Scriptures — Your Own or Someone Else's.* At various places in these chapters I have drawn on, and even recycled, portions of those earlier writings.

For quotations from the Bible other than in the context of describing and discussing one or another original version or translation, I have, in the light of the overall theme, come to the same conclusion as David Lyle Jeffrey: "Because the King James ('Authorized') Version has been the favorite text of the clear majority of post-Renaissance English authors, up to and including even modern authors such as D. H. Lawrence, James Joyce, Toni Morrison, and John Updike, it is the English Bible referred to in all quotations and references, unless otherwise noted" (Jeffrey 1992, xii), albeit in modern spelling and punctuation; we thus use, both for the body of the work and for the index of passages, its names of biblical books and its numbering of chapters and verses, in preference to those of the Septuagint and Vulgate. For the spelling of proper names I have, as is my wont, conformed to the usage of *Webster's Biographical Dictionary,* backed up when necessary by *The Oxford Dictionary of the Christian Church* and other standard reference books.

J. P.

ACKNOWLEDGMENTS

The greatest debt is to Jaroslav Pelikan, the curator of this exhibition. The exhibition is being mounted at the end of his fifty years of university teaching; it marks not only that closure but also, and more important, the continuation of his contributions to education in America. It is not by chance that this occasion is observed with a book exhibition. Professor Pelikan has been one of the most active and eloquent supporters of research libraries in America during the past half century. Every research library in this country has profited, either directly or indirectly, from his service.

The exhibition and Catalog follow a model that Bridwell Library established with its Savonarola exhibition of 1994, curated by Professor Donald Weinstein. Our goal is to organize exhibitions curated by leading scholars who can make original contributions to scholarship, while presenting important historical and artistic subjects, in an accessible format, to a general public. Such a forum, we are convinced, makes it possible to present results of complex research in the humanities to both the general public and the academic world.

A new goal, pursued under Professor Pelikan's curatorship, has been to mount an exhibition that can be shared by other research libraries. Our model, though, is not to ship an exhibition en bloc from gallery to gallery but, rather, to design it with enough flexibility to allow each institution to mount a distinctive show from its own holdings (supplemented, as necessary, with a few loans). The flexibility of the design has generated great excitement among the participants, and we anticipate with pleasure the different realizations of the exhibition.

This undertaking has depended on the goodwill and good work of many people, especially the librarians at Columbia University, Harvard University, Union Theological Seminary, and Yale University. For their assistance in verifying bibliographic data and holdings information, we thank Thomas Amos and Janet Scinto of the Houghton Library, Harvard University; Elisabeth Fairman of the Yale Center for British Art; Claudia Funke of the Rare Book and Manuscript Library, Columbia University; Milton McC. Gatch and Seth Kasten of Union Theological Seminary; Gene McAfee of the Andover-Harvard Library; and Paul Stuehrenberg of the Yale Divinity School Library. We also thank colleagues in the book world who helped us at crucial moments, especially Ken Crilly, Joshua Lipton, Kathleen McMorrow, Helmut Rohlfing, and Fred Sand.

Jean Ashton, director of the Rare Book and Manuscript Library at Columbia University, and Milton McC. Gatch, director of the Burke Library at Union Theological Seminary, made the arrangements for the joint exhibition of their holdings at Butler Library, Columbia University. Duncan Robinson, then director of the Yale Center for British Arts, offered a beautiful space at Yale University for the exhibition, where it has been mounted under Elisabeth Fairman's supervision and guidance. Charles Willard, director of the Andover-Harvard Library at the Harvard Divinity School, has supported the project since its inception, and Roger E. Stoddard, curator of rare books at the Houghton Library, made the exhibition a reality at Harvard. We also thank Richard Wendorf, director of the Houghton Library, and Ralph Franklin, director of the Beinecke Rare Book and Manuscript Library at Yale University, for their encouragement and support.

Books for the exhibition at the Yale Center for British Art come not only from the holdings of the museum's library but also from the Yale University Art Gallery, the Yale Divinity School Library, and, particularly, the Beinecke Library. Robert Babcock and Gisela Noack assisted with items from the Beinecke. At Harvard, both the Widener Library and the Andover-Harvard Library have joined with the Houghton Library to bring together all the exhibition items. Union Theological Seminary and Columbia have, of course, drawn on the extensive collections of the Burke Library and the Rare Book and Manuscript Library at Columbia University.

As a group, the participating libraries have been supported by generous loans of material from the New York Public Library, the University of Toronto, Johns Hopkins University, General Theological Seminary, the Grolier Club, and the Niedersächsische Staats- und Universitätsbibliothek. Without the assistance of these institutions, we would not have been able to include several significant books.

Almost every member of Bridwell Library's staff has been involved in this project in some way, from James Powell's dogged interlibrary loan services to Jan Sobota's seemingly miraculous conservation of several exhibition items. Jon Speck took many of the photographs for this book and installed the exhibition at Bridwell. Isaac Gewirtz arranged for several special loans and reproductions. David Lawrence attended to many details, and Page Thomas supported the effort in numerous ways. We are also deeply grateful to Evie Jo Wilson, who has provided funding for this installation and for many others at Bridwell Library.

It was possible to develop the exhibition at Bridwell Library because of the depth of its collection in fifteenth- and sixteenth-century printing, an area of collecting that has been generously supported by the J. S. Bridwell Foundation. Further, the Bible has been a special focus of Bridwell's acquisitions program for many years, especially under the stewardship of Decherd Turner, director of Bridwell Library for thirty years and its perpetual genius loci. The library also houses the Thomas J. Harrison Bible Collection (which became a permanent part of the library in 1994) and the Elizabeth Perkins Prothro Collection (which has been on deposit at the Library since 1989 and is available for use by students and scholars). The Elizabeth Perkins Prothro Collection has astonishing breadth (extending from medieval manuscript Bibles to twentieth-century fine press Bibles) but also remarkable depth, especially in sixteenth-century Bibles and in English-language Bibles.

Professor David Price of the University of Texas at Austin and I wrote the "Catalog of the Exhibition." Our collaboration has been so close that it is impossible to describe a division of labor with any exactitude. Each of us drafted roughly half the descriptions. But we assisted each other in all the research, and we undertook together several revisions of the whole, with the result that we share responsibility for each description. He and I wish to acknowledge the assistance of Professor Pelikan. Although he has taught us much in the past, we have never learned so much from him as we have through this collaboration, and we have never found a scholarly collaboration as delightful as this one has been.

Finally, we thank Jenya Weinreb of Yale University Press for her expert editing, as well as John G. Ryden and Judy Metro, also of Yale University Press, and the designer, Richard Hendel, all of whom showed enthusiasm for the project and, more important, guided us from wishful ideas to an actual book. By producing this handsome volume, they have honored Professor Pelikan's long service to the Press and to the scholarly community in general.

Valerie R. Hotchkiss
Director of Bridwell Library
Perkins School of Theology
Southern Methodist University

Adams   *Catalogue of Books Printed on the Continent of Europe, 1501–1600 in Cambridge Libraries.* 1967. Compiled by H. M. Adams. 2 vols. Cambridge: Cambridge University Press.

B   Benzing, Josef, and Helmut Claus. 1989. *Lutherbibliographie.* 2d ed. Baden-Baden: Koerner.

BMC   *Catalogue of Books Printed in the Fifteenth Century Now in the British Museum.* 1963–71. 10 vols. London: British Museum.

CR   *Corpus Reformatorum.* Edited by Karl Gottlieb Bretschneider. 1834– . Berlin and Leipzig.

Denzinger   Denzinger, Henricus, ed. 1976. *Enchiridion symbolorum definitionum et declarationum de rebus fidei et morum.* 36th ed. Edited by Adolf Schönmetzer. Freiburg: Herder.

D&M   Darlow, T. H., and H. F. Moule, eds. 1963. *Historical Catalogue of the Printed Editions of Holy Scripture in the Library of the British and Foreign Bible Society.* 2 vols. Reprint, New York: Kraus.

Goff   Goff, Frederick R., comp. and ed. [1964] 1973. *Incunabula in American Libraries: A Third Census of Fifteenth-Century Books Recorded in North American Collections.* Reprint, New York: Kraus.

GW   *Gesamtkatalog der Wiegendrucke.* 1968– . 2d ed. Stuttgart: Hiersemann.

IA   *Index Aureliensis.* 1965– . Baden-Baden: Koerner.

LW   *Luther's Works: The American Edition.* 1955–1986. Edited by Jaroslav Pelikan and Helmut Lehmann. 55 vols. Saint Louis and Philadelphia: Concordia Publishing House and Fortress Press.

McNeill   McNeill, John Thomas, ed. 1960. John Calvin. *Institutes of the Christian Religion.* Translated by Ford Lewis Battles. 2 vols. Philadelphia: Westminster Press.

OCD   *The Oxford Classical Dictionary.* 1970. 2d ed. Edited by N. G. L. Hammond and H. H. Scullard. Oxford: Clarendon Press.

ODCC   *The Oxford Dictionary of the Christian Church.* 1983. 2d ed. Edited by F. L. Cross and E. A. Livingstone. Oxford: Oxford University Press.

OED	*A New [Oxford] English Dictionary on Historical Principles.* 1884–1986. Edited by J. A. H. Murray et al. 10 vols. and Supplements. Oxford: Oxford University Press.
PG	Migne, J. P., ed. 1857–66. *Patrologia Graeca.* Paris.
PL	Migne, J. P., ed. 1878–90. *Patrologia Latina.* Paris.
PRE[3]	Hauck, Albert, ed. 1898–1908. *Realencyklopädie für protestantische Theologie und Kirche.* 3d ed. 21 vols. Leipzig: J. C. Hinrichs'sche Buchhandlung.
Schaff	Schaff, Philip, ed. 1990. *The Creeds of Christendom.* 6th ed. 3 vols. Reprint, Grand Rapids: Baker Book House.
STC (2d ed.)	*A Short-Title Catalogue of Books Printed in England, Scotland, and Ireland and of English Books Printed Abroad, 1475–1640.* 1986–91. Compiled by A. W. Pollard and G. R. Redgrave. 2d ed. begun by W. A. Jackson and F. S. Ferguson and completed by Katherine F. Pantzer. 3 vols. London: Bibliographical Society.
STC (Wing)	*Short-Title Catalogue of Books Printed in England, Scotland, Ireland, Wales, and British America and of English Books Printed in Other Countries, 1640–1700.* 1972–88. Compiled by Donald Wing. 2d ed. 3 vols. New York: Modern Language Association of America.
Tanner	Tanner, Norman P., ed. 1990. *Decrees of the Ecumenical Councils.* 2 vols. London and Washington: Sheed and Ward and Georgetown University Press.
VD16	Bayerische Staatsbibliothek in Munich, and Herzog August Bibliothek in Wolfenbüttel, ed. 1883– . *Verzeichnis der im deutschen Sprachbereich erschienenen Drucke des XVI. Jahrhunderts.* Stuttgart: Hiersemann.
WA	*Luthers Werke: Kritische Gesamtausgabe.* 1983. Weimar: Böhlau.
Br	*Briefwechsel*
DB	*Die deutsche Bibel*
TR	*Die Tischreden*

Introduction

The nineteenth century created several major testimonials to Luther and the Reformation. One of them was the editing of *Luthers Werke: Kritische Gesamtausgabe,* the so-called Weimar Edition, launched with the support of the German Kaiser for the four hundredth anniversary of Luther's birth in 1883 (and not quite complete when the five hundredth birthday came along in 1983). But another, which was dedicated on 25 June 1868, well before that anniversary (although it was not completed by the original sculptor, who had died in 1861), was Ernst Rietschel's heroic statue of the Reformer at Worms.[1] Worms was the site of Luther's courageous stand before church and empire in 1521, and of his defiant statement of rebellion and obedience: "Here I stand. I cannot do otherwise. God help me. Amen" — or whatever may have been the precise words he actually spoke. Although intended to mark that event, where Luther was probably holding his own books, which he had been ordered to recant, the statue — copies of which have since been set up in several other places, among them the United States — represents Luther with a Bible in his hand. I still remember a duet of sermons by one of my professors fifty years ago that was inspired by the copy of that statue on the campus of Concordia Seminary, Saint Louis, titled "What the Book Did for the Man" and "What the Man Did for the Book."

Of course, he was not the only man in the sixteenth century who did something for the Book; nor was he the only one whose life was fundamentally redefined by the Book (even though he violently disagreed with some of the others to whom this was happening). All across Western Christendom and even beyond, Holy Scripture became, in the words of Luther's best-known hymn, "a trusty shield and weapon" for Erasmians and Lutherans, for Calvinists and Jesuits, for Anglicans and Anabaptists, and for some who did not belong to any of those categories, to use against one another and against all other enemies. The Bible of the Reformation and the Reformation of the Bible became two sides of one coin. For the Reformation of the sixteenth century — whether Protestant, Roman Catholic, or Radical — is unthinkable apart from the Bible; and the Bible — at any rate as we know it in the realms of Western literature, culture, and faith — is almost equally unthinkable apart from the Reformation.

1. Oppermann 1875, 178–200.

This book is an examination of that symbiotic relation: across languages and cultures, between churches and theologies, through libraries and printing presses, in pulpits and lecture halls, and, to the extent that historical scholarship can gain even slight access to such mysteries, deep within the hearts of countless men and women who came to know the meaning not only of the Reformation but of reformation as such, by the power of the word of God that spoke to them through the Bible.

I : Sacred Philology

The scholarly foundations for "the Reformation of the Bible" as well as for "the Bible of the Reformation" were laid by the principles and methods of what Paul Oskar Kristeller has called "sacred philology,"[1] which became the common property of the Renaissance and the Reformation. Mutatis mutandis, therefore, Anthony Grafton's description of most humanists in the Renaissance would apply also to many scholars in the Reformation: "The men who called themselves humanists in the fifteenth and sixteenth centuries . . . hoped that they could renovate education, literature, philosophy, and theology, not by looking to an uncertain future but by turning backward to a perfect past. Convinced that they could find the best models for literature, the soundest philosophy, the most accurate history, and the best guidance for conduct in the accumulated wisdom of the Greeks and Romans, the Bible, and the writings of the fathers of the Church, they turned to books for the knowledge that they considered most worth having."[2]

Thus when Luther's junior colleague, the wunderkind Philipp Melanchthon (1497–1560), was teaching the Greek Classics and the Greek New Testament simultaneously at the young University of Wittenberg, he was quite unselfconsciously linking the Reformation and the Christian Renaissance in a relation of mutual support. Luther, too, while at the Coburg during the Diet of Augsburg in 1530, busied himself both with a task that seemed appropriate to the Reformation, translating the Book of Ezekiel from Hebrew to German, and with a task that seemed more appropriate to the Renaissance, translating the fables of Aesop from Greek to German.[3]

RENAISSANCE AND REFORMATION

Through much of the twentieth century, however, such a linkage has not suited scholarly fashion, which, to the extent that it has not subsumed them both under Early Modern social

1. Kristeller 1961, 79.
2. Grafton et al. 1993, 10–11.
3. Luther to Nikolaus Hausmann, 25.vi.1530, *WA Br* 5:385; *WA* 50:440–60.

QVATVOR EVANGELIA, AD VETVSTISSIMORVM
EXEMPLARIVM LATINORVM FIDEM, ET AD
GRAECAM VERITATEM AB ERASMO ROTE
RODAMO SACRAE THEOLOGIAE PROFES
SORE DILIGENTER RECOGNITA.

ΕΥΑΓΓΕΛΙΟΝ ΚΑΤΑ
ΜΑΤΘΑΙΟΝ.

EVANGELIVM SECVNDVM
MATTHAEVM.

Liber generatio
nis Iesu Christi
filij Dauid, Filij
Abrahã, Abra
ham genuit Isa
ac. Isaac aũt, ge
nuit Iacob. Ia
cob aũt, genuit Iudã, & fratres eius.
Iudas aũt, genuit Phares, & Zarã,
e Thamar. Phares autẽ, genuit Es
rom. Esrom aũt, genuit Aram. Arã
autem, genuit Aminadab. Amina
dab aũt, genuit Naasson. Naasson
aũt, genuit Salmon. Salmon autẽ,
genuit Boos, e Rhachab. Boos aũt,
genuit Obed, e Ruth. Obed autẽ,
genuit Iesse. Iesse aũt, genuit Dauid
regem. Dauid autẽ rex, genuit So
lomonem, ex ea q̃ fuerat uxor Vrie.
Solomon autem, genuit Roboam.
Roboam aũt, genuit Abiam. Abia
autem, genuit Asa. Asa autem, ge
nuit Iosaphat. Iosaphat autem, ge
nuit Ioram. Ioram autem, genu
A   it Oziã.

IOANNES
FROBENI
VS SVIS
TYPIS
EXCV
DE
BAT

Novvm instrumentum omne, edited, translated, and annotated by Erasmus of Rotterdam (1516), fol. A1ʳ. Item 1.16.

history, has been dictating an increasingly sharp distinction between the two movements traditionally denominated under the titles "Renaissance" and "Reformation." An instructive documentation of this shift is provided by comparing the volumes bearing the subtitle "Renaissance" in the *Cambridge Modern History* and in the *New Cambridge Modern History,* each of these being the first of the set. That volume in the *Cambridge Modern History,* written around the beginning of the twentieth century and published in 1902, contained a brace of chapters entitled, respectively, "The Classical Renaissance" (by Richard C. Jebb) and "The Christian Renaissance" (by M. R. James), with such Reformation figures as Philipp Melanchthon and Hugo Grotius (1583–1645) appearing in the first, and such Reformation works as the *Magdeburg Centuries* (1559–74) in the second; there is no genuine counterpart to either of these chapters in the revised work, which was written at midcentury. Nevertheless, whatever abiding validity there may prove to be in such a dichotomy between Renaissance and Reformation, even its most partisan defenders are obliged to recognize that there are also significant points of convergence between the two, and in some respects the growing edge of scholarship gives indications of moving back in the direction of that recognition.[4] Among such points of convergence between Renaissance and Reformation, none is of greater importance for both than sacred philology. For although the Renaissance was far more than humanism, and humanism was far more than philology, the judgment of the founder of modern Renaissance study, Jakob Burckhardt (1818–97), remains true. Burckhardt felt obliged to "insist upon it, as one of the chief propositions of this book, that it was not the revival of antiquity alone, but its union with the genius of the Italian people, which achieved the conquest of the Western world." Yet he insisted no less that his entire account of the Italian Renaissance was "coloured in a thousand ways by the influence of the ancient world; and though the essence of the phenomena might still have been the same without the classical revival, it is only with and through this revival that they are actually manifested to us."[5]

The history of the Renaissance in Italy has, with good reason, predominated in the interpretation of the Renaissance as a whole; with equally good reason, the interpretation of the Reformation as a whole has been dominated by the history of the Reformation in Germany. One unfortunate result of this division of labor, however, has been its effect on the study of the Northern Renaissance, and consequently on the interpretation of the relation between it and the Reformation.[6] The controversy over the freedom of the will in 1524–25 between Erasmus and Luther has sometimes served as the agon of the distinction. Having been one of

4. An instructive recent examination of the problematics of these issues that transcends the partisanship is the introduction to Brady, Oberman, and Tracy 1994, 1:xiii–xxiv, esp. xiii–xvi.

5. Burckhardt [1929] 1958, 1:175.

6. Among the exceptions to this are Spitz 1963 and Rice 1985.

the few scholars to have a role in editing the works both of Luther (in the American Edition of *Luther's Works,* where I had responsibility specifically for his exegetical writings in volumes 1–30) and of Erasmus (in the Toronto Edition of the *Collected Works of Erasmus,* where I served for some years on the Editorial Board), I have had repeated occasion in both contexts to lament the dichotomy, which tends to obscure Luther's dependence on the scholarship of Erasmus for his study and interpretation of the Greek New Testament, as well as Luther's major contribution, as an exegete and perhaps above all as a translator of the Bible, to the clarification and even the correction of some of the philological insights of Erasmus. In a personal sense, then, this essay is my attempt to redress that imbalance.

The most interesting venue for the study of the implications of philology for the interrelation of Renaissance and Reformation is the sixteenth-century university. Already a century before, at Oxford and then even more dramatically at Prague, universities had been the battleground of the Reformation. As a Master of Arts in the university, as university professor and preacher, and then as rector at Prague, Jan Hus (ca. 1372–1415) was able to apply critical analysis to the issues of Christian doctrine and practice, and to take advantage of the traditional, if limited, guarantees of academic freedom provided by the medieval university in articulating and defending his findings; significantly, in the standard volume on the history of Charles University an entire chapter by František Šmahel is entitled simply "The Hussite University."[7] In Italy, by contrast, the scholars of the Renaissance, for example, Lorenzo Valla (ca. 1406–57), Marsilio Ficino (1433–99), and Pico della Mirandola (1463–94), did not congregate chiefly at such universities as Bologna but did their work with the support of noble and wealthy patrons and cultivated their intellectual association through the formation of such institutions as the celebrated Platonic Academy in Florence, where the study of Greek philology — and, through it, the study of Greek philosophy — made significant advances. It is to the Florentine Academy that we owe such foundational works as a complete translation of Plato into Latin by Marsilio Ficino; the scholarly quality of the edition is evidenced by its thirty-two-page index of concepts and technical terms at the beginning [Item 1.3(1548):α5^r–γ7^r], and by Ficino's preface to his translation of *Timaeus* (replacing the Latin version of Calcidius), for example, its forty-one brief dissertations on various philological and philosophical problems of that influential Platonic dialogue [Item 1.3(1548):457–73].

The international intellectual traffic between the Northern and the Southern Renaissance is illustrated by the publishing history of Erasmus's *Hecvba, et Iphigenia in Aulide.* Between 1506 and 1518, it was published in Paris, Venice, Basel, and Florence [Item 1.2]. By contrast, at various new universities of Northern Europe the philological methodology of the new learning came into conflict both with the authority of Thomistic scholasticism and with the several

---

7. In Kavka 1964, 44–76.

varieties of nominalism and the *via moderna.* Two case studies for our purposes here are Tübingen and Wittenberg. Tübingen, in spite of its deserved reputation as a center of scholarly study, had not been hospitable to the new learning, and Melanchthon, having earned the degree of Master of Arts there in 1514 at the age of seventeen, departed for Wittenberg in 1518.[8] Once arrived there and once associated with Martin Luther, he played a major role in what has been termed the "triumph of biblical humanism in the University of Wittenberg."[9] The controversy between Erasmus and Luther (in which Melanchthon found his loyalties deeply torn[10]) did nothing to diminish Luther's admiration for Erasmus as a philological scholar, much as he condemned Erasmus (unjustly) as an Epicurean skeptic. For his part, Huldrych Zwingli (1484–1531) became the Reformer of Zurich in significant measure through the study of Erasmus, as his handwritten marginal glosses on the humanist's writings show.[11]

THE RECOVERY OF GREEK

More recent scholarship has not discarded Burckhardt's conception of "the revival of antiquity" as a category for Renaissance learning, but it has amplified and deepened it. Fundamental to that "revival" was the rediscovery of Greek. To a degree that is easy to overlook, the ignorance of Greek had been a chronic disease in the intellectual life of Western Europe during an entire millennium, from the death of Augustine in 430 to the Council of Florence in 1439. Augustine himself was, as Peter Brown has said, "the only Latin philosopher in antiquity to be virtually ignorant of Greek."[12] But he was by no means the last to suffer from such ignorance. An inability to read Byzantine Christian writers (not to mention the New Testament) with any real expertness in the original language led Thomas Aquinas astray into a dependence on misinterpretations of Eastern Christian theology, and therefore into a distortion of the differences between it and the Western church on so fundamental a point of dogma as the *Filioque.*[13] The epics of Homer were known to the Middle Ages only at second hand, so that, as one *Dantista* has put it, "Homer is present merely as a quotation in the *Vita Nuova.* . . . Of Homer, 'sovereign poet,' Dante could have no direct knowledge. . . . He knew a few quotations from Homer and Aristotle, he knew 'the matter of Troy' from the current medieval romances, and he accepted Homer's sovereignty on authority."[14] Of the Platonic corpus, the

8. On the relation between the two universities see the comments of Oberman 1977, 72–81.

9. Schwiebert 1950, 275–302.

10. Pelikan 1971–89, 4:143.

11. Farner 1946, 152–72: "Der Erasmianer."

12. Brown 1967, 36; also 271–73.

13. Pelikan 1974, 315–36.

14. Bergin 1965, 60–61.

West during most of the medieval period had little more than *Timaeus,* and that in the "crabbed"[15] Latin translation of Calcidius, necessitating the explanatory comments of Ficino mentioned earlier; but the *Republic* and even the *Apology* were largely inaccessible.[16] The preface to the edition of Homer published in 1488 presents itself as seeking to correct that "inopia librorum" [Item 1.1:fol.A1ʳ], and in a touching letter dated 10 January 1354 Petrarch had described the thrill of finally owning a manuscript of Homer in Greek — but the frustration of not being able to read it![17]

There had, of course, been exceptions all along.[18] At least three of the most influential deserve to be mentioned individually for their relevance to our subject.[19] The Greek learning of Jerome (ca. 347–ca. 419) was so substantial — indeed, Augustine called him an "expert in all three languages" because of his knowledge of Hebrew as well[20] — that he was able to translate into Latin not only the Greek New Testament but several writings of the Greek church fathers, including the treatise of Didymus the Blind, *On the Holy Spirit,* which now survives only in that translation.[21] Boethius (ca. 480–524) wanted to be seen as a faithful pupil of Augustine, bringing forth fruit from his "seeds."[22] But he far surpassed his master in philological erudition, translating the *Organon* of Aristotle into Latin and, in a celebrated poem in his *Consolation of Philosophy,* rendering a central passage of Plato's into Latin meter [Item 1.8(1501):N3ʳ–N4ᵛ].[23] And John Scotus Erigena (ca. 810–ca. 877), "one of the most remarkable phenomena of intellectual history,"[24] acquired enough sophistication in Greek to take on the translating of the pseudonymous work of the Christian Neoplatonist who around the year 500 had written under the biblical name of Dionysius the Areopagite, the Athenian convert of the apostle Paul (Acts 17:34). Despite his ignorance of Greek, therefore, Thomas Aquinas was able to draw on the work of these translators, so that, to cite the most striking instance, he quoted the Latinized *Corpus Areopagiticum* more than a thousand times in his works, including

---

15. *OCD* 226.

16. Klibansky 1939 laid the foundations for modern study of the question.

17. In Bishop 1966, 153–54.

18. See Allgeier 1943, 275–76 and 279–88, on the quality of medieval translations from Greek into Latin.

19. Lubac 1959–64, 2/1:238–62: "L'hébreu, le grec et saint Jérôme."

20. Augustine *De civitate Dei* XVIII.43.

21. Didymus *De Spiritu Sancto* (*PG* 39:1031–86).

22. Boethius *De Trinitate* pr.: "an ex beati Augustini scriptis semina rationum aliquos in nos venientia fructus extulerint."

23. Boethius *De consolatione philosophiae* III.m9, based on Plato *Timaeus* 27C–42D.

24. Schubert 1921, 467.

some crucial places in the *Summa Theologica*.[25] He also wrote a commentary on the *De Trinitate* of Boethius.

It was, however, another and more recent translator of Greek into Latin who proved to be both a major influence on the thought of Thomas Aquinas and an anticipation of the revival of Greek with which we are concerned here: his fellow Dominican, William of Moerbeke (ca. 1215–ca. 1286), who, along with other Western scholars, undertook the retranslation of Aristotle directly from Greek into Latin as a replacement for the defective and misleading translations by way of Arabic that were in circulation.[26] An elegant eventual product of this medieval process of publishing the works of Aristotle in both Latin and Greek was to be the beautifully crafted volumes of Aristotle published at Venice by Aldus Manutius (1449/50–1515) in 1495–98, the fifth volume of which contains the *Nicomachean Ethics* and the *Politics* in Greek [Item 1.4]. As Heiko Oberman has pointed out in commenting on the new edition of Aristotle that was subsequently projected by Melanchthon, such an interest in publishing an "authentic" text of Aristotle should by no means be regarded as an exclusive prerogative of humanism in its opposition to scholasticism, but represented a connection to the work of such scholars as William of Moerbeke, and thus to that of the high scholastics.[27]

For during the century and a half that followed the death of Thomas Aquinas in 1274, the knowledge and study of Greek, that is, of the Greek Classics but also of the Greek church fathers as well as of the Greek New Testament, had increased mightily in the West.[28] In part this was due to the renewal of union negotiations between the Eastern and the Western churches from the Council of Lyons in 1274 (which his death prevented Thomas Aquinas from attending) to the Council of Florence in 1439.[29] Eventually the instruction in Greek grammar that had been made available through tutoring by refugee Greeks took printed form for students in the West who knew Latin but not Greek. Constantinos Lascaris (1434–1501) was the author of the first book to be printed entirely in Greek, which appeared in 1476 and which was subsequently published by the celebrated Aldine Press at Venice in 1495 [Item 1.6].[30] His grammar contained, among other grammatical helps, explanations of the distinctive characteristics of Greek nouns and verbs and a guide to Greek prepositions; later editions had

25. Durantel 1919, 49–59: "Traductions et commentaires."

26. A brief summary of his work, with extensive bibliography, is in Chenu 1964, 215–19.

27. Oberman 1977, 75.

28. There is a large amount of biographical and bibliographical information about this development in Stinger 1977, 83–166: "The Renaissance of Patristic Studies."

29. Geanakoplos 1962.

30. Babcock and Sosower 1994, 44–45 (Item 45).

Greek and Latin on facing pages. The first Greek Classic to be printed was the 1488 edition of Homer, both the *Iliad* and the *Odyssey* [Item 1.1]. Particularly interesting as an ancestor of Renaissance interests was Plutarch, whose *Parallel Lives* had compared Greek and Roman culture as embodied in various of their great men: the edition of the *Vitae Parallelae* of Plutarch first published at Rome by Ulrich Han and later at Venice by Nicolas Jenson in 1478 [Item 1.5] documents Renaissance interest in this Greco-Roman writer, who, in the words of a modern reference book, "was in his writings an active exponent of the concept of a partnership between Greece, the educator, and Rome, the great power,"[31] thus between the ancient Hellenic culture toward which the humanists of the Renaissance were aspiring and the ancient Latin culture of which they regarded themselves as the legitimate heirs and restorers after the neglect and misunderstanding of the Middle Ages.

Neither Hellenic culture nor Latin culture, moreover, could be confined to its Classical, pagan expression. Greek had become a world language when it broke out of the confines of Attica and the Peloponnesus and when, through the historic achievements of Alexander the Great and of the Egyptian city that took his name, "Hellenism" became "Hellenistic." For "Hellenism, which is a genuine Greek word for Greek culture (*Hellênismos*), represented language, thought, mythology, and images that constituted an extraordinarily flexible medium of both cultural and religious expression,"[32] including not only the Septuagint, the writings of Philo Judaeus (ca. 13 BCE–ca. 45 CE), and the Greek New Testament, but the vast corpus of Greek patristic literature. Qualitatively similar, but quantitatively even more extensive because the missionary activity of the Western church eventually carried Latin to all parts of the earth whereas Eastern missions translated the Byzantine liturgy from Greek into such languages as Old Church Slavonic, was the *Nachleben* of the language of pagan Rome in the Vulgate and the Mass and in the still vaster corpus of Latin patristic literature, as "the new philological methods of editing and commenting which the humanists had developed in their studies of the ancient authors were also applied to the Latin Church Fathers."[33] Archaism and snobbery led some of the Renaissance humanists to a "reproduction of antiquity," which slavishly copied the Latinity of Cicero and Pliny.[34] The end result of this process was what one study has called a "maniacal Ciceronianism," which absolutized the Latin of Cicero, its constructions and even its vocabulary, as the norm for correct language.[35] Nevertheless, the books of the Greek and Latin church fathers, many of the former having become accessible for the first time in the

---

31. *OCD* 850.

32. Bowersock 1993, 7.

33. Kristeller 1961, 81.

34. Burckhardt [1929] 1958, 1:236–46.

35. James Hankins in Grafton et al. 1993, 73.

West, were accorded the same editorial care and typographical embellishment as were their non-Christian antecedents. The sheer statistics in the history of editing and publishing patristic works continue to be massively convincing,[36] but some of the individual editions make the point even more effectively. Among these, the editio princeps of Augustine's *The City of God,* produced at Subiaco in 1467 [Item 1.7] and lavishly embellished in the Bridwell and Yale copies, yields to none of the editions of the Greek and Latin Classics as a masterpiece of early printing. Such books as this laid the foundations for the publishing of patristic editions in the centuries to follow.[37]

"A FLOOD OF BIBLES"

Nevertheless, the crowning achievements of sacred philology in the age of the Renaissance, and the ones most important here because of their direct pertinence to the history of the Reformation, were of course its Bibles, so much so that a handbook published in the 1970s refers to this phenomenon as "a flood of Bibles."[38] In the West during the Middle Ages, the term *Biblia* — originally a Greek neuter plural, βιβλία, meaning "little books," but eventually used as a Latin feminine noun in the singular — had in the first instance referred to one or another Latin version, increasingly to that of Jerome, usually called the Vulgate — thus to a translation rather than to an original version. Even in the Byzantine East, which frequently preened itself on its ability to use the Greek New Testament rather than a translation, the Old Testament was likewise a translation, the Septuagint. Thus through most of the history of the church, most Christian thinkers have been obliged to base their biblical interpretation and theology, in whole or in part, on translations of Sacred Scripture! The history of the Bible in the age of Renaissance and Reformation, therefore, must include attention to these translations, the Septuagint and the Vulgate, both of which, and especially the Latin Vulgate, shaped the development of biblical study and of biblical publishing. For even as they were criticizing the Vulgate, the scholars of the Renaissance saw themselves as the legitimate heirs of Jerome, emulating his scholarship to do what he had done while coming to different results.[39] Manuscripts of the Vulgate were among the most precious elements in the medieval patrimony to

36. "Nineteen editions of *De civitate Dei,* seventeen in the original Latin, were printed in the fifteenth century. Sixteen of the Latin incunable editions are owned by Bridwell Library." Weinstein and Hotchkiss 1994, 22.

37. Jacob 1939, 191–96, illustrates the influence of such early editions by examining the publishing history of the *Historia tripartita.*

38. Tony Lane in Dowley et al. 1977, 366.

39. Rice 1985 is a brilliant examination of the reception of Jerome in the Renaissance.

which the fifteenth and sixteenth centuries fell heir, and any European library with a claim to comprehensiveness had to own one or more of these [Item 1.9].

Already in the Middle Ages, however, widespread critical attention had been paid to variations and corruptions in the text of the Vulgate, which evoked repeated programs of revision. The researches of Hans Glunz have called attention to the successive forms that such revision took in medieval biblical scholarship, particularly in the twelfth century.[40] His schematic diagram of the evolution of the Latin texts of the Bible during the Middle Ages, as recast by Raphael Loewe, graphically charts those successive texts, identified by Loewe as "1. Mixed vulgate and pre-Jerome Texts; 2. Texts essentially representative of Jerome; 3. Late and Neutral Texts."[41] A fascinating instance of the evolution of the text of the Latin Bible after Jerome, and one with intriguing connections to the history of Mariological devotion and speculation, is the protevangelium of Genesis 3:15. The New Jerusalem Bible translates it: "I shall put enmity between you and the woman, and between your offspring and hers; it will bruise your head, and you will strike its heel." But in a footnote the NJB explains: "The Greek version has a masculine pronoun ('he,' not 'it' will bruise . . .), thus ascribing the victory not to the woman's descendants in general but to one of her sons in particular, and thus providing the basis for the messianic interpretation given by many of the Fathers. The Latin version has a feminine pronoun ('she' will bruise . . .) and since, in the messianic interpretation of our text, the Messiah and his mother appear together, the pronoun has been taken to refer to Mary."

It was evidently the rendering of the Septuagint, αὐτός σου τηρήσει κεφαλήν, that underlay one of the earliest Christian applications of the text to Jesus as Messiah, that of Irenaeus of Lyons (even though we now have this only in the Latin translation of Irenaeus, the Greek original having been lost).[42] From such evidence as (1) a relatively early manuscript of Jerome's translation, the Ottobonianus, (2) his own earlier comments in the *Quaestiones Hebraicae in Genesin,* and (3) references to his translation by Pope Leo I (ca. 400–461), scholars have concluded that Jerome did render the text in Latin with the masculine pronoun: "*ipse* conteret caput tuum" (emphasis added). But soon thereafter the feminine pronoun, "*ipsa* conteret," began to appear, requiring a more subtle messianic interpretation.[43] Such early medieval interpreters as Bede and Ambrosius Autpertus took the feminine pronoun to refer to the church, but Isidore of Seville and others applied it to the Virgin.[44] By the High Middle Ages, so influential an interpreter as Bernard of Clairvaux could comment: "To whom is this victory to

40. Glunz 1933, 197–258.

41. Raphael Loewe in Lampe 1969, 103–5; Glunz 1930, 117.

42. Irenaeus *Adversus haereses* V.xi.1–2.

43. Drewniak 1934.

44. Pelikan 1971–89, 3:70–71.

be attributed, if not to Mary? Without a doubt it was she who crushed the venomous head."[45] It was, fittingly, into the mouth of Bernard of Clairvaux that Dante, in the final canto of the *Divine Comedy,* placed a hymn in praise of the Virgin Mary.

THE TEXT OF THE VULGATE

Especially important in the history of the textual criticism of the Vulgate had been the revisions and corrections developed by the Dominican and Franciscan scholars of the thirteenth century.[46] But at the end of the fifteenth and the beginning of the sixteenth century the philological enterprise of textual criticism was given a new impetus by the need to establish the correct text for the printed editions of the Latin Bible that were beginning to appear.[47] The "42-line" Latin Bible of Johannes Gutenberg (ca. 1397–1468),[48] which was the first major book to be printed from movable metal type, appears to have been published between 1452 and 1455. Jeremiah 31:33 [Item 1.10] is a text that already in the New Testament (Heb 8:10) had been taken as a prophecy of the new revelation in Christ: "Post dies illos dicit dominus dabo legem meam in visceribus eorum: et in corde eorum scribam eam: et ero eis in deum, et ipsi erunt michi in populum." By the end of that decade and the beginning of the next, other Latin Bibles were being released, including the "36-line" Bible, which may also have been by Gutenberg, and the *Biblia Latina* published in Mainz by Johann Fust and Peter Schöffer, dated 14 August 1462 [Item 1.11]. The period of the Renaissance and Reformation, which on one hand gave new impetus both to the study of the Hebrew and Greek originals and to the production of vernacular versions of Holy Scripture, nevertheless continued on the other hand the pressure for the clarification and purification of the text of the Latin Vulgate. Robert Estienne, or "Stephanus" (1503–59), was a leading figure in this enterprise, as well as in the editing of the Greek texts of both Testaments.[49] His masterpiece edition of the Vulgate, the *Biblia* in two parts, first appeared in Paris during 1527–28 [Item 1.13].

The state of the Vulgate text was a matter of special concern to the assembled council fathers at the Council of Trent, showing just how much "the Reformation of the Bible" was a part of the Catholic Reformation and not only of the Protestant Reformation. For at their fourth session, on 8 April 1546, they decreed that "from all the Latin editions of the sacred books which are in circulation" the edition that was to be regarded as "authentic" was "the old

---

45. Pelikan 1971–89, 3:166–68.

46. Denifle 1888, 471–601.

47. Metzger 1968, 95–106.

48. See the handsome volume by Ruppel 1967.

49. Armstrong 1954.

well known Latin Vulgate edition [haec ipsa vetus et vulgata editio] which has been tested in the church by long use over so many centuries" [Item 1.28:B5ʳ]. This official approval of the Vulgate could be, and was, construed by some as a declaration of its infallibility.[50] But the same session of the Council of Trent went on almost immediately to "decree and determine that hereafter the holy scriptures, particularly this ancient Vulgate edition, shall be printed after a thorough revision [quam emendatissime]."[51] That call for a thorough revision of the received text of the Latin Vulgate was taken up in earnest by Pope Sixtus V exactly forty years later, in 1586, with the appointment of a commission for the preparation of an authentic edition; it produced a printed version in 1590, which, however, proved to be so defective that it was withdrawn. Under the leadership of Pope Clement VIII, the work of the commission was continued and drastically revised, with the Jesuit scholar Cardinal Robert Bellarmine (1542–1621) bringing to the task his lifelong research on the Vulgate text.[52] The outcome was the Clementine or Sixto-Clementine edition of 1592–93, *Biblia Sacra Vulgatae Editionis Sixti Quinti Pont. Max. jussu recognita atque edita,* which acquired normative status [Item 1.14].[53] In modern times, a major contribution to the textual criticism of the Vulgate New Testament came from John Wordsworth (1843–1911), Anglican bishop of Salisbury, and Henry Julian White (1859–1934), whose edition was published between 1889 and 1954 and is conveniently available in an "editio minor," *Novum Testamentum Latine,* prepared by White and issued by Clarendon Press at Oxford in 1911, with a corrected edition in 1920. But calls for further revision and correction have continued also within Roman Catholicism, especially in the wake of the biblical encyclical of Pope Pius XII, *Divino afflante Spiritu* of 30 September 1943, which insisted that the Tridentine decree pertained "exclusively to the Western church [latinam solummodo respicit Ecclesiam]," within which the Vulgate possessed a "juridical authority [authentia iuridica]," but not a "critical authority."[54] The Second Vatican Council affirmed that the church "keeps in honour [semper in honore habet]" both the Latin Vulgate and the Greek Septuagint; but the council vigorously promoted vernacular Scriptures, as well as vernacular liturgies, and, quoting verbatim from *Divino afflante Spiritu,* urged that such translations of the Scriptures into vernacular languages be derived "especially from the original texts of the sacred books [praesertim ex

---

50. Kneller 1928, 202–24, on the canonical standing of the bull "Aeternus ille" of Pope Sixtus V; in general, see also Jedin 1961, 92–98.

51. Tanner 2:664–65.

52. Le Bachelet 1911, 107–25, reprints Bellarmine's dissertation of 1586–91, "De editione Latina vulgata," and discusses it, 13–34.

53. Baroni 1986, 216–22.

54. Pius XII, "Divino afflante Spiritu," Denzinger 754.

primigenis sacrorum librorum textibus]" rather than from either the Vulgate or the Septuagint.[55]

That twentieth-century affirmation of the prime authority of "the original texts of the sacred books" by Pope Pius XII and then by the Second Vatican Council may be seen as an ultimate vindication, more than four centuries later, of the sacred philology of the Renaissance and the Reformation. For although the humanists did urge that the corruptions of the Vulgate text, which had occurred through its transmission from one medieval copyist to another, made the production of a critical edition of the Latin text mandatory, their chief criticism was directed against the inadequacies, indeed the inaccuracies, of the Vulgate as such, which no collation of Latin manuscripts, however thorough, could be expected to set straight. In his *Collatio Novi Testamenti* of 1444, the Italian humanist Lorenzo Valla, "the first critic among humanistic historians,"[56] identified many of these inadequacies and inaccuracies.[57] Valla is probably best remembered in the history of scholarship for his critical examination of the *Donation of Constantine,* which he produced four years earlier than the *Collatio Novi Testamenti* but which was first published in 1506 and then again in a more widely circulated edition by Luther's humanistic supporter Ulrich von Hutten (1488–1523) [Item 1.15]. This medieval document had represented itself as the act of a grateful Emperor Constantine (†337), granting to Pope Sylvester I (†335) authority over "the four principal sees, Antioch, Alexandria, Constantinople, and Jerusalem," as well as over Rome, thus over all five of the patriarchal centers of the church, and over the Roman Empire.[58] In his *De Monarchia* Dante had challenged the legal right of the emperor to make any such grant.[59] Others, including Cardinal Nicholas of Cusa (1401–64), as reprinted in Hutten's edition of Valla [Item 1.15:L3r–L5r], and Bishop Reginald Pecock (ca. 1393–1461), had attacked its authenticity. But it fell to Valla to apply the philological method of Renaissance humanism to the critical examination of the *Donation,* identifying anachronisms in its terminology and in its use of geographical nomenclature and thereby demonstrating that it could not be what it purported to be.[60] But what modifications, if any, were called for in this philological method when it was applied to the biblical text if, as Valla was contending, it was necessary to turn from the Latin Vulgate to the Greek original of the New Testament?

55. Second Vatican Council, Session VIII (18 November 1965), "Dei Verbum," Chapter 6, paragraph 22, Tanner 2:979.

56. Fueter 1911, 112.

57. See Gaeta 1955, 77–126: "La nuova filologia e il suo significato."

58. In Mirbt 1924, 110.

59. Bergin 1965, 192.

60. See the Introduction and Notes to Coleman 1922.

THE GREEK NEW TESTAMENT

Valla's *Collatio Novi Testamenti* of 1444 was not published in his lifetime but lay in the library of a Belgian monastery. There it was found, and printed at Paris in 1505 with the title *Annotationes in latinam Novi Testamenti interpretationem,* at the behest of Desiderius Erasmus, for whom this was "probably the most crucial book he ever read."[61] Just over a decade later there appeared the most crucial book Erasmus ever published, the *Novum instrumentum omne* of 1516 [Item 1.16], the first of the five succeeding editions of the Greek New Testament produced by him over the next two decades, the first two of which are included in the Catalog.[62] In April 1515 Johann Froben of Basel wrote to Erasmus, urging him to produce his long-contemplated edition of the New Testament in Greek. Basing his work only on the four Greek manuscripts available to him in Basel,[63] the earliest of these dating only to the twelfth century, Erasmus produced an edition that was, he acknowledged, "more accurately called 'rushed' than 'edited' [praecipitatum verius quam editum]." Nevertheless, this volume of 1516 was the first edition ever published — though not, technically speaking, the first ever printed[64] — of the Greek text of the New Testament, together with a Latin translation. This translation was not, however, an edition of the Vulgate, even of the Vulgate with textual emendations, but a new translation into Classical, Ciceronian Latin by Erasmus himself, which he appears to have completed even before editing the Greek. In addition, Erasmus included some *Annotationes* on several passages, which were an anticipation in miniature of the far more extensive annotations and paraphrases on various books of the New Testament that he was to go on publishing for the next two decades until his death in 1536. The edition of 1518–19, now called more conventionally *Novum Testamentum,* was likewise published in Basel by Johann Froben [Item 1.17]. It was a great improvement over the first, having the benefit both of additional (and better) manuscripts and of more time for its preparation.[65] In the subsequent history of the New Testament text, as Bo Reicke has said, "Erasmus would probably have enjoyed the ironic turn of fate if he had known that his edition of the text would have inspired first biblical orthodoxy and afterwards biblical philology in such diverse ways."[66]

In importance and influence second only to Erasmus as an editor of the Greek New Testament was Robert Estienne, mentioned earlier for his 1527–28 edition of the Vulgate

61. Louis Bouyer in Lampe 1969, 494; a brief summary of Erasmus's preface to it is in Bainton 1969, 65.

62. A brief and useful overview is that of Basil Hall in Greenslade 1963, 59–61.

63. Tarelli 1943, 155–62.

64. On the New Testament text in volume 5 of the Complutensian Polyglot, which was printed in 1514 but not released until later, see Catalog Item 1.25.

65. There is a succinct and helpful summary in Bedouelle and Roussel 1989, 74–77.

66. Reicke 1966, 262.

[Item 1.13]. His first Greek Bible, the *Novum Testamentum Graece* published at Paris in 1546, was in many ways a great improvement over the editions of Erasmus; but it was his *Novum Testamentum Graece* of 1550 [Item 1.18], which included the Johannine comma (1 Jn 5:7), that formed the basis of the Greek *Textus Receptus* for, among other translations, the Authorized Version of the English Bible (see Chapter 3), which therefore included this controversial variant.

THE CHRISTIAN RECOVERY OF THE "AUTHENTIC" OLD TESTAMENT

The application of the humanistic canons of sacred philology to the earlier and larger section of the Christian Bible entailed complexities that were in some significant respects much greater than those connected with the New Testament. For although there existed far fewer manuscripts of the Hebrew Bible and although these displayed far fewer textual variants, this relative simplification of the task of textual criticism was more than compensated for by several special characteristics and problems in what Christians called the Old Testament and what Jerome had called *Hebraica veritas*. At least three of these deserve special identification because of the importance they assumed in the Renaissance and the Reformation: the study of Hebrew, the status of the Septuagint, and the Old Testament canon.

The Study of Hebrew. The most evident problem was, of course, the Hebrew language. Although the Greek of the New Testament was not identical with the Attic Greek cultivated by the humanists, nor yet with the Byzantine Greek of their refugee mentors, anyone who had learned to read Plato or Sophocles could, with some adjustments to such lexicographical peculiarities as its Hebraisms and to such grammatical idiosyncrasies as the relative absence of the optative, handle the language of the apostle Paul or the Gospels (although the reverse was not the case, as has repeatedly been discovered by those who have fallen victim to the deplorable modern tendency in schools of theology to study only the Greek of the New Testament). But no similar prehistory or context was available to them for coping with Hebrew. The study of Hebrew by the humanists and the Reformers of the fifteenth and sixteenth centuries was in fact less of an innovation than is sometimes supposed. As Beryl Smalley has pointed out in discussing the twelfth and thirteenth centuries, "Hebrew, in fact, absorbed and must to some extent have distracted Bacon's contemporaries from the study of Greek."[67] For their knowledge of Hebrew and of rabbinic exegesis, medieval Christian scholars had been obliged to learn from Jewish scholars, as had Origen and Jerome before them.[68] The same was true now of Renaissance humanists, among whom the first important

67. Smalley 1964, 338.
68. Kelly 1975, 78, 150–51.

scholar of Hebrew was Johannes Reuchlin (1455–1522). His handbook of Hebrew study is entitled to the honor of being the first significant such work by a Christian scholar, despite the book, two or three years earlier, by the ex-Franciscan Konrad Pellikan (1478–1556), with whom Luther was to correspond while he was working on Psalm 22.[69] Reuchlin's *De rudimentis hebraicis* appeared at Pforzheim in 1506, presenting the Hebrew alphabet with approximate Latin equivalents, including instructions about pronunciation, for example of the ת: "Sibilus thau lingua inter superiores & inferiores dentes inserta & ore bleso" [Item 1.19:11]; it also included a Hebrew-Latin lexicon and a grammar of Hebrew, which "adopted the system of the Classical languages as a basis for the study of Hebrew."[70] It is a pleasant conceit of this pioneering manual that its pages are numbered in reverse, that is, from right to left à la a book in Hebrew. But with their Hebrew learning, Reuchlin and other Christian Hebraists also acquired from their rabbinical mentors an acquaintance with the mysteries of the Kabbalah, which through them "found its way into the Christian world as a 'philosophy' [and] was highly appreciated both as a style of speculation and as a repository of extremely important hermeneutics."[71] In his *De arte cabalistica* of 1517, dedicated to Pope Leo X (1475–1521), Reuchlin strove to make this mysticism of the Hebrew language — thus "sacred philology" in a special sense — palatable to Christian readers, for example by explaining the mysterious meaning of the divine name (Ex 3:14): אֶהְיֶה אֲשֶׁר אֶהְיֶה [Item 1.20:LXVIʳ]. The study of Hebrew proved to be a double-edged sword in its implications for Jewish-Christian relations, however; for it provided some Christian humanists with yet another instrument in the long and painful history of intolerance and anti-Semitism, as Christians could now claim superiority to Jews even in this previously arcane knowledge.[72] An important achievement in this recovery of Hebrew was the *Biblia Hebraica* of Sebastian Münster (1488–1552), which also played a significant role in the history of translation [Item 1.22]. The Christian use of Hebrew to replace the mistakes of the Vulgate was not confined to Protestants and their vernacular versions, for Santi Pagnini (1470–1541), an Italian Dominican, produced the first printed translation of the Bible into Latin from Hebrew and Greek [Item 1.23]; it was itself impeccably orthodox, but it was to play a significant part in the Bible translation of the celebrated Protestant heretic Michael Servetus (1509/11–53) [Item 3.24].

The Status of the Septuagint. A second problem was the status of the Septuagint translation, which, in a measure not matched even by the authority that would be assigned to the Vulgate

69. Luther to Konrad Pellikan, ii.1521, *WA Br* 2:273–74.

70. Kukenheim 1951, 109.

71. Idel 1988, 263.

72. Oberman 1992, 19–34.

by the decree of the fourth session of the Council of Trent, possessed what Ludwig Diestel terms "an unwarranted esteem" in the church.[73] Indeed, it could lay claim to divine inspiration, on the basis of the Jewish legend, narrated in the *Letter of Aristeas* and repeated by some of the church fathers, about its miraculous composition;[74] the first printed text of the *Letter of Aristeas* was incorporated into the Sweynheym-Pannartz Bible of 1471, the first Bible ever printed in Italy [Item 1.12]. In addition, it was the Greek Septuagint, not the Hebrew Bible in the original, that was the Bible of most of the New Testament writers, including the apostle Paul.[75] They had based their arguments on its translations — and even its mistranslations (for example, Mt 1:23 from Is 7:14 LXX, παρθένος; Heb 1:7 from Ps 104:4 LXX, ὁ ποιῶν τοὺς ἀγγέλους αὐτοῦ πνεύματα). A comparison of the Septuagint with the Hebrew shows that in some passages the Greek translators must have had a different tradition of the vocalization of the consonants or even a different consonantal text, so that it is possible to make emendations in the Hebrew on the basis of the Greek, albeit with great circumspection.[76] For example, at Psalm 110:3, the received Masoretic text of the Hebrew reads עַמְּךָ, "thy people," but the Septuagint translates μετὰ σοῦ, "with thee," which is also followed by the Vulgate's "tecum," evidently reflecting a vocalization of the Hebrew consonants as עִמְּךָ. In a distinct category were those readings in the Septuagint, such as Psalm 22:16, which Christian exegesis had been using for its special purposes from earliest times as proof for the Crucifixion of Christ, while accusing Jewish scribes of having expunged from their text the evidence that was so supportive of Christian claims.[77] Like the Greek text of the New Testament, to which it was often joined in the manuscript tradition, the Greek text of the Septuagint had acquired many hundreds of textual variants, and it, too, was in desperate need of critical editing. Although it was in the Eastern rather than in the Western church that the Septuagint had canonical status, it was in the West that the philological study of the Septuagint moved forward. In the first Sixtine Edition of the Septuagint, *Vetus Testamentum Iuxta Septuaginta,* which was published in Rome by Francisco Zannetti in 1587, the preface of Pope Sixtus solemnly declared: "Volumus, & sancimus ad Dei gloriam, & Ecclesiae vtilitatem, vt Vetus Graecum Testamentum iuxtà Septuaginta, ita recognitum & expolitum, ab omnibus recipiatur, ac retineatur, quo potissimum ad Latinae vulgatae editionis, & veterum Sanctorum Patrum intelligentiam vtantur" [Item 1.24:a4ᵛ].

To meet those several needs as they were perceived already in the third century, Origen of

---

73. Diestel 1869, 93; also 26.

74. See, for example, Augustine *De civitate Dei* XVIII.43, but also XV.11–13.

75. Michel 1972, 55–68.

76. Ziegler 1971, 590–614, is a learned summary of the author's lifetime of Septuagint research.

77. Pelikan 1971–89, 1:19–20.

Alexandria had compiled the massive *Hexapla,* which in six columns contained the Hebrew text, a Greek transliteration of the Hebrew text, and four Greek translations: that of Aquila, the Septuagint, that of Symmachus, and that of Theodotion.[78] Although this monument had long since been lost except for fragments, it served as a model that became more practicable with the invention of printing, leading to one of the towering achievements of biblical scholarship and sacred philology in the Spanish Renaissance: the Complutensian Polyglot, *Biblia Polyglotta,* edited by Cardinal Francisco Ximénez de Cisneros (1436–1517) and printed in Alcalá by the University of Complutum between 1514 and 1517 [Item 1.25].[79] Its fifth volume contained the Greek New Testament and, having come off the presses in 1514, must be accorded chronological priority; but because Erasmus had an exclusive license, his *Novum instrumentum omne* of 1516 was the first *published,* though not the first *printed,* the Complutensian volume not having been distributed until 1522 or so. It is interesting that at Psalm 22:16 [21:17 LXX], where the Septuagint has ὤρυξαν χεῖράς μου καὶ πόδας μου, and the Vulgate "foderunt manus meas et pedes meos" (reflected in the AV's "they pierced my hands and my feet"), the reading of the Complutensian Hebrew text corresponds to the Christian, which read the text as כָּאֲרוּ ("they have pierced") rather than כָּאֲרִי ("like a lion"), as the rabbinic tradition preferred [Item 1.25:2:B1ᵛ]. In his explanation of this word, John Calvin noted that "today all the Hebrew books agree on this reading" of כָּאֲרִי, but he set it forth as "a probable conjecture that this passage was fraudulently corrupted by the Jews," and he quoted the Septuagint as proof for this emendation of the Hebrew [Item 2.10:99].[80] The format of the polyglot Bible continued to hold an appeal, and in whole or in part went on being published: the *Psalterium* published at Genoa by Pietro Paolo Porro in 1516 is a fine example [Item 1.26]. As a critical edition of the several texts in several languages, the most highly esteemed of the polyglot compilations is the London Polyglot of 1657, which included the Ethiopic and Persian texts [Item 1.27].[81]

The Old Testament Canon. A third difficulty, which became obvious from even a superficial comparison of the Septuagint with the Hebrew, was the very scope of the biblical canon; for the Septuagint contained several books — Apocryphal as Protestants have tended to call them, or Deuterocanonical as Roman Catholics have tended to call them — that were absent from the Hebrew. Being a scholar of the Hebrew, Jerome had denied them equal status; this

---

78. Field 1875.

79. On the Complutensian Polyglot see Lyell 1917, 24–52.

80. *CR* 9:228.

81. Let me add a personal note here: the first Septuagint and the first Vulgate I ever owned (both of them, to be sure, sans Apocrypha) were part of the *Polyglottenbibel zum praktischen Handgebrauch,* edited in five volumes between 1871 and 1894 by R. Stier and K. G. W. Theile, and given to me by my father when I entered seminary in 1942.

was, as Patrick Skehan has noted, "the one point on which the Church has not followed the formal teaching of her greatest Scriptural Doctor."[82] Augustine, by contrast, had accepted their authority, acknowledging that they were "regarded as canonical, not by the Jews, but by the church."[83] Throughout the Middle Ages these conflicting tables of contents had coexisted and interacted, but the Christian rediscovery of the "original" Old Testament in Hebrew and the printing of the Hebrew Bible made the issue more acute in the age of the Reformation. On both philological and theological grounds, Protestants characterized the Apocrypha as, in Luther's phrase, "not to be equated with Holy Scripture and yet useful and good to read" [Item 3.6:A1ʳ]. Also at stake was the question of the authority of the church to fix the canon of Scripture, with the Roman Catholic defenders of that authority charging that the principle of *sola Scriptura* was an argument in a circle because it depended on a prior definition of the canon by the church, and the Protestant critics of that authority maintaining that it had elevated the human opinions of bishops and councils to a level with the infallible word of God. In addition, the disputed books provided some of the best proof texts in support of such practices as the invocation of the saints and prayers for the dead, which tended to confirm the opinion of both sides about them.[84] Neither in the Augsburg Confession of 1530 nor even in the Formula of Concord of 1577 did the Lutheran Reformers go on record with a stated list of canonical books, although their position was clear from their introductions to the Bible and from their commentaries (not, however, altogether from their preaching, because they did go on basing occasional sermons on the Apocrypha, which they also went on printing, though as a separate section, in their Bibles). But at its fourth session [Item 1.28], the Council of Trent listed all the books of the canon individually, including the Deuterocanonical ones, identifying "as sacred and canonical these entire books and all their parts as they have, by established custom, been read in the catholic church, and as contained in the old Latin Vulgate edition."[85] Partly in response to Trent but also in keeping with their own definition of authority, confessions of faith in the Reformed and Calvinist tradition — which, for this purpose, must include Article 6 of the *Thirty-nine Articles* of the Anglican Church [Item 1.29] — rejected the canonicity of the disputed books and listed the narrower, "Palestinian" canon as containing "those Canonical bookes of the olde and newe Testament, of whose aucthooritie was neuer any doubt in the Churche."[86] Once again, the argument proceeded on grounds of theology, of Jewish usage, and of sacred philology — all at the same time — and thus it can be said to have led not only to the "Reformation of the Bible," but to its re-formation as well.

82. Skehan 1952, 259.

83. Augustine *De civitate Dei* XVIII.36.

84. Pelikan 1971–89, 4:209–10, 261, 263–67, 275–76.

85. Tanner 2:663–64.

86. Schaff 3:489–90.

Portrait of Martin Luther by Hans Baldung Grien. From Martin Luther, *Postil, oder vsleg der Epistel vnd Euangelien* (1522). See Item 2.4.

2 : Exegesis and Hermeneutics

Sacred philology was not an end in itself, not even for the most bookish and pedantic of Renaissance humanists, much less for Reformation theologians. "Te totum applica ad textum, rem totam applica ad te [Apply yourself totally to the text, apply its content totally to yourself]!": this winged word from the preface to the critical edition of the Greek New Testament by Johann Albrecht Bengel (1687–1752), an heir both of Reformation theology and of Renaissance sacred philology, has long served as the epigraph for the widely used Nestle edition of the Greek New Testament published by the Privilegierte Württembergische Bibelanstalt in Stuttgart. Whatever new insights into Hebrew grammar or Greek lexicography may have come from the scholars of the fifteenth and sixteenth centuries, their biblical scholarship had as its goal to derive meaning from the text — indeed, *the* meaning of the text, which each of them believed could be found, and had been found by him — and to communicate that meaning both to other scholars and theologians and to the church.[1]

What the Reformers claimed to have discovered in their study of the Bible, therefore, was not a philological insight as such, nor a historical fact as such (although it was also, to be sure, both of these), but the meaning of the Christian gospel; for it was their conviction that "the authority of a text . . . is identical with the understanding of the text," and that it could not exist apart from that understanding.[2] "Hoc est Christum cognoscere, beneficia eius cognoscere [To know Christ is to know his benefits]" was the admonition of the humanist-cum-Reformer Philipp Melanchthon, in the first systematic theology of the Reformation, his *Loci communes* of 1521 [Item 2.7],[3] which was derived from his lectures on the Epistle to the Romans, eventually published in 1522 [Item 2.8]. Similarly, as one of the wisest interpreters of another humanist-cum-Reformer, John Calvin, has summarized, "Calvin's great resource was his familiarity with the Bible and mastery of its contents. . . . His talents, training, and religious

---

1. Shuger 1994, 18–29, on "philological exegesis."
2. Grane 1975, 64.
3. *CR* 21:85.

feeling for the meaning of Scripture were such that much of his interpretation defies the acids of modern critical research."[4] Meanwhile, the Radical Reformation, as its most influential interpreter has noted, "stood for the most part with the classical Magisterial Reformation and was indeed largely dependent upon it in the recovery of the Bible and in the rejection of the medieval synthesis of Scripture, Tradition, and papal authority."[5] And the leading Thomist in the sixteenth century, who had negotiated with Luther in 1518, the Dominican Cardinal Cajetan — Tommaso de Vio (1469–1534) — had already expressed his long-standing scholarly and theological interest in biblical exegesis in his *Jentacula novi testamenti* of 1525 [Item 2.9]. The fourth chapter of this collection of exegetical disquisitions had, for example, examined the Vulgate of the Beatitudes of the Sermon on the Mount in the light of the standard medieval explanation of them as "counsels of perfection," not to be attained fully until the life to come, suggesting that "the perfections that are set forth as 'beatitudes' function in the present life as objectives [*perfectiones iste que vt beatitudines proponuntur sunt in presenti vita vt fines*]" [Item 2.9:42ʳ]. In his later years Cajetan developed many exegetical opinions that brought upon him the criticism of the traditionalists for being closer to the views of the Protestant Reformers than to those of the medieval scholastics.[6] Thus each major branch of the Reformation was, in one sense or another, what we are calling here a Reformation of the Bible, and whatever else the Reformation (or these several Reformations) may be said to have been, it was a major event in the history of the interpretation of the Bible, and it needs to be studied that way.[7] Reformation expositions of Scripture fall into several categories: learned expositions using Greek and Hebrew, annotated Bibles, sermonic expositions of individual passages or of entire sections or books of Scripture, and Bible histories and "biblical theologies."

SCRIPTURE AND TRADITION

When a medieval theologian approached the Sacred Page, he did so with the consciousness that he was only the latest in a long series of biblical expositors from previous centuries in the history of the church; thus the earliest Latin Bible printed with glosses [Item 2.1] included the *Glossa ordinaria* of a ninth-century commentary on the words of Christ to Peter (Mt 16:18–20): "Thou art Peter, and on this rock I will build my church; and the gates of hell shall not prevail against it." Therefore the recipient of the medieval academic degree of *Magister in Sacra Pagina*

---

4. McNeill 1954, 213.

5. Williams 1992, 1242.

6. *PRE*³ 3:632–34.

7. Holl [1920] 1948, 544–82, and Ebeling 1942 are two of the most fundamental such studies, to which Pelikan 1959 is deeply indebted.

(Master of the Sacred Page), which, for example, was conferred on Thomas Aquinas in 1256, carried on an activity "which, by definition, had only a measure of originality," as Père Chenu has described it, but which in Thomas's case "must certainly have extended over the whole of his teaching career since commenting on the Bible was the prime task of the master in theology."[8] Out of his many sets of exegetical works, the most influential was the *Catena Aurea super quattuor evangelistas* — or, as he himself called it, *Expositio continua in Matthaeum, Marcum, Lucam et Johannem,* which dates from 1262–64; our examples, all from the "cradle of printing," document its popularity in the Renaissance [Item 2.2]. The "measure of originality" in this work was, at one level, absolutely nil, for the book consisted entirely of Thomas's compilation of quotations from patristic and other sources in explanation of the text of the four Gospels. But there was a significant element of originality nevertheless; for those patristic sources extended beyond the customary dependence on Augustine and other Latin fathers to include newly available writings of the Greek church fathers, who were assuming a new importance because of the efforts connected with the upcoming Council of Lyons in 1274 to repair the schism between East and West. "That this commentary may be more complete and have more continuity," Aquinas explained in the dedication of the second part, "I have had many works of the Greek doctors translated into Latin, and I have added extracts of them to the commentaries of the Latins, being careful to place the names of the authors before their testimonies."[9] It is instructive and striking to compare the exegetical method at work in the *Catena Aurea super quattuor evangelistas* of Thomas Aquinas with that of a Reformation commentary which initially appears to be somewhat similar, but which on closer inspection proves to be dramatically different: the *Harmonia ex tribus Evangelistis composita, Matthaeo, Marco et Luca: adiuncto seorsum Iohanne, quod pauca cum aliis communia habeat / cum Iohannis Calvini Commentariis* [Item 2.11]. Both Thomas and Calvin were convinced that the accounts in the several Gospels do not contradict each other, and in this sense they were following one whom each of them, albeit for rather divergent reasons, claimed as his master, Augustine, who had written "the first comprehensive treatment of this problem," *De consensu Evangelistarum libri IV.*[10] But that is essentially where the similarity ends. For example, in explaining the statement of Christ to Peter, Aquinas in the *Catena Aurea,* on the basis of Augustine,[11] conceded that "Peter" could be a figurative name for the church, or that "the rock was Christ, whom Peter confessed" [Item 2.2(1493):67r]. But for Calvin this concession took the polemical turn that because "non alibi posse fundari Ecclesiam quam in Christo solo," it followed that "non sine sacrilega blasphemia aliud

---

8. Chenu 1964, 243; the entire section "Magister in Sacra Pagina," 242–49, is very helpful.

9. Translation from Chenu 1964, 249.

10. Merkel 1971, 218.

11. Augustine *Retractationes* 51.

fundamentum Papa commentus est. Et certe quantopere vel vno hoc nomine tyrannidem Papatus detestari nos deceat, nullis verbis exprimi satis potest, quod in eius gratiam sublatum fuerit Ecclesiae fundamentum, vt apertus inferni gurges miseras animas absorbeat" [Item 2.11:258].[12]

In addition to the legacy of the church fathers, however, other exegetical traditions were at work already in the Middle Ages, which then in the age of the Reformation would supply some of the context for the interpretation of the Bible. Among these, none is more intriguing than the rabbinic tradition.[13] As noted in Chapter 1, Jerome and Origen had been instructed by rabbis. For Reformation exegesis, however, the most important source of information about the rabbinic tradition was the Franciscan Nicholas of Lyra (ca. 1270–1349), who has been characterized by a modern reference book as nothing short of "the best-equipped Biblical scholar of the Middle Ages"[14] and who was also useful in the Reformation's turn to the literal sense of Scripture. Between 1350 and 1450 seven hundred manuscripts of his *Postilla litteralis* were produced, in whole or in part, and it was the first commentary on the Bible to be printed, at Rome in 1471–72 and several times soon thereafter [Item 2.3]. Because of his ample citations from rabbinic exegetes, notably from Rashi — Rabbi Salomo ben Isaac (1040–1105) — as a result of which he came to be called (unfairly) "Rashi's ape,"[15] Nicholas of Lyra became a valuable resource in the Reformation's study of the Hebrew Bible, to, for example, Martin Luther. During the editing of the eight volumes of the English translation of Luther's *Lectures on Genesis* from 1535 to 1545 in the American Edition of *Luther's Works,* consequently, it was necessary to keep Lyra continually at hand, in order to identify not only the many explicit references to Lyra but the unacknowledged borrowings by Luther — or perhaps by the compilers of Luther's *Lectures on Genesis*[16] — from this source. Thus it would seem to have been from Lyra's account of "the many ways in which the Jews attempt to subvert the interpretation" of Genesis 49:10 as a prophecy of the coming of Christ [Item 2.3:ad locum] (as well as from other sources) that Luther learned about the rabbinic exegesis that he refuted in his account of this verse.[17] Nevertheless, this process of editing the *Lectures on Genesis* in English translation has also confirmed how much of an exaggeration, indeed a *dicton absurde,*[18] it is to say, in the doggerel verse of Luther's detractors, that "Si Lyra non lyrasset, Lutherus non

---

12. *CR* 45:476.

13. Smalley 1964, 149–72, is basic.

14. *ODCC* 972; see the trenchant account of Lubac 1959–64, 2/2:344–67.

15. Hailperin 1963, 145.

16. Meinhold 1936 is the most complete investigation of the question; but see Pelikan 1959, 90–91.

17. *WA* 44:753–59; *LW* 8:238–45.

18. Smalley 1964, xvi.

saltasset [If Lyra had not played his lyre, Luther would not have danced]"; for the most impressive feature of Luther's exposition of Genesis, whether it be construed as a strength or a weakness, is its originality in comparison with patristic and medieval exegetes, including Nicholas of Lyra, not its dependence on any of them.[19] A vast amount of learning and lore from this tradition was collected and printed in the *Magna Biblia Rabbinica* first published at Venice by Daniel Bomberg in 1516–17, which contained the Bible in pointed Hebrew but the rabbinic materials in unpointed text [Item 1.21].

Both the patristic tradition and the rabbinic tradition, as mediated also through medieval thought, thus made their mark on the Reformation interpretation of the Bible. But it is a commonplace of the theological and historical literature, going back to the Protestant Reformers themselves, that the sole authority of Scripture, sola Scriptura, was one of the fundamental principles of Reformation theology, to which the authority of tradition had to yield, and that therefore the Reformers no longer regarded Scripture and tradition as two sources of divine revelation, nor even as a single source in two modalities.[20] The confusions at work in this conventional wisdom have received helpful clarification through Heiko Oberman's distinction between "two concepts of Tradition. . . . We call the single-source or exegetical tradition held together with its interpretation 'Tradition I' and the two-sources theory which allows for an extra-biblical oral tradition 'Tradition II.'"[21] With the implications of this issue of Scripture and tradition for the doctrine of authority and for the defense of the catholicity of the church in Reformation teaching we cannot be concerned directly here,[22] but only with its bearing on the theory and practice of biblical exegesis. As the earlier comparison between Aquinas and Calvin in the exegesis of the Gospels suggests, it truly was the case, according to Luther and Calvin, that compiling or counting votes from the church fathers did not decide the meaning of a passage of Scripture contrary to its clear grammatical and literal sense, and therefore that even Tradition I had a limited claim of authority, while Tradition II was a presumptuous arrogation of the authority of the Bible to fallible human beings, "teaching for doctrines the commandments of men," as stated in a passage from the Gospels and originally from the prophets (Mt 15:9; Is 29:13 LXX) that Calvin and the other Reformers quoted against such presumption.[23] Thus at the Leipzig Debate of 1519, Luther's opponent Johann Eck (1486–1543) marshaled some of the same evidence of tradition from the church fathers and the canonists that appears in the *Catena Aurea* to support his interpretation that

---

19. Pelikan 1959, 89–108; see 89, n 1.

20. Holl [1920] 1948, 558–63; Pelikan 1959, 71–88 — both with representative quotations from Luther.

21. Oberman 1963, 371; also 390–93.

22. Pelikan 1971–89, 4:262–74.

23. Calvin *Institutes* IV.10.23–24 (*CR* 2:884–86; McNeill 2:1201–3).

Matthew 16:18 pertained to the Church of Rome, but Luther refused to be bound by that exegetical tradition.[24] Similarly, Heinrich Bullinger of Zurich (1504–75), in the seventy-fourth of his *Hvndred Sermons vpon the Apocalips of Iesu Christe,* which was translated from German into English during his lifetime and published at London in 1561, defied the entire medieval exegetical tradition to identify the Whore of Babylon in chapter 17 of the Book of Revelation as "the very citie of Rome, and euen the popish and Romish church, and the pope himself with all his creatures and chapplaynes" [Item 2.12:510].

THE REPUDIATION OF ALLEGORISM

In 1512 Martin Luther, monk of the Augustinian Order of Hermits, received the degree of *Doctor in Biblia,* in obedience to his religious superiors.[25] This degree provided him with the academic credentials, but the oath he took upon receiving the degree also imposed on him the official responsibility, to engage in the exposition of Scripture as a professor at the recently established University of Wittenberg. Years later, he would invoke that official responsibility as the moral obligation that had made him a reformer of the church. In his *Commentary on Psalm 82* of 1530, for instance, posing the question being raised by his opponents, "Why do you, by your books, teach throughout the world, when you are only preacher in Wittenberg?" he replied: "I have never wanted to do it and do not want to do it now. I was forced and driven into this position in the first place when I had to become Doctor of Holy Scripture against my will. Then, as a doctor in a general free university, I began, at the command of pope and emperor, to do what such a doctor is sworn to do, expounding the Scriptures for all the world and teaching everybody. Once in this position, I have had to stay in it, and I cannot give it up or leave it yet with a good conscience."[26]

Clearly, one of the major differences between being a Magister in Sacra Pagina in the medieval context and being a Doctor in Biblia in the Reformation context was a changed definition of hermeneutics, the art and science of interpretation. Gerald L. Bruns has formulated that difference sharply in *Hermeneutics Ancient and Modern:*

> If one were to look for a symbolic moment of transition between ancient and modern hermeneutics, one might choose the winter semester of 1513–14, when Martin Luther began preparing his first lectures as professor of theology at the University of Wittenberg. He was to lecture on the Psalms and wanted each of his students to have a copy of the scriptural text to consult. Luther therefore instructed Johann Grunenberg, the printer for

24. *WA* 2:272, 286–87.

25. Steinlein 1912, especially 22–33.

26. *WA* 31/1:212; *LW* 13:66.

the university, to produce an edition of the Psalter with wide margins and lots of white space between the lines. Here the students would reproduce Luther's own glosses and commentary, and perhaps (who knows?) they would have room for their own exegetical reflections as well. At all events Luther produced for his students something like a modern, as opposed to a medieval, text of the Bible — its modernity consisting precisely in the white space around the text. In a stroke Luther wiped the Sacred Page clean as if to begin the history of interpretation over again, this time to get it right.[27]

Fortunately, this Copernican revolution in hermeneutics brought about by Luther and the Reformation was able, as Karl Holl has said, to find "in the second generation a successor who managed to grasp by intuition what [Luther] in his genius had achieved and to work it up into a technical methodology of interpretation,"[28] Matija Vlačić-Ilirik, or as he was usually known by his Latinized name, Matthias Flacius Illyricus (1520–75).[29] This "technical methodology of interpretation" he systematized in his masterful, if nearly impenetrable, work, *Clavis scripturae sacrae seu de sermone sacrarum literarum,* first published in 1567 in two massive volumes [Item 2.14].[30] Medieval hermeneutics was dominated by a reliance on, and a quest for, the multiple sense of Scripture. Eventually the theory of the many senses was codified in the concept of the fourfold sense; its development has been definitively studied by Henri de Lubac, who quotes a Latin verse that summarizes the fundamental assumption of the "mystical" sense:

> Hujus festi sacramentum
> Licet per integumentum
> Et figurae velamentum
> Sparsim vetus Testamentum
>   Mystice significat.[31]

Or, in the standard verse formula, elaborating all four senses,

> Littera gesta docet. quid credat allegoria.
> Moralis quid agat. quo tendat anagogia.

---

27. Bruns 1992, 139–40.

28. Holl [1920] 1948, 578.

29. Mirković 1980, 2:160–63, on his "independent contribution to linguistics [samostalni Vlačićev prinos lingvistici]."

30. Moldaenke 1936 is still the most authoritative study of Flacius and of the *Clavis,* but recent attention to hermeneutics, also among literary scholars, would suggest the need for further investigation.

31. Lubac 1959–64, 2/2:208.

Thus, in the example usually given, the name "Jerusalem" referred in the literal sense to the physical "metropolis in the kingdom of Judea," in the moral sense to "the faithful soul," in the allegorical sense to "the church militant," and in the anagogical sense to "the church trium-phant" [Item 2.3:1:(2ʳ)]. By breaking with this fourfold sense in order "this time to get it right," the Reformers strove to come up with an interpretation that was (to cite some of the various ways it could be designated) grammatical, literal, and historical, but not — or at least not necessarily and not usually — allegorical.

The Grammatical Sense. In the hermeneutics and exegesis of the Reformation, the sacred philol-ogy of the Renaissance became part of the standard equipment of the theologian and even of the parish pastor and preacher. As reformers of education no less than reformers of the church, such figures as Melanchthon (to whom the title Preceptor of Germany was soon applied), Calvin, and Calvin's colleague and Academy successor, Théodore de Bèze (1519–1605), recast the curriculum of the secondary schools along humanistic lines, requiring not only Latin but also Greek and Hebrew and requiring them, moreover, not only of future clergy but of laymen. Students were, therefore, expected to come to the study of theology and specifically to the exegesis of Scripture with the requisite philological and grammatical prepa-ration for the responsible scrutiny of the Bible in its original languages. The annotations attached to the *Testamentum Novvm* of Bèze, which was published at Geneva by Henri Estienne in 1565 and then in 1589, were in the first instance grammatical and lexicographical [Item 2.13], as was the entire first volume of the *Clavis* of Flacius. For example, as Lorenzo Valla had already pointed out, the Pauline characterization of matrimony by the Greek word μυστήριον (Eph 5:32) — the term employed in the Greek Orthodox tradition for "sacrament" — did not, as the Vulgate translation "Sacramentum hoc magnum est" implied, rank it with Baptism, the Eucharist, and the other sacraments of the church (whichever and howsoever many these may have been), even though matrimony was in fact the only one of the seven to be explicitly so designated in the New Testament.[32] Hence Flacius concluded on the basis of these words from Ephesians: "Nowhere in Holy Writ is this word 'sacrament' employed in the strict sense in which it is now used, to refer to the sacred ritual of Baptism and the Eucharist" [Item 2.14(1628):1:1061]. This was, therefore, a qualified answer of yes to the question cited in Chapter 1 from such humanists as Valla as to whether the explication of the biblical text was governed by the same philological principles as that of any other text. For whatever else the explication of the biblical text had to be in addition — above all of course the Chris-tianized explication of the biblical text of the Hebrew Bible, which Jewish exegesis was explaining in a radically different fashion — it could not be less than grammatical.

---

32. Pelikan 1971–89, 4:308–9, 257, 295; 3:209–14.

The Literal Sense. In Reformation exegesis the terms "grammatical sense" and "literal sense" sometimes appeared to be virtually interchangeable, especially when it was disengaging itself from medieval allegorical exegesis or associating itself with the increased emphasis on the literal sense practiced by Nicholas of Lyra and his *Postilla litteralis.* But the adherence of the Reformers to the literal sense was never as simple as that. In his *Institutes of the Christian Religion,* therefore, Calvin attacked medieval exegesis (as well as the kind of Protestant exegesis that appeared to him to be slavishly following medieval exegesis), not this time for its allegorism but for its excessive literalism in the interpretation of the words of institution of the Eucharist, "This is my body."[33] Conversely, Luther, who was at least the indirect target of this criticism — the direct target being the Lutheran polemicist Joachim Westphal (1510–74) — attacked his opponents, Roman Catholic and especially Protestant, for being excessively literal in their exegesis of the biblical term "the right hand of God," which, he insisted, must be freed of its literal and spatial connotations, not to mention its anthropomorphic ones.[34] An additional stipulation to the term "literal sense" pertained especially to the exegesis of the Old Testament and is summarized in Luther's concept of the literal-prophetic sense.[35] Thus in an exegesis of the fifty-third chapter of Isaiah that its English translator, Leroy Nixon, has aptly entitled *The Gospel According to Isaiah,* Calvin simply took it for granted that "the Prophet speaks in the same manner as Saint Paul spoke from him" and that the only acceptable exegetical method was to "join what is proposed in Saint Matthew with what the Prophet Isaiah wished to affirm."[36] He defended the thesis that when the New Testament applied these verses to an event that occurred many centuries after the verses were written by Isaiah, that is, to the suffering and death of Christ (Mt 8:17; Acts 8:26–35; 1 Pt 2:21–25), this meant that "the prophet, in His Name, speaks of the total situation of our Lord Jesus Christ."[37] This was not a figurative use, much less an allegorical interpretation, but was in fact "the intention of the Prophet [l'intention du Prophete]"[38] and the meaning of these verses all along, hence the only way they could be taken. Similarly, because Christ on the cross had quoted from Psalm 22:1, albeit in Aramaic or "Chaldaean" (Mt 27:46; Mk 15:34), that — and only that — was, in Luther's phrase, the "literal prophetic meaning" of that psalm, which implied (in relation to the example cited in Chapter 1) that the Hebrew of Psalm 22:16, as a reference to the history of the Crucifixion, should read כָּאֲרוּ, not כָּאֲרִי.

---

33. Calvin *Institutes* IV.xvii.23 (*CR* 2:1021–22; McNeill 2:1388–90).

34. Pelikan 1959, 148–51.

35. Bornkamm 1969, 87–101.

36. *CR* 35:672, 629–30; Nixon 1953, 112, 57.

37. *CR* 35:617; Nixon 1953, 41.

38. *CR* 35:631; Nixon 1953, 59.

The Historical Sense. But could this also be termed the "historical sense" of Psalm 22, and did the Hebrew text of the Bible possess any meaning within its own historical context, a meaning that the contemporaries of the psalmists and the prophets could understandably and legitimately have attributed to it, prior to and apart from its christological interpretation? Despite the great preponderance of the messianic interpretation, there are occasional hints in Reformation exegesis of an identification of this kind of "historical sense," as for example in Luther's interpretation of Psalm 111.[39] More usually, however, the historical sense referred to what I have elsewhere called the Reformers' interest in "the history of the people of God."[40] According to the chronologies compiled by the Reformers, the history narrated in the New Testament covered only one century, from the birth of Christ to the death of his "beloved apostle," Saint John the Divine (identified as the author of the Fourth Gospel, the three Catholic Epistles bearing his name, and the Apocalypse), whereas the history narrated in the Old Testament covered several millennia, from the creation of the world to the last of the prophets:[41] the "Chronologia Sacra" of the London Polyglot [Item 1.27:1ESup:] follows the chronology of one of its contributors, Archbishop James Ussher (1581–1656), in dating the death of Antiochus Epiphanes (1 Mc 6:16), which took place in 164 BCE, at 3940 in the history of the world. Quantitatively at any rate, therefore, the history of the people of God referred above all to the history of the patriarchs and the history of Israel. Although individual commentaries on the historical books of the Old Testament such as Kings and Chronicles were greatly outnumbered by commentaries on Genesis, the Psalms, and the Prophets — just as within the New Testament, for that matter, commentaries on the Book of Acts were far less frequent than commentaries on the Gospels and the Pauline Epistles — the attention to the historical sense led to an effort to do justice to the historical framework of the prophetical books. The typological use of Jonah's three days in the belly of the whale as an event prophetic of the resurrection of Christ, which had the highest possible warrant in Christ's own words in the Gospel (Mt 12:40), was not to be permitted to reduce the rest of the history of Jonah and the city of Nineveh to mere scenery. For the history, according to Luther, "eyn tref-flichs/ sonderlichs/ tröstlichs exempel des glaubens/ vnd ein gros mechtigs wunderzeychen gottlicher guete/ aller welt fur tregt" [Item 2.6:A2ᵛ];[42] by contrast, Luther was quite prepared to accept the explanation of the Book of Judith as "kein geschicht/ sondern ein geistlich schöne gedicht" [Item 3.6:A1ᵛ].[43] Calvin's explanation of the harmony of the Gospels, in

---

39. See my introductory comments, *LW* 15:xii.

40. Pelikan 1959, 89–108.

41. *WA* 53:22–184.

42. *WA* 19:186; *LW* 19:36.

43. *WA DB* 12:4–6; *LW* 35:338–39.

which several Reformers of the second and third generations followed his example,[44] reflected this same methodology of taking sacred history seriously and yet critically *as history*. Therefore it was an "extremely trivial and frivolous argument [nimis leve ac friuolum argumentum]" [Item 2.11:84][45] to take the Sermon on the Mount in Matthew 5 and the Sermon on the Plain in Luke 6 as separate accounts. Christ told parables, not all of which necessarily had to be true stories; but he did not live a parable, because the accounts in the Gospels did have to be true stories.[46] Similarly, the history of Abraham — his journey to an unknown land, his visions of the Almighty, and above all the Akedah, the Binding of Isaac — carried an impact that had the makings of high drama, as Théodore de Bèze's play of 1550, *Abraham Sacrifiant* [Item 4.11], showed both on the page and on the stage[47] (and as, three centuries later, Søren Kierkegaard's "knight of infinite resignation" was to show again). But for Reformation exegesis it was real history before it became drama.[48]

A Limited but Legitimate Allegorical Sense. Yet the Bible itself said about that history of Abraham, in its only use of the technical term, "which things are an allegory [ἅτινά ἐστιν ἀλληγορούμενα]" (Gal 4:24). It said this, moreover, not in some obscure passage but in the Reformers' own beloved Epistle to the Galatians.[49] For a long time in the history of Christian exegesis, indeed even in the exegetical practice of Judaism before the rise of Christianity, the crucial test case for this issue of allegorical interpretation had been not the history of Abraham but the Song of Songs. This was not a question of imposing an allegory on a primary sense of the sacred text that was literal or historical; but, as Ann Matter has put it, "the inclusion of the Song of Songs in the [Jewish] canon of Scripture was based on the assumption of a recognized and accepted allegorical reading," and it was already as an allegory that it came from the Jewish canon into the Christian canon of Scripture, and as an allegory that it had been consistently read in Christian exegesis.[50] An exegesis that was consistently and rigorously "grammatical, literal, and historical" would have to read the erotic language of this poem, with its highly explicit attention to sexual love, as the celebration of the physical union between a man and a woman. In the history of monastic exegesis, the Song, read of course as an allegory, had been "the book which was most read, and most frequently commented in the medieval cloister," as

44. Theodor Zahn in *PRE*³ 5:653–61.

45. *CR* 45:160.

46. Köhler 1917 is a delightful collection of quotations on this subject.

47. Shuger 1994, 160–62; see also Jeffrey 1992, 380 (Camille R. LaBossière).

48. Lerch 1950, 156–202; see especially 158–63 on "das Einmalige" in the narrative.

49. See Luther's attempt to deal with this by reducing it to "a kind of illumination of an oration or of a case that has already been established on other grounds" (*WA* 40/1:657; *LW* 26:433–34).

50. Matter 1990, 51.

Dom Leclercq has said.[51] But a close reading of medieval exegesis of the Song, for example that of Bernard of Clairvaux (1090–1153), has demonstrated that, contrary to the Reformers' disparagement of allegory as arbitrary and subjectivist, it proceeded by explicit rules, which did significantly limit what the exegete could or could not do with the text. When the Reformers turned to the Song, even they could not have interpreted it literally and yet have been able to justify its retention in the biblical canon; and when Sebastian Castellio (1515–63) did take it literally, that was one of the grounds for Calvin's attack. With the exception of the Mariological interpretation that had become quite popular in the twelfth and thirteenth centuries,[52] each of the possible variations on the theme of its allegorical application found resonance somewhere in Reformation exegesis:[53]

(a) the interpretation of the Song as a loving exchange in which, as the heading of the first chapter in the King James Version explains [Item 3.14(OT):Lll4ʳ], "the Church and Christ congratulate one another," an interpretation that is reflected in the illustration and description provided by Corrozet's verses in *Icones historiarum Veteris Testamenti,* where the theme of the Song is said to be

> Salomon Roy au liure des Cantiques
> Propos d'amy uers une amie expose,
> L'amour couurant soubz parolles mystiques
> De Christ enuers l'Eglise son espouse [Item 4.6(1547):K4ᵛ];

(b) the mystical reading of it as the dialogue of the soul with Christ, which had been "a secondary possibility for the text throughout the long tradition of ecclesiological exegesis" in the Middle Ages but "came into its own in the twelfth century,"[54] and which then found an echo in Reformation hymnody and devotional literature, for example in the well-loved eucharistic hymn "Schmücke dich, o liebe Seele," which has been characterized as "perhaps the finest of all German hymns for the Holy Communion,"[55] and in the Bach cantata "Wachet auf" (*BWV* 140), the major portion of which, apart from the chorale, consists of a loving exchange between Christ as Bridegroom and the soul as bride;[56]

(c) the transfer of the venue of the Song to the covenantal relation between God and Israel, as "a song in which Solomon . . . gives [God] thanks for his divinely established and

---

51. Leclercq 1962, 90.

52. Astell 1990, 48–50.

53. Pope 1977, 89–229, "Interpretations of the Sublime Song," is a historical account rich in detail.

54. Matter 1990, 123.

55. Julian [1907] 1957, 1014.

56. It has been closely analyzed by Jost Casper in Petzoldt 1985, 49–76.

confirmed kingdom and government," an exegesis that can perhaps be seen as express-ing the determination that, if there had to be an allegorical exegesis, it nevertheless would be just as historical as possible.[57]

Distinguishing between typology and allegory [Item 2.14(1628):2:341–42], Flacius system-atized the Reformation approach to allegory by identifying three reasons that could prompt the necessity of invoking it: "when the Scriptures present a falsity unless you accept the presence of a trope"; "when the words of Scripture taken in the grammatical sense produce an absurdity"; "when the grammatical sense conflicts with sound doctrine or is opposed to proper morality" [Item 2.14(1628):2:76–77].

THE ANALOGY OF FAITH

That third stipulation of sound doctrine or proper morality by Flacius indicates that although the Reformers rejected simultaneously both the binding authority of tradition and the validity of unbridled allegorization, this was significantly qualified, above all in their exegetical practice but even in their hermeneutical theory, by another principle: *analogia fidei,* the analogy of faith. The original provenance of this phrase was biblical, in the prescription of the apostle Paul that prophesying be κατὰ τὴν ἀναλογίαν τῆς πίστεως (Rom 12:6). This is the only passage of the New Testament to employ the Greek word ἀναλογία, "analogy" or "proportion," which by its appearance (in the adverbial form ἀναλόγως) in such an influential passage of the Apocrypha as Wisdom 13:5 had provided part of the biblical justification for natural theology in patristic thought.[58] But no less crucial in determining the meaning of this prescription is the other Greek word, ἡ πίστις, "faith" or "*the* faith" with a definite article. Does it apply here to the act or state of believing, the subjective *fides qua creditur* as the heirs of the Reformation would call it, as it apparently does in Romans 10:17, the passage that was the origin of the Reformation emphasis on *fides ex auditu*?[59] Or does it apply to the object of faith and the content of the act of believing, the objective *fides quae creditur,* as Jude 3 speaks of it when referring to "the faith once delivered to the saints [τῇ ἅπαξ παραδοθείσῃ τοῖς ἁγίοις πίστει]"?

The very translation of κατὰ τὴν ἀναλογίαν τῆς πίστεως in the Vulgate, in Reformation Bibles, and in later versions documents just how multi-layered its meaning could be: Vulgate, "secundum rationem fidei"; Tyndale and the Great Bible, "that it be agreynge unto the fayth"; Geneva Bible and King James, "according to the proportion of faith"; Bishops' Bible, "after the measure of faith"; Rheims, "according to the rule of faith"; Revised Version, "according to

57. *WA* 31/2:586–769; *LW* 15:189–264.

58. Pelikan 1993, I, 71, 213.

59. Bizer 1958.

the proportion of our faith"; Revised Standard Version, "in proportion to our faith."[60] The New Jerusalem Bible renders it "We should prophesy as much as our faith tells us," but then it supplies "another translation, less likely," in a footnote: "'according to the rule of faith,' that is, the common teaching of the Church, as in 1 Cor 12:3, where the 'confession of faith' is the criterion of 'authentic gifts of the Spirit.'" The history of its use in Christian theology and exegesis, and even in Reformation theology and exegesis, however, has been less equivocal. Thus Melanchthon in his *Annotationes* of 1522 on Romans took this to mean that prophecy, "whether it be that by which future events are predicted or that by which the Scriptures are expounded [siue qua futura praedicantur, siue qua exponuntur scripturae]," in either case "should not depend upon human conjectures, human wisdom, or human judgment, but on the judgment of faith [non debet pendere ex humanis coniecturis, humana sapientia, humano iudicio, sed iudicio fidei]" [Item 2.8:K3^v–K4^r].[61] John Calvin, in the preface to his *Institutes,* addressed to Francis I (1494–1547), the king of France, equated "the analogy of faith" with "the rule of faith."[62] In keeping with that equation, the Calvinist theologian William Bucanus (fl. 1591–1603) gave the following definition of *analogia fidei,* with which Flacius's definition agrees almost verbatim [Item 2.14(1628):1:36]: "the constant and perpetual sense of Scripture expounded in the manifest places of Scripture and agreeable to the Apostles' Creed, the Ten Commandments, and the general sentences and axioms of every main point of divinity."[63] It was on the assumption of the presence of such a constant and perpetual sense of Scripture that Augustine in his trinitarian hermeneutics had repeatedly invoked what he called the *canonica regula* as an exclusionary rule, to reject as unacceptable any exegesis of a particular passage, above all of such sayings of Christ as "the Father is greater than I" (Jn 14:28), that might have seemed to be valid according to the grammar but that led to error in dogma.[64]

In their systematic theologies, beginning with the *Loci communes* of Melanchthon from 1521 through its successive and expanded editions, and then with the *Institutes of the Christian Religion* of Calvin from 1536 through its successive and expanded editions, the heaping up of proof texts became the standard method of verifying the scriptural character of a teaching about doctrine or life. In some of the Reformed confessions of the sixteenth and seventeenth centuries, for example in the Scottish Confession of 1560[65] and perhaps above all in the Westminster Confession of Faith of 1647,[66] this method of prooftexting often took the form

---

60. Weigle 1961, 902–3.

61. *CR* 15:708 (wording somewhat different).

62. *CR* 2:12–13; McNeill 1:12–13.

63. Quoted in McNeill 1:12–13 n, in explanation of Calvin's use of the phrase.

64. Pelikan 1990b, 329–43.

65. Schaff 3:437–79.

66. Schaff 3:598–673.

of citing chapter (and verse) numbers in notes rather than of quoting the passages themselves in the body of the articles of the confession, with the collation and doctrinal application of the texts left to the treatises of the theologians. Although the method at work in the biblical commentaries of the Reformed and Lutheran theologians who wrote the confessions and the dogmatics shows some of the same tendency, the format of a consecutive explication de texte seems to have dictated a closer attention to the passage at hand and the use of parallel passages — and, in the case of the New Testament, the use of the Old Testament passages being quoted by the New Testament at this particular place — as a key to the exposition. In his *Annotationes* of 1589 on John 5:39, "Search the Scriptures," Bèze took the Greek verb ἐρευνᾶτε as an indicative, not an imperative as "many" had interpreted it, but went on to denounce those "who approach the reading of Scripture, not with an interest in seeking the truth that is there, but with prejudged opinions or something even worse; therefore they do not see when they see, nor hear when they hear, nor learn when they read [qui ad scripturarum lectionem, non veritatis inde inquirendae studium, sed praeiudicatas opiniones aut aliquid etiam deterius adferunt: ideoque nec videndo vident, nec audiendo audiunt, nec legendo discunt]" [Item 2.13:1:359]. It definitely was not to be thought of as such a "prejudged opinion" when the analogy of faith played a decisive role in this searching of the Scriptures, though often as an invisible hand, directing the choice from among parallel passages and (as in the case of κατὰ τὴν ἀναλογίαν τῆς πίστεως in Romans 12:6 itself) from among alternative meanings of a Greek or Hebrew vocable. Ironically, therefore, the resultant Protestant "biblical theology" often bore a striking family resemblance to the Catholic tradition of creed and dogma whose formal authority as *norma normata* (the norm that is itself subject to another norm) Reformation polemics had subordinated to that of Scripture alone as *norma normans* (the norm that regulates all other norms).

COMMENTARY AND CONTROVERSY

That irony or inconsistency in the Magisterial Reformation was not lost either on the Roman Catholic "defenders of the faith" (which was the title, *Defensor Fidei,* that Pope Leo X conferred on King Henry VIII of England in 1521 for his vindication of Roman Catholic teaching against Luther [Item 3.10:✠2ʳ]) or on the thinkers of the Radical Reformation, especially the opponents of the orthodox Nicene doctrine of the Trinity. The exegesis and hermeneutics of the Reformation must, then, be viewed in the light not only of commentaries based on the Bible as a source but of controversies in which the Bible was, essentially, a weapon of defense and of attack. From the point of view of those wielding the weapon, this did not represent a distortion of the biblical message at all but was to be seen as a clarification of insight that had been made necessary by the false teachers, in obedience to the admonition "be ready always to give an answer to every man that asketh you a reason of the hope that is in you" (1 Pet 3:15) — an admonition that meant to Luther that "wenn man dich angreyfft vnd fragt/ wie eyn ket-zer/ warumb du glewbist/ das du durch den glawben selig werdest/ da antwort/ Da hab ich Gottis wort vnd klare sprüche der schrifft" [Item 2.5:T4ʳ]. Many of the church fathers of both East and West, for example Gregory of Nazianzus and Augustine of Hippo, had freely admitted that the rise of controversy had sometimes compelled the church to clarify the meaning of passages of Scripture that had previously been obscure or neglected, on such central teachings as the doctrine of the Holy Spirit and the doctrine of Original Sin.[67] In such cases — whatever the validity of the theological explanation that the doctrine had been implicit all along but had eventually been made explicit[68] — the historical explanation sug-gests that there has been a dialectical relation between commentary and controversy, with each evoking and defining the other at various stages.

Although the several fronts of the controversies over the real presence of the body and blood of Christ in the Eucharist are in many ways the most productive case study for an examination of this dialectical relation between commentary and controversy in the age of the Reformation,[69] the related issue of Christology is no less interesting. It may be even more pertinent to the various concerns of Reformation exegesis and hermeneutics, because this issue presents itself as a problem in the exegesis of many times more passages than does the eucharistic issue, and because the dogma of the Council of Chalcedon in 451 performed an explicit function as an accepted traditional norm for most of the parties.[70] On every page of the Gospels it was necessary, for the lay reader no less than for the professional clergyman and theologian, to ask how the text was related to that Chalcedonian doctrine of Christ as both totally divine and totally human. "Is the Divine that has appeared on earth and that has reunited men with God identical with the Supreme Divine that rules heaven and earth, or is it a demigod?" had been, in the succinct summarization of Adolf von Harnack, the decisive question in the Arian controversy of the fourth century.[71] In various permutations this continued to be a decisive question for the Reformation. Should the One in whom "dwelleth all the fulness of the Godhead bodily" (Col 2:9) be called "God" in an unequivocal or even a metaphysical sense — and did the New Testament ever call him that? The exegetical and even the textual answer to that second question is far from unambiguous; for it is striking, although on further thought not entirely surprising, to note how many of the standard proof texts

---

67. Gregory of Nazianzus *Orationes* XXXI.27; Augustine *De praedestinatione sanctorum* xiv.27; *De dono perseverantiae* ii.4.

68. Thomas Aquinas *Summa Theologica* I.Q.36.A.2 *ad* 2.

69. Pelikan 1959, 137–254.

70. Pelikan 1971–89, 4:158–61, 350–62.

71. Harnack 1905, 192.

concerned with this issue are textually doubtful: Matthew 24:36 (NRV), "About that day and hour no one knows, neither the angels of heaven, *nor the Son,* but only the Father" (emphasis added), where "nor the Son" is omitted by the Vulgate, as well as by the *Textus Receptus* (and therefore by the AV); John 1:18, which usually appears as "the only begotten Son" but which has enough manuscript evidence for "the only begotten God [μονογενὴς θεός]" to appear that way in modern critical editions of the Greek New Testament and in footnotes to some modern translations (for example, RSV); Acts 20:28, "to feed the church of God, which he has purchased with his own blood," where many manuscripts avoid attributing "blood" to "God" by reading κυρίου rather than θεοῦ; 1 Timothy 3:16, where ὅς may also be θεός; and the most celebrated of all, the Johannine Comma of 1 John 5:7,[72] "For there are three that bear record in heaven, the Father, the Word, and the Holy Ghost: and these three are one," which Erasmus omitted from his first two editions of the Greek New Testament [Item 1.16; Item 1.17] and then, responding to criticism, added in later editions, so that Estienne included it in what eventually became the *Textus Receptus* [Item 1:18].

But it is instructive to consult the treatment of such passages in two of the Bibles of the Radical Reformation, that of Michael Servetus published in 1542 [Item 3.24] and that of Sebastian Castellio in 1551 [Item 3.25], which followed the translation of the Italian Dominican Santi Pagnini [Item 1.23]. These opponents of the dogma of the Trinity set forth what George Williams has called a "reasoned intrascriptural construct evolved largely in freedom from the constraints and the conventions interwoven in Tradition I, that is, the exegetical and hermeneutical tradition from patristic times of interpreting Scripture from within itself, but not each exegete wholly on his own but by building on antecedent commentary and discussion."[73] Nevertheless, Acts 20:28 is translated "ad regendum ecclesiam *dei* quam acquisiuit sanguine suo" in Servetus [Item 3.24:234ʳ] and "ut *dei* pascatis ecclesiam, quam ipse suo sanguine comparauit" in Castellio [Item 3.25(NT):163] (emphasis added); and most surprising of all, considering its sixteenth-century history, the Johannine Comma appears in both [Item 3.24:255ᵛ; Item 3.25(NT):264]. For these antitrinitarian biblicists, the first of whom was executed for his heresy, the rules of sacred philology were clearly too authoritative to be violated in a translation if that was the way the texts read; and it was up to exegesis rather than translation — not to mention textual conjecture — to repair the damage of preceding centuries and to explain the real meaning of the text, "as if to begin the history of interpretation over again, this time to get it right."[74]

72. See *ODCC* 741.

73. Williams 1992, 1165–66.

74. Bruns 1992, 140.

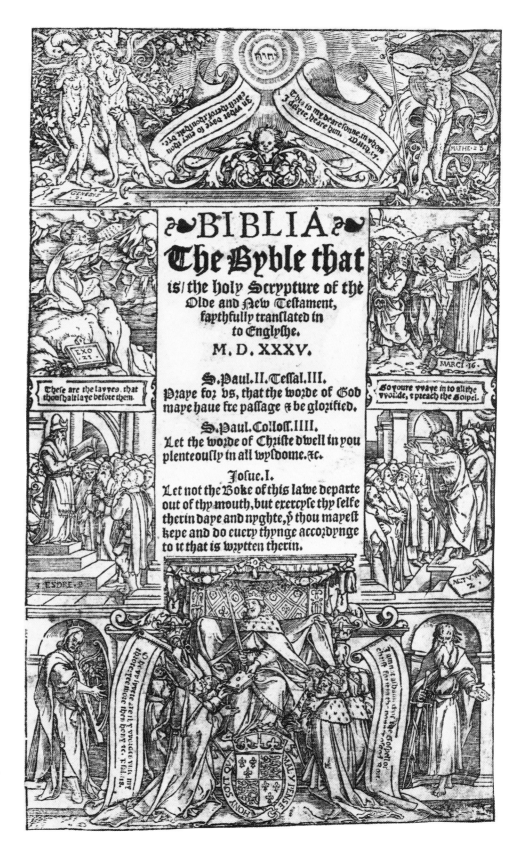

"English"
title page
of Coverdale
Bible (1535).
By permission
of H. P. Kraus,
Rare Books and
Manuscripts,
New York.
See Item 3.10.

3 : Bibles for the People

The most challenging assignment faced by the Reformation interpreters of the Bible was not exegesis but translation, as it would in turn become their most enduring monument. Biblical exegetes could, and often did, elide their way around obscure or difficult passages, but biblical translators could not get away with that: they were expected to do it all, word by word and phrase by phrase. A translator faithful to the principles of the Reformation had to be an exegete first, using the tools of sacred philology in Hebrew and Greek to discover the correct reading of the text and then its correct meaning. After that, he had to become a philologist of the vernacular, probing the strengths and weaknesses of the language of the common people as a medium for articulating biblical truths that for centuries had been most familiar in their Latin formulations and that had now become accessible in the sacred languages of their originals. Just over two centuries before the Reformation, the defense of the vernacular as a fitting vehicle for expressing ideas and sentiments that had been reserved to the Classical languages had received its most eloquent statement ever, which, significantly, had itself to be written in Latin:[1] the treatise *De vulgari eloquentia,* published by Dante Alighieri probably in 1303–4. "It may be fairly said," Thomas Bergin has written of it, "that no comparable study of language and 'eloquence' had preceded Dante's work. Certainly no vernacular had been given the 'scholarly' treatment implied in Dante's deliberate choice of Latin for his essay."[2] And despite some inconsistencies he put his poem where his treatise was: having considered the use of Latin for the writing of the *Divine Comedy,* he went on to compose and complete it in Italian,[3] thereby effectively codifying the Italian language and virtually creating Italian literature.

---

1. Shapiro 1990, 8, 92.

2. Bergin 1965, 154.

3. See the familiar explanation by Boccaccio of why Dante wrote the *Divine Comedy* in Italian rather than Latin, in Toynbee 1965, 212.

REFORMATION THEORY AND PRACTICE OF BIBLICAL TRANSLATION

It is an almost irresistible contrast with Roman Catholic Italy to point out that in the German, English, and Czech homelands of the Protestant Reformation that honor of having effectively codified the vernacular language must be awarded, in significant measure, to Reformation translations of the Bible, namely in those three cases, Luther's German Bible [Items 3.4–3.6], the Authorized or King James Version of the English Bible [Item 3.14], and the six-volume Bible of Kralice of the Hussite *Unitas Fratrum* [Item 3.16b]. And in those Reformation lands, accordingly, the nearest equivalents to Dante's *De vulgari eloquentia* were the defenses of the vernacular not as the language of poetry but as the language of biblical faith. Among the most influential of these defenses were Luther's *Sendbrief von Dolmetschen,* published at Wittenberg and elsewhere in 1530 [Item 3.2];[4] followed by his *Summarien über die Psalmen und Ursachen des Dolmetschens* of 1531–33;[5] and the prefaces to English translations of the Bible, beginning with Tyndale's and climaxing in the classic "The Translators to the Reader" of the King James Bible in 1611 [Item 3.14].

That preface of 1611 spoke for all the Reformers when it declared: "But how shall men meditate in that, which they cannot vnderstand? How shall they vnderstand that which is kept close in an vnknowen tongue? as it is written, 'Except I know the power of the voyce I shall be to him that speaketh, a Barbarian, and he that speaketh, shalbe a Barbarian to me.' The Apostle excepteth no tongue; not Hebrewe the ancientest, not Greeke the most copious, not Latine the finest" [Item 3.14:A4ᵛ]. Characteristically, Luther articulated the theoretical principles underlying his practice of biblical translation in detail only a posteriori, when he felt provoked and compelled to do so by the attacks from the critics of his translations of the Bible, the "know-it-alls [klüglinge]" as he dubbed them, who delighted in a nitpicking criticism over one missing or misinterpreted word. "For who," he asked, "will be so bold as to claim that he has not missed a single word, as though he were Christ and the Holy Spirit himself?"[6] Luther's response to these know-it-alls concentrated on two issues, corresponding to the themes of our first two chapters, "Sacred Philology" and "Exegesis and Hermeneutics," as those issues affected concrete decisions in translating the Hebrew and Greek of the Bible. The first of these themes involved the effort to understand the difficult vocabulary and grammar of the original text. For example, like earlier translators of the Book of Job, Luther compared the difficulties of its language to the sufferings of Job, declaring with typical hyperbole that he and his colleagues had "during four days barely been able to complete three lines."[7] But once the biblical scholar

---

4. *WA* 30/2:632–46; *LW* 35:181–202.

5. *WA* 38:8–69; *LW* 35:209–23.

6. *WA* 38:16; *LW* 35:221.

7. *Sendbrief WA* 30/2:636; *LW* 35:188.

had accomplished the task of applying sacred philology to the Hebrew or Greek and had "understood" the original text, there arose the perennial dilemma faced by any translator from any language into any language in any age, the dilemma of literalism versus license:[8] "The rule is that we have sometimes adhered strictly to the words and at other times have given only the sense."[9] Or, more fully: "Where the words can permit it and provide a better understanding, we have not allowed ourselves to be constrained by the grammatical rules of the rabbis to provide a lesser or a different understanding; for as all the schoolmasters teach, meaning is not to serve and follow the words, but the words are to serve and follow the meaning." The question a translator had to ask, he continued, was, "How does a German speak in such a case?"[10] Needless to say, this was at the same time also a question of "How does a Christian speak in such a case?" because, for example, the "mountain" in Psalm 68:15–16 referred to "Christendom, which is the mountain of God."[11] Following the example of Augustine and other early Christian writers,[12] therefore, Luther quoted the words of Paul (2 Cor 3:15), "Even unto this day, when Moses is read, the vaile is upon their hearts," to prove that the Jews understood the prophets "only a little and very seldom," in spite of all their technical grasp of Hebrew philology.[13] What they were missing was the "literal-prophetic sense" as this referred to the coming of Jesus as the Messiah.

In keeping with this conception of the prerequisites for understanding and therefore translating a biblical text, Luther took the distinction between the law and the gospel to be the key to the understanding of Scripture, not only for the exposition of the Epistles of Paul, from which the distinction had come, but for the explanation of, for example, the Gospel for the Third Sunday in Advent (Mt 11:2–10). "Any law, and especially the divine law," he said in providing that explanation, "is a word of wrath, the power of sin, the law of death," whereas the gospel "is a word of grace, life, and salvation, a word of righteousness and peace, altogether contrary to the law, and nevertheless completely in agreement with it at the same time" [Item 2.4:F3ᵛ–F4ʳ]. Therefore Luther brought his own understanding of a text to bear on his own translations, and in the *Sendbrief von Dolmetschen* he presented an apologia for the boldest — or, in the eyes of his opponents, the most flagrant — instance of this principle of biblical

---

8. Barnstone 1993, 25–27; because Barnstone's discussion throughout this provocative book concentrates on the Bible as the primary exemplar of the problems of translation, it bears on the discussion in this chapter at many points, even where his approach and mine are diametrically opposed.

9. *WA* 38:17; *LW* 35:222.

10. *WA* 38:11; *LW* 35:213–14.

11. *WA* 38:12; *LW* 35:214.

12. Augustine *De civitate Dei* XVII.7.

13. *WA* 38:11; *LW* 35:213.

translation, his rendering of Romans 3:28 in the September Testament of 1522 [Item 3.4:a3ʳ]: "So halten wyrs nu/ das der mensch gerechtfertiget werde/ on zu thun der werck des gesetzs/ *alleyn durch den glawben* [Therefore we maintain that man is justified without doing the works of the law, *through faith alone*]" (emphasis added).[14] For, as his critics gleefully reminded him, the Greek instrumental dative πίστει had nothing in it corresponding to his "alleyn," which was then an unwarranted interposition of the Lutheran doctrine of justification by faith alone (sola fide) into the German translation of the New Testament. In his polemical response Luther challenged his adversaries: "Ich kan Psalmen vnd Propheten auslegen/ Das können sie nicht. Ich kan dolmetschen/ Das können sie nicht. Ich kan die heiligen schrifft lesen/ Das können sie nicht. [I know how to expound Psalms and Prophets, they do not. I know how to translate, they do not. I know how to read Holy Scripture, they do not]" [Item 3.2:B1ʳ]. And if it came to that, he even knew their dialectical technique and their beloved Aristotle better than they![15] Therefore he did not need them to inform him that "alleyn" or "the four letters 'sola'" were not in the original Greek text. But in keeping with the question "How does a German speak in such a case?" he insisted that it was the German way of speaking to add the word "alleyn" when one thing was being affirmed and the other negated, as, for example, "The peasant brings grain *alone,* and no money." William Tyndale was more circumspect about substituting eisegesis for exegesis, regarding it "better to put a declaration in the margin, than to run too far from the text."[16] At Romans 3:28, therefore, he translated, "We suppose that a man is justified by faith without the deeds of the law," and in the margin he added, "Faith justifieth," and even there without any "alone"; in the 1537 edition, the phrase "faith *alone*" did appear in the marginal note.[17] Melanchthon, already in his commentary of 1521, published in 1522, interpreted these words to be saying, quite unambiguously, "Sola itaque fides saluat, nullorum operum neque bonorum neque malorum respectu" [Item 2.8:C3ᵛ]. Cassiodoro de Reina's Spanish translation of 1569, by contrast, deleted the πίστει from the verse altogether and translated, "Determinamos ser el hombre justificado sin las obras de la Ley" [Item 3.23:k2ᵛ].

CHOICES FACING BIBLICAL TRANSLATORS

As George Steiner has said, "much of the Western theory and practice of translation stems immediately from the need to disseminate the Gospels, to speak holy writ in other tongues."[18]

---

14. See Bluhm 1984, 106–10.

15. *WA* 30/2:635; *LW* 35:186.

16. "W. T. unto the Reader," Daniell 1989, 3.

17. Daniell 1989, 228.

18. Steiner 1992, 257.

Throughout the history of Bible translation, that need and the search for adequate equivalents have engaged anyone who took up the task. Three illustrations may suffice to identify the nature of the search: vocabulary, grammar, and syntax.[19]

The most obvious problem was *vocabulary*. When missionaries were translating the Bible into a new language, were they to employ the ready-made religious terms that were familiar to their prospective converts on the basis of their pagan tradition, as the translators of the Septuagint had done in rendering אֱלֹוהִים with ὁ θεός (though not with the equivalent plural, οἱ θεοί), thus risking confusion between the old and the new faith (as Sebastian Castellio was accused of having done in his translation [Item 3.25])? Or were they to transpose, or even transliterate, the technical terms of the original or of an older version into the new version — as, for example, John Eliot was to do in the century after the Reformation, in the very title of the translation he prepared in the Natick-Algonquin language, *Up-Biblum God* [Item 3.21]? Or were they to invent a brand-new set of words and phrases for their new church — as, in a sense, the Vulgate did when it used the neo-Latin "Christus" to translate not only the ὁ Χριστός of the Greek New Testament throughout but also the מָשִׁיחַ of such passages as Psalm 2:2 (although it did not use the name of the supreme God of the Romans, Jove, to render יהוה, despite the deceptive assonance)? An amusing variant was Luther's practice of rendering biblical proper names in German with Latinate endings: "Jesus" as a fourth-declension noun whose dative was "Jesu," but "Christus" as a second-declension noun with "Christo" as the dative. The history of biblical translation has been marked by each of these several solutions, and by various combinations of them.

Reformation translators, to be sure, were not facing precisely that challenge, for their peoples had been "converted" long since and already had in their own languages words for biblical concepts, some more satisfactory than others. Ever since Valla and Erasmus, scholars and theologians had been aware of the inadequacy of "poenitentiam ago" or "poenitentiam facio," "I do penance," as a translation for μετανοέω and its cognates. Luther reflected that awareness in the first of his Ninety-Five Theses of 1517: "When our Lord and Master Jesus Christ said, 'Poenitentiam agite,' he willed the entire life of believers to be one of repentance," rather than that one must perform individual acts of penance.[20] That distinction in English between "penance" (as the Roman Catholic sacrament) and "repentance" or "penitence" (as the Protestant summons to a break with the past and a new beginning) carried over, though

19. It will be evident that throughout this section I have benefited from the essays in Brower 1959, especially from that of Eugene A. Nida, "Principles of Translation as Exemplified by Bible Translating," 11–31, and the brief comments of Roman Jakobson, "On Linguistic Aspects of Translation," 232–39.

20. *WA* 1:233; *LW* 31:25.

not with complete consistency, into biblical translations.[21] Thus Luther in the September Testament [Item 3.4:a2ᵛ] had John the Baptist (Mt 3:2) call out: "Bessert euch." In his "prologe to the reader" Miles Coverdale explained the "maner haue I used in my translacyon, callyng it in some place pennaunce, that in another place I call repentaunce, and that not onely because the interpreters haue done so before me, but that the aduersaries of the trueth maye se, how that we abhorre not this word penaunce" [Item 3.10:✠6ᵛ]. For some biblical terms, however, English vocabulary possessed impressive advantages. The outstanding example was the word "gospel" as a native term for the Greek εὐαγγέλιον, which in almost every other language was simply transliterated instead of being actually translated as it could be in English and had been at least since the *Lindisfarne Gospels*.[22] Another was the word "worship," instead of the variations on the Latin "cultus" or on "divine service" used in other tongues.

A second issue for the translator was *grammar*. On one important point of grammar, most (though not all) of the vernaculars of the Reformation boasted a feature that was important in Greek but that the Vulgate had notoriously lacked, the definite article.[23] "Latin has no definite article" is listed as the first of the "Disadvantages of Latin as Compared with Greek" in the modern dictionary of the Vulgate by G. C. Richards.[24] Therefore it is defined in Lascaris's *Institutiones* [Item 1.6(1510):A4ᵛ] as "De Articulo [Περὶ ἄρθρου]. Articulus est pars orationis declinabilis praeposita declinationi nominum et postposita." The absence of the definite article in Latin grammar had been a handicap to translators from the Greek since Classical antiquity. For the New Testament, it repeatedly affected Vulgate renderings. In the Latin term "filius Dei," the Vulgate's rendering of the title for Jesus Christ that a standard modern concordance to the Greek New Testament identifies as "ὁ υἱός (κατ᾽ ἐξοχήν),"[25] there was no way to tell from the Latin whether such a phrase meant "*a* son of God" among others or "*the* Son of God" uniquely as the Only-Begotten or ὁ μονογενής. Augustine had taken great efforts to find a theological compensation for this grammatical disadvantage.[26] Significantly, the Romance languages, which descended from Latin, acquired definite articles, forming them from the Latin demonstrative pronoun "ille," so that they were in a position to make the distinction. By contrast, the Slavic languages have remained like Latin and used a similar technique in translating the Greek and Hebrew definite article, and the Czech version of 1506 [Item 3.16a:Bb5ʳ] was obliged to say only "syn božij."

---

21. *OED* P:642–43; P:632–33; R:464–65.

22. *OED* G:308–9.

23. Kukenheim 1932, 115–24.

24. Richards 1934, vi–vii.

25. Schmoller 1949, 493.

26. Pelikan 1990b.

A subtler choice for the translator involved *syntax.* If, in answer to the question quoted earlier from Luther's *Ursachen des Dolmetschens,* "How does a German speak in such a case?" the answer was that in rendering the syntax of some passage a German speaker (or a speaker of any other vernacular language) not only would use a native word but would prefer to resort to another part of speech, the next question was whether the translation, instead of rendering a preposition with a preposition, should accommodate itself to this preference of the vernacular. The most arresting illustration of this issue in my recollection appears not in any of our Reformation translations but in a twentieth-century version, the New Testament of the New English Bible, which was published jointly by Oxford University Press and Cambridge University Press in 1961 — and which, incidentally, reveals its venue in a seafaring nation when Jesus commands Peter, "Shoot the net to starboard" (Jn 21:6). A literally faithful translation of the Greek prepositional phrases of Romans 11:36, ἐξ αὐτοῦ καὶ δι' αὐτοῦ καὶ εἰς αὐτὸν τὰ πάντα, would be, as the AV has it, "For of him, and through him, and to him, are all things," a translation that is matched by the other Reformation versions being dealt with here. But the NEB, presumably on the grounds that, by contrast with Greek prepositions as Lascaris had already described them [Item 1.6], English prepositions tend to be somewhat feeble, took the bold step of changing the syntax and of rendering the prepositional phrases with monosyllabic nouns: "Source, Guide, and Goal of all that is." (In the Revised English Bible, this imaginative translation was retracted in favor of the more cautious and conventional "From him and through him and for him all things exist.")

THE WORD OF GOD, THE PEOPLE OF GOD —
AND THE SEVERAL PEOPLES OF GOD

Two of the most powerful factors at work in promoting Reformation translations of the Bible, one of them theological and the other cultural, were the central Reformation doctrine of the universal priesthood of believers and the coming-of-age of the vernacular languages. The priesthood of believers did not mean, as some of its individualistic interpreters in the nineteenth century maintained, that believers were to be their own priests, as William James in a celebrated definition described religion as "the feelings, acts, and experiences of individual men in their solitude, so far as they apprehend themselves to stand in relation to whatever they may consider the divine."[27] Rather, Christian believers were to be one another's priests within community, mediating the word of God and the grace of God to fellow members of the church as the people of God; as Luther explained the key chapter of the New Testament on

27. James [1902] 1990, 36.

this concept (1 Pt 2): "Nu ist Christus der hohe vnd vbirster prieste von Gott selbs ge-salbet/ Hat auch seyn eygenen leyb geopffert fur vns/ wilchs das höhiste priester ampt ist/ Darnach hat er am Creutz fur vns gebeten/ Zum dritten hatt er auch das Euangelion verkundiget/ vnd alle menschen geleret/ Got vnd sich erkennen. Diese drey ampt hat er auch vns allen geben/ Drumb weyl er priester ist/ vnd wyr seyne brüder sind/ so habens alle Christen macht vnd befelh/ vnd müssens thun/ das sie predigen vnd fur Gott treten/ eyner fur den andern bitte/ vnd sich selbs Gotte opffere" [Item 2.5:K2ʳ].[28]

To carry out this spiritual priesthood, lay people who were engaged in workaday voca-tions — "at the plow," as was often said, or in the home — needed to be able to read and understand the Scriptures for themselves, without the interposition of clerical authorities. To the lay confessors of the Reformation who at the Diet of Augsburg in 1530 presented their Confession in both Latin and German, or to the "consuls and Senate of the celebrated city of Frankfurt" to whom Calvin dedicated (in Latin) his *Harmonia* [Item 2.11:¶2ʳ],[29] it was neces-sary to have the word of God in their own language, not least because they could be obliged to place their lives on the line for it. Yet sometimes, ironically, the combination of the principle of sola Scriptura with the insistence on the primary authority of the Hebrew and Greek originals of that Scriptura could put into the hands — or the mouth — of the Protestant minister in the pulpit an authority matching or even exceeding that of the medieval priest. For not only were women to "ask their husbands at home" (1 Cor 14:35) about theological questions; the husbands, too, ultimately had to defer to the superior knowledge of those who could read the Scriptures in the original languages. And when the authority of the Scriptures pertained to civil government and the ordering of society, as it did above all in the Reformed and Calvinist tradition, the outcome could be a theocratic or bibliocratic clericalism, for which, to borrow Perry Miller's phrasing, "religion is revealed in Scripture, but it is proposed to the mind by the ministry."[30]

The trenchant aphorism of Sir Maurice Powicke, "The one definite thing which can be said about the Reformation in England is that it was an act of State,"[31] has as its corollary the principle codified (but not invented) by the Religious Peace of Augsburg of 1555: "cuius regio, eius religio." For in one country after another the Reformation appealed to the rising tide of national consciousness, as when Luther permitted himself to claim the title "the prophet of the Germans."[32] Nothing, moreover, expressed that national consciousness more effectively than

28. *WA* 12:307–8; *LW* 30:53–54.
29. *CR* 15:710–12.
30. Miller 1961, 1:68.
31. Powicke 1961, 1.
32. Pauck 1939, 297.

BIBLES FOR THE PEOPLE 49

the vernacular language, and nothing more fervently symbolized that attachment to the vernacular than the translation of the Bible into the language of the people. Thus the Danish translation of the Bible commissioned by King Christian III (1503–59) and published in 1550 contained not only his portrait and coat of arms but his official letter of endorsement [Item 3.17]. When the Reformation came to a new land, for example to King Christian's Denmark, it united itself to the drive for nationhood: the church and clergy were no longer to be answerable to a foreign potentate, the bishop of Rome, but were accountable to their own nation and to its temporal rulers; and the language of the people was to replace a foreign tongue, the Latin of the Mass and of the Vulgate, as the medium both for public worship and for the communication of the word of God. The newly empowered laity of the Reformation churches were able, as they had not been before, to read and interpret the word of God in the Bible. But in an age when the means of communication and of transportation were becoming increasingly international, the replacement of Latin by the several vernaculars could — and did — set up new barriers. It has often been claimed that the Latin Mass made it possible for a traveler to attend worship anywhere in the world, but the waggish observation often accompanying that claim, that such travelers would understand the Mass as little elsewhere as they did at home, reinforces the Reformation case for the "Englishing"[33] (or "das Verdeutschen") of both the Bible and the liturgy.

For the history of that process, especially in the Reformation of the sixteenth century and its aftermath, the German Bible and the English Bible have a special significance both intrinsically and statistically, as well as because of their implications for the spread of the Bible in other nations, through such agencies as the British and Foreign Bible Society (whose catalog, by Darlow and Moule, is a fundamental reference tool for any study of the history of the Bible, including this one).

THE GERMAN BIBLE

Partisans of Martin Luther and of his Reformation have sometimes given the impression that the translation of the Bible into German begins with him, an impression that his remark that the Bible had been lying "under the bench [unter der Bank]" before the Reformation seemed to foster. The historical situation is, of course, quite otherwise. Because the entire development of the German Bible before the Reformation is not our subject here, one outstanding example may perhaps suffice: the *Biblia Germanica* published at Strasbourg in 1466 by Johann Mentelin (ca. 1410–78) [Item 3.1].[34] This German version was based on the Latin translation

---

33. *OED* E:180, where the first instance of this as a verb is from Wycliffe.
34. On Mentelin and this Bible see Schorbach 1932, 176–80 and Plate VIIIb.

rather than on the Hebrew and Greek originals. Nevertheless, it deserves pride of place as the first printing of a Bible in the German language, by contrast with Gutenberg's editions of the Vulgate. It was followed by seventeen other printed High German and Low German Bibles that appeared before Luther's September Testament of 1522.[35]

When all of that has been said and duly noted, however, the fact remains that the history of the German Bible and the history of the German Reformation are so intertwined that neither history can be understood without the other.[36] Two centuries after the Reformation, the most celebrated of all German writers, in the most celebrated of his works, could have his protagonist take the Greek New Testament in hand and declare his intention "to translate the sacred original into my beloved German,"[37] which every reader would be sure to recognize as the reenactment of what Luther had done at the Wartburg in 1521. Luther was both a practitioner and an advocate of the sacred philology described in Chapter 1, as he declared unequivocally in 1524, speaking about Hebrew and Greek (as well as Latin) as "*the* languages" in a special sense: "Although the gospel came and still comes to us through the Holy Spirit alone, we cannot deny that it came through the medium of languages, was spread abroad by that means, and must be preserved by the same means. . . . In proportion as we value the gospel, let us zealously hold to the languages. For it was not without purpose that God caused his Scriptures to be set down in these two languages alone — the Old Testament in Hebrew, the New in Greek. Now if God did not despise them but chose them above all others for his word, then we too ought to honor them above all others."[38]

Nevertheless, he had simultaneously been engaged in producing, as preliminary samples, individual translations of the Bible, often in conjunction with his printed sermons on a text, such as his translation of Luke 17:11–19, the Gospel lesson for the fourteenth Sunday after Trinity, *Euangelium Von den tzehen auzsetzigen,* published at Wittenberg by Melchior Lotter in 1521 [Item 3.3].[39] But later in that same year,[40] the second segment of his time of protective custody at the Wartburg in the aftermath of the Diet of Worms enabled him, in a white heat of production that took a mere eleven weeks, to complete *Das Newe Testament Deûtzsch,* which

---

35. Listing in Reinitzer 1983, 85.

36. Reu 1934 remains a useful compilation in English of the state of research at that time, but the most thorough and up-to-date such compilation is now to be found in the material of the several historical introductions to the *Die Deutsche Bibel* volumes of the Weimar Edition of *Luthers Werke,* much of which has been brought together in the elegant and useful volume of Reinitzer 1983, prepared for the five hundredth anniversary of Luther's birth.

37. Goethe *Faust* 1217–23.

38. *WA* 15:37; *LW* 45:358–59.

39. *WA* 8:340–97.

40. See Luther's letter to Johann Lang, 18.xii.1521 (*WA Br* 2:413; *LW* 48:356–57).

was published by Melchior Lotter the Younger at Wittenberg in September 1522 and is generally identified as the September Testament [Item 3.4]. It was based on the 1519 edition of Erasmus's Greek New Testament (which lacked 1 Jn 5:7) and was supplied with prefaces, also to individual books, and with marginal glosses. By December of the same year he was able to put out a revised and corrected version (December Testament) of the New Testament, and for the quarter century until his death in 1546 he never flagged, even amid all the other duties and controversies occupying his attention, in his devotion to the task of translating and retranslating the Bible into German, as a chronology and a complete list of the Bibles issued in whole or in part during that period amply demonstrate.[41]

Even as the September Testament was in the press, therefore, he had been working on the much more daunting task of translating the Hebrew Bible into German, beginning with the Pentateuch: *Das Allte Testament deutsch* published at Wittenberg by Melchior Lotter in 1523 [Item 3.5]. This was followed early in 1524 by *Das Ander teyl des alten testaments,* comprising the books from Joshua to Esther, and in October of that year by *Das Dritte teyl,* containing the Poetical Books. The principle of asking "How does a German speak in such a case?" required him, in translating the roster of the menagerie of unclean animals in Leviticus 11, to inquire of both Jewish and Christian scholars as to the identity of all these creatures and their German names (if any!). That obligation of Luther the translator was not obviated by the insistence of Luther the theologian that these regulations were not binding on Christians, an insistence that he spelled out in a brief but hard-hitting treatise of 1525–26, *Eine Unterrichtung, wie sich die Christen in Mose sollen schicken.*[42] At the same time, the translation of the Decalogue (Ex 20:2–17) in the 1523 rendering of the Pentateuch also served as a trial run for the most influential translation from the Hebrew that Luther ever undertook, in the *Small Catechism* of 1529,[43] complete with the controversial (and often misleading) numbering of the Ten Commandments according to the Roman Catholic system (with the prohibition of graven images, Ex 20:4–5, being treated not as the Second Commandment but as an appendix to the First Commandment), rather than the Hebrew system (with the entire prohibition of coveting being counted as the Tenth Commandment), which was adopted by most other Protestant groups and by Eastern Orthodoxy.[44]

These four separate volumes of translations, with further corrections and revisions by Luther in collaboration with his "Sanhedrin" of scholars and colleagues, came together in 1534, with the publication of *Biblia/ das ist/ die gantze Heilige Schrifft Deudsch,* issued at

41. Reinitzer 1983, 114–25.

42. *WA* 16:363–93; *LW* 35:161–74.

43. *WA* 30/1:243–47.

44. *PRE*[3] 4:561.

Wittenberg by Hans Lufft in 1534 and again in 1535 [Item 3.6]. Luther's process of correction and revision was unceasing; and even after his death on 18 February 1546 its results were visible, with the publication later in that year of a two-volume version into which Luther's collaborator and editor of his lectures, Georg Rörer (1492–1557), incorporated changes that the Reformer had authorized but that could not appear until this posthumous edition.

In a separate category of the history of the Bible in German was *Das naw testament,* published at Dresden by Wolfgang Stöckel in 1527 and translated by Luther's longtime adversary, Hieronymus Emser (1478–1527) [Item 3.7].[45] The title "translator" was, however, one that Luther was not willing to grant to Emser, whom he accused, with a considerable measure of justification, of having plagiarized his translation — and of having, moreover, botched the plagiarism! The translation was preceded in 1524 by Emser's *Annotationes vber Luthers naw Testament gebessert und emendirt.*[46] As these two titles indicate, Emser's version was intended to correct Luther's mistranslations and to bring the German version of the New Testament into harmony with the teachings of the church.

THE ENGLISH BIBLE

The staggering number of versions of the Bible in English, which continues to grow at the end of the twentieth century, makes the evolution of the English Bible perhaps the most thoroughly studied chapter in the history of biblical translation.[47] It is also a major chapter in the history of the Reformation; for despite the English translations of the Bible in whole or in part undertaken during the Middle Ages, notably the Wycliffite *New Testament,* shown as Item 3.8 in a fifteenth-century English manuscript on vellum, with a prologue in English inserted before the opening of the Gospel of Matthew, it is not until the Reformation of the sixteenth century that the history of the English Bible as we know it actually begins.

The New Testament of *William Tyndale* (ca. 1494–1536), a scholar trained at Oxford who had developed his translating skills by rendering into English the Greek of the Classical orator Isocrates and the Latin of Erasmus's *Enchiridion,* was a translation directly from the Greek original (with considerable debt to Luther's translation, particularly in the prefaces to the various books of the New Testament) rather than from the Vulgate, as its predecessors had

---

45. Strand 1982, 6–7, 13–30, plates 1–98, gives a good view of Emser's translation.

46. See Reinitzer 1983, 195–99 (nos. 110–13).

47. Of the many histories of the English Bible that have been and continue to be published in the twentieth century, the increase in which likewise shows no sign of abating, Greenslade 1963, 141–74, is outstanding; also of great value are Bruce 1978 and Metzger et al. 1991.

been; it was first published in 1525–26.[48] Tyndale followed this with translations from the Hebrew Old Testament — the Pentateuch in 1530, Joshua to 2 Chronicles in 1537 (printed posthumously as part of "Matthew's Bible" [Item 3.9]), and Jonah probably in 1531.[49] He did not finish the entire Bible, not, at any rate, in his own name. But there is much to be said in favor of attributing to Tyndale the folio Bible that appeared at Antwerp in 1537, the year after Tyndale's martyrdom, under the name of Thomas Matthew [Item 3.9]; that was almost certainly a pseudonym of Tyndale's friend John Rogers (1500–1555), who edited the book, primarily on the basis of Tyndale's work.[50] Tyndale's modern editor, David Daniell, has noted "that Tyndale, from an intimate and craftsmanly knowledge of all three languages, believed passionately that Hebrew went better into English than into Latin (where, one might say, it had been in hiding for a thousand years)"; and therefore, according to Daniell, Tyndale "has produced a translation that goes some way to rendering in English the rawness of the original."[51] As for Tyndale's New Testament, Daniell makes the point even more forcefully: "It is commonly said that Luther's 1522 New Testament gave Germany a language: it ought to be said more clearly that Tyndale's 1534 New Testament gave to English its first classic prose. Such flexibility, directness, nobility and rhythmic beauty showed what language could do."[52] Or, as Daniell has said elsewhere, "he made a language for England."[53]

The translation of *Miles Coverdale* (1488–1568), published in 1535 [Item 3.10], although it included the entire Bible, was based on other translations rather than directly on the Greek and Hebrew texts, or, in his own words, "out of five sundry interpreters," namely, as Mozley has enumerated them, and with illustrative examples: "Vulgate, Pagninus, Luther, the Zurich Bible in the 1531 and 1534 editions, and Tyndale [or perhaps Erasmus's Latin version]."[54] The translation was dedicated to King Henry VIII, with the reminder that Pope Leo X, without realizing the full implications of what he was doing, had in 1521 designated him "Defendour of

---

48. This is available to modern readers in Daniell 1989.

49. Such is the table of contents of the edition in Daniell 1992. On "the historical books from Joshua to 2 Chronicles," Daniell 1994, 334, comments that they "seem to have come from nowhere; except that in the treatment of both Hebrew and English, they match exactly the methods of Tyndale in the Pentateuch," from which Daniell concludes that it is "almost completely certain that the historical books in 'Matthew's Bible' are by Tyndale."

50. The chapter "Matthew's Bible," Daniell 1994, 333–57, is a weighing of the evidence; see also Greenslade 1963, 150–52.

51. Daniell 1992, xiv–xv.

52. Daniell 1989, xxx.

53. Daniell 1994, 3.

54. Mozley 1953, 78–109.

the Fayth" [Item 3.10:⊞2ʳ], a title whose full implications he was now in a position to exercise. "What is now the cause of all these vntollerable and nomore to be suffred abhominacions?" Coverdale asked in the dedication. "Truely euen the ignoraunce of the scripture of God. For how had it els ben possyble, that such blyndnes shulde haue come in to the worlde, had not the lyghte of Gods worde bene extyncte?" [Item 3.10:⊞3ᵛ]. It is a curiosity in the history of the Englishing of the Bible that the Song of Songs is called in English "The Ballet of Balettes [that is, the ballad of ballads]"⁵⁵ and interpreted allegorically as "a mysticall deuyce of the spirituall and godly loue / betwene Christ the spouse / and the churche or congregacyon his spousesse" [Item 3.9:245ᵛ].

Circulation of these and other translations of the Scriptures during the sixteenth century caused a demand for a version of the Bible that would have the sanction of ecclesiastical authorities. In response to this demand an official commission prepared the so-called *Great Bible* of 1539, printed again in 1540, with a preface by Archbishop Thomas Cranmer (1489–1556) [Item 3.11a]. It was designed for use on the lecterns of churches, and the leaders of church and state sought to enforce it as the only permissible version of the Scriptures: "The Bible in English, that is to say the content of all the holy scripture, both of the old and new testament, truly translated after the verity of the Hebrew and Greek texts, by the diligent study of diverse excellent learned men, expert in the foresaid tongues."

Dated "From Geneua. 10. April. 1560" [Item 3.12:pr.3ᵛ], the *Geneva Bible* was guided by explicit principles of translation. Its translators, addressing some of the problems of language I outlined earlier, explained, "Now as we haue chiefely obserued the sense, and laboured alwaies to restore it to all integritie: so haue we moste reuerently kept the proprietie of the wordes, considering that the Apostles who spake and wrote to the Gentiles in the Greke tongue, rather constrayned them to the liuely phrase of the Ebrewe, then entreprised farre by mollifying their language to speake as the Gentils did" [Item 3.11:***4ʳ]. At their hands the opening words of Psalm 46 became "God *is* our hope and strength, & helpe in troubles, readie to be founde" [Item 3.11:Pp4ᵛ]. This Bible features maps, which strove for geographical accuracy and completeness — another implication drawn from the Reformation's emphasis on the historical sense of the Scriptures, as discussed in Chapter 2.

The continuing popularity of this and other versions made some revisions of the Great Bible seem desirable for use in the churches; these were incorporated into the Bishops' Bible, *Holie Bible,* published at London by R. Jugge in 1568, with the prologue by Thomas Cranmer. The scene in the Garden of Eden shown in the Catalog [Item 3.11b:A2ʳ] depicts Adam and Eve at peace in the natural world of hares and horses, with יהוה, the Tetragrammaton of the divine name, emblazoned overhead. In the preface the translators presented themselves as

---

55. *OED* B:639.

following the example of the "olde forefathers that haue ruled in this realme, who in their times, and in diuers ages did their diligence to translate the whole bookes of the scriptures, to the erudition of the laytie, as yet at this day be to be seene diuers bookes translated into the vulgar tongue, some by kynges of the realme, some by bishoppes, some by abbottes, some by other devout godly fathers: so desirous they were of olde tyme to haue the lay sort edified in godlynes by reading in their vulgar tongue" [Item 3.11b:★2ʳ]. Even these revisions did not go far enough, and the Bishops' Bible did not succeed in establishing itself among the people or even in the churches. England needed a new translation that would incorporate the best features of earlier translations but recast them.

Such a new translation was provided by the *Authorized or King James Version* of 1611 [Item 3.14]. Its dedication to King James I (1566–1625) is an acknowledgment of the central role played by the monarch in its preparation [Item 3.14:A2ʳ], and its "The Translators to the Reader," quoted earlier in this chapter, was an extensive justification of the principles of translation at work in its composition. Although the Authorized Version has never lacked critics, it has, as I noted in the Preface by means of a quotation from David Lyle Jeffrey, so embedded itself in the religious and literary history of the English-speaking peoples that for most of its history its secure place has been challenged only by revisions of it, not by replacements for it — of both of which there have been, and continue to be, many.

Of the translations of the Bible into English coming out of the Roman Catholic Reformation, the most influential was the *Reims-Douai Bible* of 1582–1610, more commonly known as the Douai Version. The New Testament was "printed at Rhemes by Iohn Fogny 1582" [Item 3.13]. In accordance with the decree of the Council of Trent quoted in Chapter 1, it was based on the Vulgate. Picking up on the controversies over the words of Christ to Peter (Mt 16:18), as discussed in the preceding chapter, including the passage from Augustine's *Retractations* in the *Catena Aurea,* the annotations to this passage explained, "And though S. Augustine sometimes referre the word (*Petra*) to Christ in this sentence (which no doubt he did because the terminations in Latin are diuers, and because he examined not the nature of the original wordes which Christ spake, nor of the Greek, and therefore the Aduersaries which otherwise flee to the tongs, should not in this case alleage him) yet he neuer denieth but Peter also is the Rocke and head of the Church" [Item 3.13:46]. Twentieth-century studies have demonstrated many instances of the influence of the Douai Version on the Authorized Version.[56]

56. Carleton 1902, 84–250, is a careful tabulation of that influence.

OTHER PEOPLES, OTHER TONGUES, OTHER BIBLES
IN THE REFORMATION

From its very beginnings the Reformation was an international movement. When Luther at the Leipzig Disputation of 1519 declared that some of the teachings for which Jan Hus had been condemned a century earlier had been Christian and Catholic, he received congratulations from the followers of Hus in the Czech lands. First at the University of Wittenberg and a generation later in Geneva, foreign students imbibed Reformation teachings and then returned to their home countries to propagate them. This was true already of the Lutheran Reformation, although it continued to be most heavily represented in German and Scandinavian territories. By contrast, the Calvinist Reformation — or, more precisely, those who defined themselves as "Reformed, in accordance with the word of God ['Gereformeerden' or 'nach Gottes Wort reformiert']" — spread almost immediately to a truly international venue. The Lutheran confessions in the *Book of Concord* of 1580 were all German in provenance;[57] but the confessions that Philip Schaff (1819–93) assembled under the heading "the Evangelical Reformed Churches" came from Switzerland, Germany, France, Belgium, Scotland, England, Ireland, and the Netherlands,[58] and he could have (or perhaps should have) added confessions from Hungary, Poland, and Bohemia, which have appeared in other collections of Reformed statements of faith. In all those countries, the coming of the Reformation prompted new attention to several aspects of Christian faith and life, such as preaching, vernacular liturgy and hymnody, catechesis, and church discipline — and to the teaching and reading, and hence the translating and publishing, of the Bible. Even beyond all those territories, moreover, the religious impulses set into motion by the Reformation, often in conjunction with the sacred philology of the Renaissance and with the growth of the technology of printing, aroused interest in making vernacular Bibles available to other peoples in their own tongues. What follows is an alphabetical catalog of some of these other peoples, other tongues, and other Bibles in the Reformation.[59]

Arabic. The period of the Reformation in Central Europe was also marked by a heightening awareness of Islam — and with good reason. In 1526, at the Battle of Mohács, Christian Hungary had fallen to the Turkish armies, who went on in 1529 to put Vienna under siege. At the Imperial Diet of Augsburg in 1530, the two major items on the agenda were the Protestant Reformation and the Turkish threat; Luther in turn linked "des Papsts und Türken Mord" as

---

57. Schaff 3:1–189.

58. Schaff 3:191–704.

59. The book-length collection of individual articles under the heading "Bibelübersetzungen," *PRE*[3] 3:1–179, a number of them by the eminent New Testament textual scholar Eberhard Nestle, can still be used with profit.

major threats in his hymn "Erhalt uns Herr."[60] He also wrote *Vom Kriege wider die Türken* in 1528–29, *Eine Heerpredigt wider den Türken* in 1529, and *Vermahnung zum Gebet wider den Türken* in 1541.[61] But beyond these political and military responses to the Muslim threat, he undertook in 1542 to publish in German translation the *Confutatio Alcorani* of the thirteenth-century Dominican, Ricoldo Pennini de Monte Croce (ca. 1243–1320).[62] In addition to such defenses against Islam, Christians were concerned to counterattack by bringing the gospel — and the Gospels — to the Muslim world. Although modern writers sometimes speak about Arabic translations of the Bible before the rise of Islam, no authenticated fragments of these appear to have survived. What we do have are translations from Hebrew, from Greek, from Syriac, from Coptic, and from Latin. The Arabic *Evangelium sanctvm domini nostri Iesu Christi* shown in the Catalog [Item 3.15] was printed at Rome by the de' Medici Press in 1590–91.[63] It depicts the scene in which Mary Magdalene recognizes the risen Christ but is told "Touch me not; for I am not yet ascended to my Father," and is then dispatched to bring the message of the resurrection to "my brethren" (Jn 20:17).

Czech. Of the vernacular Bibles in this list, only the 1506 Czech Bible antedates the outbreak of the Reformation as we usually speak of it, because the Czech Reformation also antedates the outbreak of the Reformation as we usually speak of it. Without settling the mooted question of how much originality to attribute to Jan Hus in relation to John Wycliffe,[64] it does have to be conceded that Hus's movement did — and that Wycliffe's movement did not — found a church, in fact, more than one. That implied, among other things, that the Hussites produced hymnals (in both Czech and German) and catechisms, as well as translations of the Bible.[65] The most successful of these, the Bible of Kralice [Item 3.16b], which owed much of its initiative to "the humanistic Renaissance in the Unity of Czech Brethren" led by Jan Blahoslav (1523–71),[66] came at the end of the sixteenth century, with its large-format six-volume edition appearing in 1579–93/94, and the final revised version of its New Testament in 1613, at almost exactly the same time as the Authorized Version in English. This was the Bible that refugees after the Battle of White Mountain (1620) took with them into exile. But among its predecessors, the edition of the Czech Bible published in Venice in 1506, *Biblii Cžeská* [Item

60. *WA* 35:467; *LW* 53:304–5.

61. *WA* 30/2:107–48 (*LW* 46:161–205); 30/2:160–97; 51:585–625.

62. *WA* 53:272–396.

63. D&M 1637.

64. Spinka 1941 strives to be a balanced assessment.

65. Segert 1994, 131–38, is a discussion by a distinguished Czech scholar of Semitic languages; Pelikan 1946 includes a review of earlier translations as background for the Bible of Kralice.

66. Jakubec 1929–34, 1:666–76.

3.16a], may claim a special place.[67] It includes a Czech translation of the letter of Paulinus to Jerome, which appeared at the beginning of many editions of the Vulgate, but which (in accordance with the position of Jerome identified earlier) is being used here to justify a vernacular version: "Žádosti weliké byl nieyaký Paulin. kniez pocztiwý aby mohl rozumieti pijsmuom swatým. a od tohoto se swieta odtrhnúti. Y psal k swatému Jeronýmowi" [Item 3.16a].

Danish. The Danish Reformation was in considerable measure prepared for by the work of biblical humanists, among whom the most significant was Hans Tausen (1494–1561), "the Danish Luther," who had studied in Wittenberg in 1523–24 and who in 1526 took the lead of the Reformation movement at Viborg, in the territory of Jutland. In 1529 he was appointed to the Church of Saint Nicholas in Copenhagen. King Christian II (1481–1559) had himself visited Wittenberg in 1524 and had become a Lutheran, as a result of which he could not return to Denmark. (He later turned back to Roman Catholicism.) The new king, Frederick I (1471–1533), eventually granted freedom to the Reformation party, in his oft-quoted statement of 1527 to the Roman Catholic bishops: "The Christian faith is free. None of you desires to be forced to renounce his faith, but you must also understand that those who are devoted to the Holy Scriptures, or to the Lutheran doctrine as it is called, will no more be forced to renounce their faith. . . . Therefore shall every man conduct himself in a way which he can justify before Almighty God on the Day of Judgment, until a final decision is made for all Christendom." With the death of Frederick I in 1533 and after an interregnum, Christian III became king. It was at his initiative that Luther's colleague and pastor, Johannes Bugenhagen "Pommeranus" (1485–1558), was summoned to Denmark to reform the church; during Bugenhagen's absence from the pulpit in Wittenberg, Luther preached the sermons that became his *Commentary on the Sermon on the Mount.*[68] The Danish scholar N. K. Andersen, on whose succinct narrative of the Danish Reformation this account is largely based, concludes it with this assessment: "The most important and permanent heritage which the Reformation left for posterity was the simple Danish service and the uncomplicated Christianity of the catechism on which the coming generations were raised. For its most significant monument we have the great *Christian III's Bible* of 1550, the first Danish translation of the Bible in its entirety."[69] And that "most significant monument" is likewise what we have here: *Biblia/ Det er den gantske Hellige*

67. D&M 2180.

68. *WA* 32:299–544; *LW* 21:3–294. On Bugenhagen's trip to Denmark see my introduction, *LW* 21:xix–xxi, with quotations from Luther's letters.

69. In Elton 1962, 142.

Scrifft, issued at Copenhagen by Ludwig Dietz in 1550 [Item 3.17]. This edition's portrait of Christian III, its patron, is shown in the Catalog.

Dutch. The eventual outcome of the Reformation in the Netherlands was one of the most pluralistic in Europe — including Roman Catholics, Orthodox Calvinists adhering to the Synod of Dort, Arminians, and Anabaptists — but initially its most distinctive expressions were part of the Radical Reformation. "In the Netherlands," George Huntston Williams has said, "Anabaptism was the first major onslaught of organized popular reformation. It preceded revolutionary-nationalist Calvinism by more than a generation."[70] Menno Simons (1469–1561) was a Roman Catholic priest from 1524 to 1536, when, by accepting believers' baptism and severing his ties to Roman Catholicism, he assumed leadership of the Dutch Anabaptist community that eventually came to be named for him. Because Emperor Charles V (1500–1558), as heir of Burgundy, had been nominal ruler of the Netherlands since 1506 and remained so until 1555, opposition to him and to the House of Habsburg became the political and military focus of the Reformation in the Netherlands, for which therefore the Dutch language assumed a position of major importance, even among those who remained true to Roman Catholicism. In his enumeration of the several "Dutch versions" of the Bible printed in the sixteenth century,[71] S. Van der Woude cites, in a footnote: "Another translation of the New Testament based on Erasmus appeared in 1524 at Delft, printed by C. H. Lettersnyder. It was often reprinted." That is the translation presented as Item 3.18: *Dat Niewe Testament.* It contains the Johannine Comma: "Getuych geuen wten hemel/ de vader/ twoert/ end die heylige geest/ end dese drie zijn een" [Item 3.18:O8ᵛ].

French. More perhaps in France than in any other country of Europe, there is a direct line from biblical humanism to the vernacular Bible. For "in the history of the French Bible," as R. A. Sayce has pointed out, "there is no Authorized Version, no Luther, no translation which has achieved anything like the universal authority of the standard versions in England and Germany."[72] In France itself, the Reformation party, the Huguenots, were a minority, and often a persecuted minority, and the principal strongholds of French-speaking Protestantism were Strasbourg and then Geneva. But unlike the Reformer of Wittenberg, the Reformer of Geneva, although he was in many ways better trained as a humanistic scholar than Luther, did not manage to impose his French translation of Holy Scripture on succeeding generations as a

70. Williams 1992, 527.

71. S. Van der Woude in Greenslade 1963, 122–25.

72. In Greenslade 1963, 113.

model both for the language of faith and for the language of poetry.[73] If, accepting the validity of Sayce's generalization, one had nevertheless to select the one French translation that approaches most nearly to that universal authority although falling far short of it, it would have to be the Neuchâtel Bible of 1535: *La Bible Qui est toute la Saincte escripture. En lanquelle sont contenus, le Vieil Testament [et] le Nouueau, translatez en Francoys* [Item 3.19]. It was the work of John Calvin's cousin, Pierre Robert, who came to be called Robert Olivétan (ca. 1506–38) and who in his brief life worked in Strasbourg, in Piedmont, and in Geneva. His translation of the New Testament and the Apocrypha leaned heavily on the work of the French humanist Jacobus Faber Stapulensis, or Jacques Lefèvre d'Etaples (ca. 1455–1536), but his translation of the Old Testament was far more his own work.[74] The history of its subsequent editions and revisions, some of which were by Calvin himself, is the mainstream of the career of the French Bible in the sixteenth century. Another chapter in the history of the French Bible is provided by the French Psalter by Clément Marot (ca. 1496–1544) and Bèze, *Les Psaumes de David, mis en rime françoise* [Item 4.16], which, as an important document in the history of the "poetry of the Bible," will be discussed in the next chapter.

Italian. Italy, the home of the Renaissance Papacy, was also the home of Renaissance humanism, and the early history of the Bible in Italian was caught between these two forces. Antonio Brucioli (ca. 1495–1566) published an Italian New Testament at Venice in 1530, and an entire Bible two years later; it was indebted to the Latin translation of Santi Pagnini [Item 1.23], especially for its rendering of the Hebrew. In 1562 Brucioli's translation of the Old Testament was combined with the Italian New Testament of Massimo Teofilo, the sometime Benedictine from Florence, and published under Protestant auspices in Geneva. But the most important figure in the history of the Italian Bible was the Calvinist theologian and scholar of Hebrew, Giovanni Diodati (1576–1649), who was born in Geneva of Protestant parents and who taught Old Testament there, becoming the successor of Théodore de Bèze in 1609 and continuing as professor of theology for the next forty years. The editio princeps of Diodati's Italian Bible was published at Geneva in 1607: *La Bibbia* [Item 3.20].

Natick-Algonquin. The age of the Reformation was also the age of exploration and then of conquest and colonization, above all in the Western hemisphere. One of the justifications — or, perhaps, rationalizations — for this expansion of European hegemony, adduced by both

73. See the discussion "Jean Calvin et la Bible," in Bedouelle and Roussel 1989, 240–45, and the bibliography, 776–78.

74. On Lefèvre d'Etaples and Olivétan see R. A. Sayce in Greenslade 1963, 116–20.

Roman Catholics and Protestants, was the intention to Christianize the heathen peoples. Jesuits and Franciscan missionaries brought Christian Latin to their converts, among them Native Americans across the new continent from Quebec to California. But for Protestants, the program of conversion necessitated the translation of the Bible into native tongues, which often required the creation of an alphabet and a written language. The first Bible printed in North America was the translation into the Natick-Algonquin language of Native Americans in Massachusetts by John Eliot (1604–90), often identified as "Apostle to the Indians"; the New Testament was first published in 1661, the Old Testament in 1663 [Item 3.21].

Portuguese. Concerning the place of Portugal in the age of the Reformation, every schoolchild knows — or at any rate used to know, when geography and history were required subjects — about the Papal Line of Demarcation of 1493 as a result of which Brazil became Portuguese-speaking, about Portuguese voyages to East Asia under royal patronage, and about the Portuguese colony in Goa. As for religious history, the Portuguese navigators, traders, and soldiers were followed by missionaries, above all the members of the newly formed Society of Jesus; for ecclesiastical history, these achievements were consolidated with the establishment of the archbishopric of Goa in 1557–58 and the coming of the Inquisition. The principal connection of Portugal with the Protestant Reformation was brought about through the work of Damião de Goes (1502–74), the author of the *Chrónica do felicíssimo rei Dom Manuel.* In 1536, it was he who cradled the head of the dying Erasmus in his arms. During those years Damião de Goes was in contact not only with various humanists but with Protestant Reformers in Wittenberg and elsewhere, as a result of which he was accused of Lutheranism and arrested. There had been interest in a Portuguese Bible already at the beginning of the sixteenth century, and various portions of the New Testament did appear. But the prohibition of vernacular Bibles by the Inquisition in both Portugal and Spain meant that such translations could not be published there. The translation of the New Testament into Portuguese was carried out by João Ferreira d'Almeida [Item 3.22], and its first edition appeared at Amsterdam in 1681. This edition, *O Novo Testamento,* was published at Batavia by João de Vries in 1693. It was based on a form of the Greek text that incorporated the Johannine Comma (1 Jn 5:7): "Porque tres sam os que testificam 'no ceo, o Pae, a Palavra, e o Espirito Sancto: e estes tres saõ hum" [Item 3.22:552].

Spanish. Sixteenth-century Spain is known as the land of the Inquisition, not of the Reformation; but what is less well known is that one of the most magnificent monuments of biblical scholarship and publication in the entire age of the Reformation, the Complutensian Polyglot [Item 1.25], owed its existence to the Grand Inquisitor of Spain, Cardinal Francisco Ximénez de Cisneros. As the home base of Emperor Charles V, before whose imperial diets Luther was summoned in 1521 and the Augsburg Confession was presented in 1530, Spain symbolized Roman Catholic opposition to the Reformation movement. Indeed, its most important contribution to the Reformation — and eventually to biblical study — was almost certainly the rise of the Society of Jesus, which cultivated biblical "lectures" that consisted, as John W. O'Malley's fine study of Jesuit beginnings has put it, of "a loose concatenation of philological information, patristic commentary, medieval spiritual teachings, scholastic divisions of materials, digressions, and sage reflections into which were injected specific and practical applications to different groups of people that might be in the audience."[75] But, for those very reasons, Spain was repeatedly the object of Protestant agitation and infiltration, part of which was the production of a Spanish Bible by Cassiodoro de Reina (ca. 1520–94) and then by Cyprian de Valera (1532–1602): *La Biblia,* which was issued not in Spain but in Switzerland, at Basel, by Thomas Guarin in 1569. The translators explicitly differentiated it, therefore, from Roman Catholic translations based on the Vulgate: "Primeramente declaramos no auer seguido en esta Translacion en todo y portodo la vieja Translacion Latina, que está en el comun vso: porque anque su autoridad por la antiguedad sea grande, ni lo vno ni lo otro le escusan los muchos yerros que tiene, apartandose del todo innumerables vezes de la verdad del texto Hebraico" [Item 3.23:**1ᵛ–2ʳ]. Therefore the title page contains, in unpointed Hebrew (Is 40:8), דבר אלהינו יקום לעולם, "La Palabra del Dios nuestro permanece para siempre."

---

75. O'Malley 1993, 109; on Jesuit attitudes toward the Bible see also 256–59.

4 : The Bible and the Arts

The rediscovery of the Bible by the Reformation of the sixteenth century was, as Karl Barth's similar rediscovery of "the strange new world within the Bible" in the twentieth century has been called, a "bomb that fell into the playground of the theologians." But it is not an inappropriate extension of this metaphor to add that the explosion of that bomb in the sixteenth century also produced a cultural fallout that continued into the following centuries. Like a nuclear fallout, the cultural fallout was in some ways incidental to the main purpose of the bombardment, but that did not make it any less powerful. For according to a formula of Wilhelm Dilthey, which dealt specifically with the Lutheran Reformation but could be extended to the Reformation in all its branches, "The religiosity of Lutheranism cannot be completely recognized on the basis of its works of dogmatics, but its documents are the writings of Luther, the chorale, the sacred music of Bach and Handel, and the organization of church life."[1] The cultural significance of the Reformation, as it was charted by Karl Holl, affected several major areas: popular education, the study of history, philosophy, literature, and art.[2] Now, it would surely be misleading to assume that all these areas of art and culture were related to "the Reformation of the Bible" in the same way, because some of them have only a distant connection with the biblical revival of the Reformation.

In the history of architecture, for example, the initial connection during the sixteenth century was minimal; for although Romanesque and Gothic churches were not built chiefly for preaching or even for frequent communion receiving both the host and the chalice, and therefore had to be rearranged inside for the new forms of worship, it seems to have been only when, after the devastation of the Thirty Years' War, Protestants were compelled to design and build their own churches that the opportunity came to express the architectural implications of Reformation beliefs in real buildings constructed from the ground up. As Karl Holl said in the lecture cited earlier,

---

1. Dilthey 1964, 515.
2. Holl [1918] 1959, 109–52.

"Magnificat" from *The booke of Common praier noted* (1550), fol. E2ʳ. Item 4.15.

If Protestantism lagged for such a long time in the one art whose work is most visible, in architecture, there were special reasons. First of all, the existing churches that Protestantism took over sufficed for its needs. For centuries there was no occasion to build new ones. But at this point there was also an inner obstacle. The fact that in the worship service Luther had not really created anything new, but had been content with a purification of tradition, long prevented Protestantism from reaching clarity over the purpose of the church building. What ends should it really serve? It could not be a house of God in the Catholic sense. For there was here no sacrament to be revered. Should it then be a preaching place or a place for meditation? Or both together? So long as these questions were not decided, indeed, not even discussed, Protestantism was not in a position to give artists assured direction.[3]

The biblical source and inspiration, however, would appear to have been historically incontestable practically from the outset for at least three areas of culture and the arts: the visual arts, literature, and music. But even for these three areas the importance of the Reformation for the history of culture is by no means the same from one country to another, nor (and perhaps more important) from one Reformation tradition or confession to another. The purpose of this brief chapter is to examine both the effect of the Bible on culture and the arts that was common to the entire Reformation and some of the several forms of that effect that were concentrated within one or another of the confessions.

ILLUSTRATIONS OF THE BIBLE AND ILLUSTRATIONS FROM THE BIBLE

It seems fair to estimate that no area of culture occasioned deeper disagreement and greater variety of outlook among Reformation parties than the visual arts. This tendency of the attitude toward the visual arts to become a point of cultural and even theological differentiation between churches had been a phenomenon of long standing in the history of Christianity. The most notable instance of it was unquestionably the distinctive apologia for icons developed by Byzantine thought in the eighth and ninth centuries on the basis of the Incarnation, as this justification for making the Invisible visible was definitively legislated into dogma by the Second Council of Nicea in 787.[4] That way of validating the use of images had found an occasional echo in the West, but despite its conciliar validation it had also often been misun-

3. Holl [1918] 1959, 148.
4. Pelikan 1990a, 67–98.

derstood there.[5] In the Western tradition during the Middle Ages, nevertheless, the visual arts of painting, sculpture, and stained glass had been one of the most important media for transmitting the Bible and its message, especially but not exclusively to the illiterate. Thus, apparently reflecting a childhood memory, Luther spoke of a medieval picture of Christ seated at the end of the rainbow, judging the quick and the dead.[6]

This diversity within the Reformation was such that in certain respects there can be said to have been deeper affinities between some of the Reformation churches (most notably, perhaps, the Lutheran Church) and the Roman Catholic Church with which they broke than between those Reformation churches and some other Reformation churches. For example, Luther refused to let medieval abuse nullify the legitimate use of the visual arts; and when his sometime colleague Andreas Rudolf Bodenstein von Carlstadt (ca. 1480–1541) led the attack against pictures in church as idolatrous, Luther counterattacked in his *Widder die hymelischen propheten von den bildern vnd Sacrament* of 1525; a major section of it bore the subtitle "Von dem Bildsturmen" [Item 4.1:B1ʳ].[7] In Zurich, as the leading student of Zwingli's attitude toward the arts has summarized "the war against the idols" waged there by Zwingli,

> the committee as a body went into every church in Zurich. Once inside, they locked the doors behind them, and then, free from all disturbance from the curious crowds without, began to dismantle the church. . . . Every standing statue was removed from its niche or its base and, together with the base, taken out of the church. It was then either broken up by the masons, if made of stone or plaster, or burned, if made of wood. Every painting was taken down from the altars and burned outside. All murals were chipped away or scraped off the walls. The altars were stripped of all images and vessels, all votive lamps were let down and melted outside, and all crucifixes were removed.[8]

And, as a more recent study by Lee Palmer Wandel has shown, not only Zurich but Strasbourg and Basel "differ significantly from Wittenberg," and "they provided important examples . . . [for] John Calvin . . . to spread in midcentury a conception of the 'Reformed' Church in which there were no images."[9] By contrast, as Carl C. Christensen has said, "if the Reformation in Germany resulted in the tragic destruction of countless ancient monuments, it also was partly responsible — at least in Lutheran areas — for the creation of a significant and interesting

5. Chazell 1992–93, 53–76.

6. Bainton 1950, 30–31.

7. *WA* 18:67; *LW* 40:84.

8. Garside 1966, 159.

9. Wandel 1995, 21–22.

body of new art objects," among which he lists in first place "Protestant Bible and book illustrations."[10]

In this case of such Protestant Bible and book illustrations, where the danger of idolatrous worship addressed to images was not as serious as it was with statues and paintings in churches, the printed Protestant Bibles of the Reformation often not only went along with the medieval practice but in some ways took the lead in redefining it. The medieval *Biblia Germanica* printed by Anton Koberger at Nuremberg [Item 4.2] in the year Martin Luther was born, 1483, illustrated major incidents of biblical history in woodcuts designed to be colored. Of special interest because it was to be a major theme both in the biblical theology and in the artistic creativity of the Reformation is the depiction of the Binding of Isaac, the Akedah (Gn 22:1–14), in a scene complete with a windmill. The same scene is the subject of a woodcut in Luther's Pentateuch of 1523 [Item 3.5]. Once again manifesting the combination of continuity and discontinuity between the Reformation and the later Middle Ages, Luther's *Passional,* which has been called "the prototype of a picture Bible," has been shown to have set a pattern for artistic representations of the sufferings of Christ, as well as of the Akedah.[11] That pattern had already begun to make itself evident somewhat earlier in such a masterwork as Albrecht Dürer's *Large Passion.* It was published in 1511 and included his 1510 portrayal of the Last Supper [Item 4.3], which is then recalled antiphonally by his portrayal in the *Small Passion* of 1511 of the Disciples at Emmaus, where the risen Christ "was known of them in breaking of bread" (Lk 24:35) [Item 4.4]. Interestingly, Dürer's depiction of the Last Supper from 1523 has been interpreted as "utraquistic," because it shows the apostles receiving the Sacrament *sub utraque specie* in both the host and the chalice [Item 4.5], in accordance with the insistence of the Reformers, beginning with Jan Hus and his followers (one party of whom came to be called Utraquists for that reason), that the Lord's Supper had been instituted for the laity as well as the clergy to receive under both kinds.

In the *Historiarum veteris instrvmenti icones,* issued at Lyons by Jean Frellon in 1538 [Item 4.6a], Hans Holbein's woodcuts are accompanied by Latin texts. French poems were added in later editions. An especially striking "icon," or picture, shows the battle between David and Goliath described in 1 Samuel 17,[12] with this French poem in the 1547 edition [Item 4.6b:F2ᵛ]:

> Dauid occit Goliath d'une pierre,
> Sans estre armé, en Dieu se confiant.

10. Christensen 1979, 110.
11. Van der Coelen 1994, 7.
12. Jeffrey 1992, 314–15.

> Par un enfant legeant mis par terre,
> Des Philistins l'ost retourne fuyant.

The Latin superscription says the same thing in prose, explaining in addition that David had gone into battle with Goliath "Saulis armis reiectis."

Some of the best-known artists of the period of the Reformation in addition to Dürer also made significant contributions to this genre of the illustrated Bible, sometimes by providing vivid graphic expression for Reformation polemics, including the Reformers' designation of the Pope as the Antichrist and "man of sin" (2 Thes 2:3–12), which is sharply portrayed in the pictures and prose of the *Passional Christi und Antichristi* of 1521.[13] Thus in Luther's September Testament [Item 3.4], Lucas Cranach the Elder (1472–1553) had depicted the Whore of Babylon (Rv 17)[14] with a triple tiara, in keeping with the standard Reformation identification of the Whore, quoted earlier from Heinrich Bullinger, as standing for "the very citie of Rome, and euen the popish and Romish church, and the pope himself with all his creatures and chapplaynes" [Item 2.12:510]. The same Cranach woodcut appeared in Luther's December Testament, but this time without the tiara. By a process whose details remain historically puzzling, the Roman Catholic antidote to Luther's translation of the New Testament into German, described in the preceding chapter, *Das naw Testament,* prepared by Hieronymus Emser and published at Dresden by Wolfgang Stöckel in 1527 [Item 3.7], which Luther denounced as a piece of plagiarism, contained all but two of these illustrations by Lucas Cranach — including the Whore of Babylon, but of course without the tiara! In the Emser volume are other illustrations by Georg Lemberger, especially for the Gospels.[15]

Lucas Cranach the Elder also provided the illustrations for a collection of images with the text of the Apostles' Creed, published in 1549, *Der heiligen XII. Aposteln ankunfft/ beruff/ glauben/ lere/ leben vnd seliges absterben,* by one Johannes Pollicarius, who identified himself on the title page as "Prediger zu Weissenfels": having abolished the cult of the saints, the Reformers nevertheless — or, more precisely, therefore — continued to be devoted to the apostles, and Cranach's final portrait shows the favorite apostle of the Reformers, Saint Paul [Item 4.7]. Soon thereafter there appeared seventy-eight illustrations by "Jost Amman/ Bürgern zu Nürnberg" in *Künstliche Vnd wolgerissene figuren,* which appeared at Frankfurt in 1579. As in the Lyons *Icones historiarum veteris testamenti* of 1547, these figures bear a Latin superscrip-

---

13. *WA* 9:701–15, with the pictures in an appendix; Scribner 1981, 148–89.

14. Reinitzer 1983, 139–41, on Dürer; Jeffrey 1992, 826–28 (Ronald B. Bond) traces this theme in English literature.

15. Reinitzer 1983, no. 111.

tion and a vernacular verse underneath (this time, however, in German). The orthodox trinitarian exegesis spoken of in Chapter 2, which the mainstream of the Reformation shared with the Tradition I of the fathers East and West, is reflected in an illustration of the prologue to the Gospel of John [Item 4.8:L1ʳ], whose verse paraphrase reads as follows:

> Christus Gotts Son das Wort erlesen/
>> Für der Welt anfang ist gewesen.
> Mit Gott dem Vatter vnd dem Geist/
>> Gleich ewig Christus allzeit heißt.
> Ein vnderschiedenlich Person/
>> Vom Vatter ist das Wort/ der Son.
> Nicht daß der Son vnd Vatter sey
>> Vermischt/ lehrt jedes Ampt gar frey.

Although belonging to a later generation, the engravings by Matthäus Merian (1593–1650) in *Icones Biblicae,* published from 1625 to 1627, with verses by Johann Ludwig Gottlieb, are also a kind of polyglot Bible in miniature, being accompanied by captions in Latin, German, and French verse [Item 4.9]. The French version for the story in Daniel 3 explains the picture:

> O Iouuenceaux heureux, pour n'auoir à l'Image
> Ni plié le genoil, ni fait aucun hommage,
> Vous estes enfournés dans vn feu plein d'horreur:
>> Mais par l'Ange se vid la flamme tost esteinte,
> Vostre chair ne fut pas de la chaleur atteinte,
> Mais vos bourrcaux bruslés donnent au Roy terreur.

Such works demonstrate what a dangerous and unjust oversimplification it would be to generalize about Reformation attitudes toward representational art on the basis of the reaction of the first generation against what was perceived to be an idolatrous use of sacred images.

POETRY OF THE BIBLE AND POETRY FROM THE BIBLE

Yet this genre of illustrations with poetic annotations already suggests that among all the arts, none was more obviously central to the Bible, and therefore more essential to the work of the biblical interpreter and translator, than poetry and drama. "We can," it has been observed by one of the few distinguished New Testament scholars to have been also a serious published poet, "call most of these texts 'poetry' if we are willing to include not only those which are evidently hymns but also those of a recitational character."[16] Martin Luther, in keeping with his espousal of the theory, quoted in Chapter 2, that the Book of Judith was not history but poetry, suggested that the Jews "solch geticht gespielet haben . . . Damit sie jr volck vnd die jugent lereten / als jnn einem gemeinen bilde" [Item 3.6:A1ʳ–ᵛ].[17] Thus he provided some of the same justification for biblical poetry and literature that he supplied for visual art in his treatise *Against the Heavenly Prophets,* quoted earlier in this chapter, and without the same ambivalence. It was a sound principle of biblical translation, which had evidently been at work in the Septuagint and then even more in the Vulgate, as Jerome's prefaces to the several books also attest, that the literature and language of the Bible must not be homogenized but that each of the several literary forms of the Bible deserved to be reproduced distinctively in the new language. It would not do to have Queen Jezebel reciting sublime poetry or the Blessed Virgin Mary sounding prosaic! A more subtle corollary of this principle was the question whether the translation should reflect not only the literary diversity between biblical books but the linguistic diversity as well. Should the differences between the Greek of the Gospel of Mark and that of the Gospel of Luke, so obvious to anyone coming to the Greek New Testament from a background in the Classics, be made evident to the reader of a vernacular version, and if so, how could that be accomplished? A persistent criticism of the King James Version of the Bible has been that in its striving for a dignified rendering of the Greek and Hebrew originals, sometimes referred to pejoratively as "dainty English," it had gone too far and thus had lost what Daniell calls "the rawness of the original."[18] At the very minimum, however, it was a legitimate requirement of the biblical translator, be he Jerome or Martin Luther, that he make the poems of the Bible sound poetic. And that is how they did sound, for example in Luther's poetic rendering in 1523 [Item 3.5] of the triumphant paean of the prophetess Miriam and her brother Moses with the children of Israel, recorded in Exodus 15:21 and 15:1 — the sequence having been transposed into that order by George Frideric Handel (1685–1759) in his *Israel in Egypt,* in order to make Miriam the choragus:

Vnd MirJam die prophetyn Aarons schwester nam eyn paucken ynn yhr hand/ vnd alle weyber folgeten yhr nach hynaus mit paucken am reygen/ Vnd MirJam sang yhn fur/ Last vns dem HERRN singen/ das er herlich gehandellt hat/ man und ross hat er yns meer gestortzt.

Da sang Mose vnd die kinder Jsrael dis lied dem HERRN und sprachen.

16. Wilder 1964, 115.

17. *WA DB* 12:4–6; *LW* 35:338–39.

18. Daniell 1992, xiv–xv.

Ich will dem HERRN singen/ denn er hatt herlich gehandellt/ Ros vnd wagen hat er gestortzet yns meer.

Such a cultivation of beautiful language by translators could, however, go only so far in expressing, for one national group after another, the literary and linguistic dynamism that had been articulated in Dante's *De vulgari eloquentia* for Italian and that had been documented in the several vernacular versions of Holy Writ, as this dynamism has been examined in the preceding chapter. As Johannes Quasten showed in the case of the early church, speaking about music, "The earliest of the Church Fathers frequently emphasized the beauty and euphony of the human voice, . . . [but] in contrast to the Christian people's joy in singing and the growing melodic development of liturgical song, many ecclesiastical writers of the fourth and fifth centuries began to fear that the prayerful character of singing could suffer because of too great an artistic elaboration."[19] In keeping with that dialectical attitude toward sacred music (to be discussed below), which parallels the even deeper ambivalence toward images or what I have elsewhere called "the ambiguity of the iconographic tradition,"[20] the contribution of the Bible in the age of the Reformation, particularly to the poetics of the languages and the lands that it helped to reshape, far transcended the important but limited task of the translator; rather, it went on to provide a new impulse to the poet. An intriguing example, of Roman Catholic provenance, is a "poema eroico" by an Italian noblewoman and member of a distinguished Florentine family, Maddalena Salvetti Acciaiuoli (†1610), *Il David Perseguitato o vero fuggitivo,* in which the scene shown earlier from 1 Samuel 17 is described in these heroic lines:

> Egl' è pur quel, che'l fier Golia trafisse,
>   E che de' Filistei l'armate squadre,
>   Con la man valorosa, in fuga misse,
>   E mill' altre fe poi proue leggiadre;
>   Ch'hor in vil seruitù sarieno affisse
>   Le forze d'Israel misere, & adre,
>   Se lui non era, hor tal premio si rende
>   A quel, che vita, e libertà difende? [Item 4.12:11^r]

It would almost be possible to print her lines in conjunction with the illustration of this scene in the *Icones historiarum veteris testamenti* [Item 4.6b:F2^v].

To document this literary development fully would require nothing short of a special

19. Quasten 1983, 92, followed by illustrative quotations from Chrysostom and Augustine.

20. Pelikan 1990a, 41–66.

historical reference book, with many such examples of various themes, for each of the several national literatures affected. As David Lyle Jeffrey has said in his preface to the very model of such a historical reference book, "Cynewulf's adaptations of New Testament narrative further exemplified a tradition extending through Chaucer, Shakespeare, Milton, Bunyan, and Defoe, as through Hawthorne, Melville, Whitman, and Dickinson, to Eliot, Auden, MacLeish, and Nemerov. As a result, contemporary readers of English literature for whom the Bible itself remains a closed book, even a 'dead' book, continue to 'hear' it persistently, inter alia. Whether or not the Bible's literary presence comes to be reckoned with cogently is a question upon which, it seems, much else depends — even, perhaps, the probable shelf life of a substantial body of our most accomplished literature."[21] For our more limited purposes in this chapter, one of these examples from English literature cited by Jeffrey may perhaps suffice, particularly because of the stature of the poet: John Milton (1608–74). Milton's prowess as a biblical interpreter has long been known from the study of some of his prose works dealing with the fine points of marriage and divorce, where he carefully analyzed the appropriate biblical passages. His prowess as an innovator in biblical theology, by contrast, had remained largely unknown, until the publication of his *Christian Doctrine* a century and a half after his death, in 1825, made it clear, with a shock to some of his readers, that he had gone far beyond the "magisterial Reformers" to challenge the orthodox Christian dogmas of the Trinity and the person of Christ, and that he had done so by questioning not merely the rationality of these doctrines but their biblical foundations. For like the antitrinitarians of the Reformation, with their "Christocentric Unitarian position without that terminology . . . [which was] reached in the sixteenth-century devolution of the Nicene doctrine on the basis of the quest for scriptural sanctions,"[22] Milton claimed to have fought his way through from Nicene orthodoxy, which the Anglican Reformers and the Puritan divines continued to profess (inconsistently, according to his judgment), to the authentic teaching of Scripture. His new position was, he claimed in *Christian Doctrine,* the logical outcome of the Reformation doctrine of sola Scriptura, which Reformers like Luther and Calvin had enunciated in the abstract but had not applied thoroughly to the creedal tradition that they had received from the Greek and Latin church fathers of Christian antiquity.

For most present-day readers outside the scholarly circles of specialists in Puritanism and historians of theology, of course, Milton's standing as an interpreter of the Bible derives almost exclusively from his three biblical epics, *Paradise Lost* in 1667 [Item 4.13a], *Paradise Regained* in 1671, and *Samson Agonistes* also in 1671 and published in the same volume with *Paradise Regained* [Item 4.13b]. In these epics and in Bunyan's *Pilgrim's Progress,* as Christopher Hill has pointed

21. Jeffrey 1992, xiii.
22. Williams 1992, 476.

out, "Milton and Bunyan did not reproduce Biblical stories, as earlier verse paraphrases had done: they re-imagined the myths in the light of the problems of their own society."[23] *Samson Agonistes* combines in the two words of its title the Classical and the biblical sources of Milton's inspiration; that combination is carried out on its title page, which we have reproduced in the Catalog, by a quotation, in Greek and then in Latin, of the famous passage from chapter 6 of Aristotle's *Poetics* (1449b): "Τραγοιδία μίμησις πράξεως σπουδαίας [Tragedy is the imitation of an action that is serious]." By common consent, *Paradise Lost* is the greatest of the three poems, both in its literary power and in its psychological-religious insight: Milton's Satan is, with Shakespeare's (and Verdi's) Iago, one of the great evil spirits of all literature. Yet considered only on the basis of its biblical derivation, this account of the Fall and this portrait of Satan rest on a rather narrow foundation, namely, the story of the temptation of Adam and Eve in the third chapter of Genesis, with some assistance from other portions of the Bible, especially the prologue in heaven that introduces the Book of Job and the story of the temptation of Christ. Although no one would presume to put *Paradise Regained* on the same level as an epic poem, it is far more than a mere sequel even when considered as literature; and when considered as a biblical drama it embraces a far more inclusive body of material from the Bible: by implication all the sources that contributed to *Paradise Lost,* plus the red thread of salvation-history that runs from Genesis to Revelation. It has been suggested that "Milton, throughout the *Christian Doctrine,* and by inference, in his other works, referred as often to the Hebrew text as to any other version, and always, when the possibility of doubt concerning a given passage might arise, went direct to the Hebrew original."[24]

Working from such a knowledge of the original languages, therefore, Milton in *Paradise Regained* was able to concentrate on the corresponding temptation story, the account of the temptation of Christ. Because the Gospel of Luke, as Frank Kermode has said, "powerfully links the Temptation with the climax of the whole story, the Crucifixion, . . . it is hardly to be wondered at that Milton, in *Paradise Regained,* based his own interpretative narrative mainly on Luke's."[25] Thus the response of Christ to the second temptation in Luke 4:5–8 — which is the third temptation in Matthew 4:8–10 and which would go on to inspire other great literature, such as the Legend of the Grand Inquisitor in Dostoevsky's *The Brothers Karamazov* two centuries later — became, in Milton's hands, a heroic period beginning this way in lines 43 to 48 of Book Three of *Paradise Regained* [Item 4.13b:56]:

> To whom our Saviour calmly thus reply'd.
> Thou neither dost perswade me to seek wealth

23. Hill 1993, 372.
24. Fletcher 1926, 72.
25. In Alter and Kermode 1987, 397.

> For Empires sake, nor Empire to affect
> For glories sake by all thy argument.
> For what is glory but the blaze of fame,
> The peoples praise, if always praise unmixt?

The expansion of Luke's version of the dialogue between tempter and tempted continued for many more lines, until at Book IV, line 363, Satan was "quite at a loss, for all his darts were spent" [Item 4.13b:97]. And through this victory of the tempted over the tempter Paradise was regained, as it had originally been lost through the victory of the tempter over the tempted.

SONGS OF THE BIBLE AND SONG FROM THE BIBLE

As is evident from the example of Zwingli, who destroyed images and statues but loved music,[26] music occupied a special place among the arts for the Reformers. And a special category of the "poetry of the Bible" had always consisted of those poetic passages from both the Old Testament and the New Testament that were intended for use in community worship, such songs as the Magnificat of the Virgin Mary (Lk 1:46–55), the Benedictus of Zacharias (Lk 1:68–79), and the Nunc Dimittis of Simeon (Lk 2:29–32), all from the first two chapters of the Gospel of Luke, and above all, of course, the songs from the Book of Psalms. All these biblical songs had long since been set to music, perhaps even originally in the case of the New Testament canticles and almost certainly so in the case of the Psalter. The leading neo-Latin poet Helius Eobanus Hessus (1488–1540) produced his own poetic rendering of Psalm 46, though not with a musical setting:

> Robur et auxilium est nobis deus ipse repertus,
> Per mala quae passi perniciosa sumus [Item 4.10(1544):144].

Humanist that he was, Hessus translated into Latin not only the Psalter (in 1538), but the *Iliad* of Homer (in 1540); and his Classical humanistic training comes through in the marginal gloss to those lines of Psalm 46: "Laeta uox exultantis cordis ob praesentiam Dei. Est autem enthimema, primo Minorem post conclusionem ponit," the "enthymeme" to which that explanation refers being a rearrangement of the traditional order of the syllogism, from major premise–minor premise–conclusion to major premise–conclusion–minor premise.

In their effort to be faithful to the authority of the letter of Scripture in its musical use as

---

26. Garside 1966 is an examination of this contrast between music and other arts in Zwingli, which the author's early death prevented him from expanding into the full-scale examination of the Reformers and the arts that he was planning — and which continues to be needed.

well, therefore, the Reformers were concerned to probe and determine the meaning of the notations and prescriptions that appeared in some of the Psalms, for example "Selah [סֶלָה]," which occurred seventy-one times in the Hebrew Bible and had been translated in the Septuagint as διάψαλμα. Flacius, citing as authorities both Jewish and Christian writers, expressed his preference for the meaning "that in the singing of the adjoining verse there was to be an intensification both of the voice and of the mind" [Item 2.14(1628):1:1114]. Such a probing of Hebrew musical annotations, which in most Reformation translations of the Bible (for example, in the German translation of Psalm 46:3 by Luther, quoted below) nevertheless left the Hebrew word transliterated but not translated, acquired special urgency for those confessions in which the Book of Psalms as such acquired the standing of *a* or *the* Christian hymnbook. The rationale behind this privileged position accorded to the Psalms was quite explicitly the emphasis of the Reformation on the authority of the Bible. In the poetic introduction that he appended to the French Psalter by Clément Marot (ca. 1496–1544) and himself, *Les Psaumes de David, mis en rime Françoise,*[27] Théodore de Bèze combined references to the Classical Muses with references to David the Psalmist, in order to explain and exhort:

> Or donc afin que pas vn n'eust excuse
> De louer Dieu, Marot auec sa Muse
> Chanta iadis iusqu' au tiers des Cantiques
> Du grand Dauid, qui en sons Hebraïques
> Sa harpe fit parler premierement
> Et puis choisit la plume de Clement,
> A celle fin que du peuple François
> Dieu fust loué & de coeur & de voix [Item 4.16(1642):c2ʳ].

Each psalm is accompanied by a musical setting: that of Psalm 46, "Des qu' aduersité nous offense, Dieu nous est appui & defense," appeared in the Huguenot Psalter [Item 4.16(1642):D9ᵛ–D10ʳ].

An early edition of the prayer book of the Church of England, *The booke of Common praier noted,* which appeared as early as 1550, listed "iiii. sortes of notes" to indicate how the Psalms were to be sung: "The first note is a strene note and is a breue. The second a square note, and is a semy breue. The iii. a pycke and is a mynymme. And when there is a prycke by the square note, that prycke is halfe as muche as the note that goeth before it. The iiii. is a close, and is only vsed at the end of a verse" [Item 4.15:A2ʳ]. The Genevan translator of the Italian Bible mentioned in the preceding chapter, Giovanni Diodati (1576–1649), appended a metrical and

---

27. See the careful and thorough discussion in Douen 1878–79.

rhymed version of the Psalms to his *La Sacra Bibbia* of 1641, with a free rendering in paraphrase that falls somewhere halfway between a translation and a new poetic composition:

> Alto ripar die guerra,
> Epossa inuitta in perigliosa proua,
> Ecci quel gran Signor, che cielo, e terra,
> Sotto le leggi de l'imperio serra [Item 3.20(1641):B5ᵛ].

This tradition of metrical (and often rhymed) translations of the Psalms for use in common worship reached one of its summits in the hymnody of Isaac Watts (1674–1748). There is a straight line from the medieval practice of singing the Lesser Doxology, the Gloria Patri, at the conclusion of a psalm to make it into a Christian hymn,[28] to "Old Hundredth," often called the Common Doxology, sung at the end of a metric psalm (and still one of the best known of all Christian songs in the English-speaking world), written by Bishop Thomas Ken (1637–1711):[29]

> Praise God from whom all blessings flow,
> Praise him, all creatures here below.
> Praise him above, ye heavenly host,
> Praise Father, Son, and Holy Ghost.

But just as the Reformation impulse to biblical poetry could not content itself with translating the poetry of the Bible but had to go on to compose original poetry that came from the Bible and was inspired by the Bible, so it was to be a fortiori with biblical song, which became, already in Luther's hands, more than poetic translation of the Bible, more even than poetic paraphrase, but the free outpouring of the biblical message in creative new forms. The New Testament itself had prescribed, "Let the word of Christ dwell in you richly in all wisdom; teaching and admonishing one another in psalms and hymns and spiritual songs, singing with grace in your hearts to the Lord" (Col 3:16). The Geneva Bible commented on this verse, "Psalmes properly conteine complainings to God, narrations, & expostulations: hymnes, onely thankes giuing: songs conteine praises, & thankes giuing, but not so largely and amply, as hymnes do" [Item 3.12:AAa2ᵛ]. These words were a prescription, and therefore a legitimation, which did seem to go well beyond the metrical Psalters of the Reformation, to include the latter two categories, hymns and spiritual songs, which were then understood to refer to original, postbiblical compositions. In a typical bon mot, Luther averred that the devil should

---

28. *ODCC* 572.

29. Julian [1907] 1957, 616–22.

not have all the pretty melodies, and he made his contribution to redressing that unfavorable balance by publishing or at least sponsoring a series of hymnals, beginning with the *Achtlieder-buch* of 1524 [see Item 4.14].[30] Seen as part of the impact of the Bible on the arts in the Reformation, Luther's hymns take the work of the biblical translator beyond translation to a new level of creativity, as can be perceived most strikingly in the best known of them all, the first stanza of "Ein feste Burg ist unser Gott." That hymn is shown here along with Luther's translation, from his Bible of 1534, of the first verses of Psalm 46 — verses that are clearly the inspiration of the hymn but just as clearly are not its source in any simple literal sense:

Gott ist vnser zuuersicht vnd stercke/	EIn feste burg ist unser Gott,
Eine hülffe jnn den grossen nöten/	Ein gute wehr und waffen.
die vns troffen haben.	Er hilfft uns frey aus aller not,
Darumb fürchten wir uns nicht/	die uns jtzt hat betroffen.
wenn gleich die welt vnter gienge/	Der alt böse feind
Vnd die berge mitten jnns meer süncken.	mit ernst ers jtzt meint,
Wenn gleich das meer wütet vnd wallet/	gros macht und viel list
Vnd von seinem ungestüm die berge	sein grausam rüstung ist,
einfielen. Sela.	auff erd ist nicht seins gleichen.[31]

It was John Milton's almost exact contemporary, Paul Gerhardt (1607–76), who, a century after the Reformation, came to occupy, in the history of the biblical hymnody of the German Reformation, a position analogous to Milton's position in the history of the biblical poetry of the English Reformation.[32] Passing through the fiery trial of the Thirty Years' War, Gerhardt found his religious and poetic voice in chorales that were existential in their intense subjectivity and yet utterly objective in their ground of faith. This was the very combination of objectivity and subjectivity that the faith and theology of the Reformers had found in the Bible itself and that in turn the Bible had stamped on their spirituality. Sometimes the biblicism of Gerhardt's hymns was quite overt, as in his twelve-stanza hymn of 1656, "Befiehl' du deine Wege," sung to the melody of Hans Leo Haßler's (1564–1612) "Herzlich thut mich verlangen," whose stanzas open with consecutive words and phrases from Luther's translation of Psalm 37:5: "Befehl dem HERRN deine wege/ Vnd hoffe auff ihn/ er wirds wol machen."[33] Sometimes the biblical inspiration was more indirect, as in his best-known hymn:

---

30. W. Lucke's introductions, *WA* 35:1–87; on the collections, *WA* 35:314–99.

31. *WA* 35:455–57; *LW* 53:284–85.

32. Julian [1907] 1957, 409–12.

33. Ibid., 125–26, including a list of English translations.

O Haupt voll Blut und Wunden
Voll Schmerz und voller Hohn!
O Haupt, zu Spott gebunden
Mit einer Dornenkron'!
O Haupt, sonst höchst gezieret
Mit höchster Ehr' und Zier,
Jetzt aber hoch schimpfieret:
Gegrüsset seist du mir![34]

This was sung to the same melody by Haßler, and the immediate source of the text was the medieval "Salve caput cruentatum," which was probably written by the thirteenth-century Cistercian, Arnulf of Louvain (†1248). But the full biblical context of Gerhardt's hymn was supplied only after yet another century, in the 1740s, when it became the recurring leitmotiv and, in these words of its first stanza, an emotional climax for the definitive version of *The Passion of Our Lord According to Saint Matthew* (*BWV* 244) of Johann Sebastian Bach (1685–1750).[35] Bach's own relation to the Reformation — and to the Bible of the Reformation[36] — in both text and music was profound and complex. Luther's "Ein feste Burg" served as the basis for his chorale prelude settings of that chorale (*BWV* 302, 303) and for his Reformation Cantata of the same name (*BWV* 80). And yet another century later, just at the time when Felix Mendelssohn-Bartholdy (1809–47) was preoccupied with the church music of Bach, leading up to his revival of the *Passion According to Saint Matthew* on 11 March 1829, he composed his *Fifth Symphony* in D major, the "Reformation Symphony," whose fourth movement is a fugue-like elaboration of Luther's chorale "Ein feste Burg." That also was — and is — an authentic part of the history of the cultural fallout from the Reformation of the Bible, as well as an abiding resonance from the Bible of the Reformation.

34. Ibid., 835.

35. Pelikan 1986, 81–88.

36. Various aspects of the biblical exegesis and hermeneutics at work in the compositions of Bach have been examined in Petzoldt 1985.

Catalog of the Exhibition

A NOTE ON THE CATALOG OF THE EXHIBITION

Bibliographic information for each item has been simplified, although references have been provided, wherever available, to standard bibliographies that supply full descriptions. Brackets are used for imprint information not derived explicitly from the title page or colophon. Names of authors, printers, and publishers are given according to the native language of each, except in some cases where English usage is extremely powerful (as for John Calvin or Aldus Manutius) and in other cases where the obscurity of the name has left no option but adopting the (usually latinate) spelling of the imprint. It proved to be impractical and unwieldy to provide copy-specific information and collations because participating libraries use largely their own holdings. Occasionally a library exhibits an alternative edition for an item; this is indicated under "Exhibition."

For those books that either lack title pages or, as often happens with early printed books, have titles that differ substantially from modern usage, it has been necessary to provide a uniform title. When a title or passage is cited from an imprint, however, original orthography has been used, despite inconsistencies. The capitalization of Latin titles and quotations has been regularized. Original capitalization has been retained for all other languages, except that only the initial letter is capitalized for words originally in solid capitals. Ligatures and abbreviations have been resolved for all languages.

The descriptions of the items place them in the context of early modern culture, with special attention accorded, as appropriate, to the history of books and printing. Moreover, we have tried to give a feel for the books by quoting characteristic or impressive passages and by including images of most of the items. The references at the ends of the descriptive passages are sources for the descriptions and are also intended as aids for further research on the issues the item raises.

Unless otherwise indicated, the illustrations are from the holdings of Bridwell Library or from the Elizabeth Perkins Prothro Collection on deposit at Bridwell Library.

ΥΠΟΘΕCΙC ΤΗC Α ΟΜΗΡΟΥ ΟΔΥCCΕΙΑC·

ἐῶν ἀγορὰ γίνεται περὶ τοῦ τὸν Ὀδυσσέα ἐξ Ἰθάκης τε
ἐκπεμφθῆναι ἀπὸ τῆς Καλυψοῦς νήσου, μεθ' ἣν ἡ Ἀθηνᾶ
ἐς Ἰθάκην παραγίνεται πρὸς Τηλέμαχον, ὁμοιωθεῖσα
Μέντη τῷ βασιλεῖ Ταφίων· γενομένης δὲ ὁμιλίας παρορ-
μήσασα ἡ Ἀθηνᾶ Τηλέμαχον παρασκευάσασθαι διὰ τὴν τοῦ
πατρὸς ζήτησιν· εἰς πύλον μὲν, πρὸς νέστορα· ἐς Σπάρτην
δὲ, πρὸς Μενέλαον ἀπαίρει· ἐμφασιν Ἀθηνᾶς οὔσης ὡς θεὸς ἦν
καὶ τῶν μνηστήρων γίνεται λωχία.

ΟΔΥCCΕΙΑC Α ΟΜΗΡΟΥ ΡΑΨΩΔΙΑC·

Α θεῶν ἀγορή, ὀτρυνεὶ δ' Ἀθήνη παλλάδ' Ἀθὶ θάρσος.

α

ἄνδρα μοι ἔννεπε μοῦσα πο-
λύτροπον ὃς μάλα πολλὰ
πλάγχθη, ἐπεὶ Τροίης ἱερὸν
πτολίεθρον ἔπερσε.
πολλῶν δ' ἀνθρώπων ἴδεν
ἄστεα, καὶ νόον ἔγνω.
πολλὰ δ' ὅ γ' ἐν πόντῳ πάθεν
ἄλγεα ὃν κατὰ θυμόν,
ἀρνύμενος, ἥν τε ψυχὴν καὶ
νόστον ἑταίρων.

ἀλλ' οὐδ' ὣς ἑτάρους ἐρρύσατο ἱέμενός περ.
αὐτῶν γὰρ σφετέρῃσιν ἀτασθαλίῃσιν ὄλοντο
νήπιοι· οἳ κατὰ βοῦς ὑπερίονος ἠελίοιο
ἤσθιον· αὐτὰρ ὁ τοῖσιν ἀφείλετο νόστιμον ἦμαρ.
τῶν ἁμόθεν γε θεά θύγατερ Διὸς εἰπὲ καὶ ἡμῖν.
ἔνθ' ἄλλοι μὲν πάντες ὅσοι φύγον αἰπὺν ὄλεθρον
οἴκοι ἔσαν πόλεμόν τε πεφευγότες ἠδὲ θάλασσαν.
τὸν δ' οἶον νόστου κεχρημένον ἠδὲ γυναικός,
νύμφη πότνι' ἔρυκε Καλυψὼ δῖα θεάων
ἐν σπέσσι γλαφυροῖσι, λιλαιομένη πόσιν εἶναι.
ἀλλ' ὅτε δὴ ἔτος ἦλθε περιπλομένων ἐνιαυτῶν,
τῷ οἱ ἐπεκλώσαντο θεοὶ οἶκόνδε νέεσθαι
εἰς Ἰθάκην· οὐδ' ἔνθα πεφυγμένος ἦεν ἀέθλων.
καὶ μετὰ οἷσι φίλοισι· θεοὶ δ' ἐλέαιρον ἅπαντες,
νόσφι Ποσειδάωνος· ὁ δ' ἀσπερχὲς μενέαινεν

AA1

1.1, fol. AA1ʳ,
beginning of the
Odyssey

I. SACRED PHILOLOGY

I.I

Homer. *Opera.*

Edited by Demetrios Chalcondyles.
2 vols. Florence: [Bartolommeo di Libri with]
Demetrios Damilas for Bernardo and Neri Nerli,
9 December 1488.
BMC 6:678–79 (IB.27657a); Goff H-300.

The recovery of Greek literature in the Renaissance included religious, philosophical, historical, and poetic works. It is fitting, and not surprising, that the first Greek classics to be printed were Homer's *Iliad* and *Odyssey.* After all, the *Iliad* was the central literary text in the Byzantine curriculum, and Western humanists, beginning with Petrarch, had long regretted having no direct access to Homer's poetry.

The editio princeps (which, in addition to the epics, includes the *Batrachomyomachia* and the *Homeric Hymns*) was edited by Demetrios Chalcondyles (1423–1511), one of several important Greek scholars who pursued careers in Italy with the collapse of the Byzantine Empire. After studying in Rome, he held a series of teaching positions. From 1463 to 1472 he was professor of Greek at Padua; from 1472 to 1491 he taught at the Florentine *Studio,* where Johannes Reuchlin (1455–1522), Thomas Linacre (1460–1524), Giovanni Pico della Mirandola (1463–94), and Giovanni de' Medici (1475–1521), the future Pope Leo X, were among his students. In part enticed by opportunities to edit Greek texts, he took a professorship at Milan in 1491 and stayed there, with brief interruptions, until his death.

The work is dedicated to Piero de' Medici (1471–1503). In the introductory letter "To Piero, son of Lorenzo de' Medici," the publisher Bernardo Nerli explains that the lack of Greek books in Italy inspired him to engage Chalcondyles, an Athenian, and to choose Homer, "as the oldest and greatest poet, with a certain divine genius, and the spring from which all literature has flowed" (fol. A1ʳ).

The typeface is derived from the design of Demetrios Damilas (fl. 1476–88) for Lascaris's *Epitome* of 1476, which, in turn, is thought to have been based on the handwriting of Michael Apostolis (Barker 1992, 30–31). On the basis of the roman types used, Proctor assigned the work to the press of Bartolommeo di Libri. Nerli, however, acknowledges Damilas's "skill" ("Demetriique Cretensis dexteritatem"; fol. A1ʳ) but does not mention any participation by di Libri.

References: Barker 1992, 30–37; Cammelli 1954, 88–92; Harlfinger 1989, 6, 40–49; Proctor [1900] 1966, 66–69.
Exhibition: Bridwell, 06355–56; Harvard, Inc/6343.5; Union/*Columbia,* Inc/H-300; Yale, YCBA/Early Eng. 57.

1.2, title page.

By permission of the Houghton Library, Harvard University.

I.2

Euripides.

Hecvba, et Iphigenia in Aulide.

Translated by Erasmus of Rotterdam. Venice: Aldus Manutius, December 1507.
Adams E-1045.

Hecuba and *Iphigenia* were, respectively, the second and third Greek works that Erasmus (1466/69–1536) translated, although they were the first to appear in print. In 1503, he prepared translations of three speeches by Libanius, which were not printed until 1519. Between 1502 and 1504 he translated *Hecuba* and in 1506 *Iphigenia,* both of which were first published by Badius Ascensius (1462–1535) in an edition dedicated to William Warham (ca. 1456–1532), archbishop of Canterbury.

Disheartened by mistakes in Badius's printing, Erasmus arranged for a subsequent edition at the Aldine press in 1507. Aldus Manutius (1449/50–1515), who had printed Euripides's plays in Greek in 1503, was authorized by Erasmus to correct the text. Further emendations were made, under Erasmus's supervision, in the Froben editions (1518, 1524, and 1530), which also include the original Greek text on pages facing the metrical Latin renderings.

Erasmus's work is the first complete translation of a Greek tragedy ever printed. Before him, Francesco Filelfo (1398–1481) had translated only the prologue to *Hecuba,* an effort that Erasmus criticized sharply. Erasmus probably selected *Hecuba* because it had held an important place in the Byzantine school curriculum.

In the dedicatory letter, he says that he undertook these translations as preparatory exercises for greater tasks to follow, meaning, most scholars agree, his edition and translation of the New Testament.

References: Bigliazzi et al. 1994, 98; Renouard 1825, 1:222; Rummel 1985, 28–47; Waszink 1972; Wilson 1973.
Exhibition: Bridwell showing Florence: Heirs of Filippo

Giunta, December 1518 (AER4453); Harvard, *NC5/
Erl53/506eb; Union/*Columbia* showing Basel: Froben, 1524
(Lodge/1524/Eu73); Yale, Beinecke/Gfe86/ff507.

1.3

Plato. *Opera.*

Translated by Marsilio Ficino. 2 vols. Florence:
Lorenzo di Alopa, [May 1484–before April 1485].
BMC 6:666 (IB.27995); Goff P-771.

The only writings of Plato available to medieval
readers were Latin translations of *Phaedo* and *Meno*
and partial translations of *Timaeus* and *Parmenides.*
That changed dramatically in the early Renaissance
with the efforts of Manuel Chrysoloras (ca. 1350–
1415), Leonardo Bruni (1369–1444), and Uberto
Decembrio (†1427), all of whom translated numerous dialogues, and then with the publication of
the first complete Latin version of the dialogues by
Marsilio Ficino (1433–99) in 1484/85.

Ficino made use of earlier translations, especially
for his version of the *Republic,* which relies heavily
on those by Chrysoloras and Decembrio. In the
preface, he acknowledges that he also consulted
with Chalcondyles and Angelo Poliziano (1454–94),
among others. Nonetheless, he also studied Greek
manuscripts of Plato carefully, four of which have
been identified (Sicherl 1962, 53). As early as 1462,
Cosimo de' Medici (1389–1464) gave him a complete Greek manuscript of the dialogues.

In *Platonic Theology,* Ficino published a successful
compendium of Platonic thought. He emphasized
the immortality of the soul in Plato and, generally,
sought to reconcile Platonism and Christianity,
viewing Plato as a *medicus animorum* (doctor of souls),
whose works could inspire conversion to a life of
virtue. Ficino also established an academy, modeled
after Plato's Academy, where he lectured informally
on philosophy and politics, mainly to young men of
Florence's ruling families.

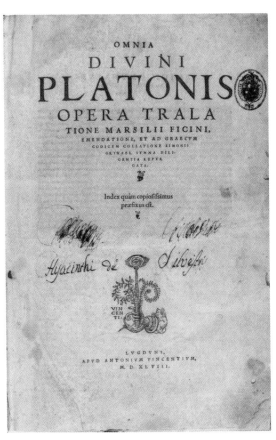

1.3, title page (1548 edition).

References: Hankins 1990, 267–359, 456–85; Kristeller 1974–
76, 1:50–68 and 2:101–14; Sicherl 1962.

Exhibition: Bridwell showing Lyons: Antoine Vincent, 1548
(184.1/P718/1548); Harvard, Inc/6405*; Union/*Columbia,*
Inc/P-771.

1.4, vol. 5: fol. αααα2ʳ, beginning of *Nicomachean Ethics*

1.4

Aristotle. *Opera.*

5 vols. Venice: Aldus Manutius,
1 November 1495–June 1498.
Goff A-959; *GW* 2334.

The edition of the complete works of Aristotle helped establish Aldus Manutius's reputation as the most distinguished printer of Greek texts in the Renaissance.

The fifth volume, shown here, contains the only incunabular Greek printing of the *Nichomachean Ethics,* which was probably the most influential Aristotelian text during the Renaissance. It had, however, been printed in Latin in some twenty-five separate editions before 1501, the most important Latin versions having been composed by Leonardo Bruni and Joannes Argyropoulos (1393/94–1487). Although Aristotle was probably more often read in Latin, several of his works were used as school texts in the original Greek. For example, Johannes Sturm (1507–89) made the *Nicomachean Ethics,* in Greek, a core text for his pedagogical program at Strasbourg.

For the complete edition, the Aldine press developed a new font, relying, almost certainly, on the skill of Francesco Griffo (now considered the leading type-cutter of his era). It is an elaboration of the first Aldine Greek font, the "Lascaris font" (so named for its use in the printing of Lascaris's grammar [see Item 1.6]), which was itself relatively complex (Lowry 1979, 130–31). The several forms for the same letters, the many ligatures, and the cursiveness make Aldine fonts difficult to read, despite their beauty.

References: Cranz 1971, 122; Lowry 1979; Schmitt 1983, 34–88; Sicherl 1976.
Exhibition: Bridwell, 06045; Harvard, WKR/2.5.5; Union/*Columbia,* Inc/A-959.

I.5

Plutarch.

Vitae illustrium virorum.

2 vols. Rome: Ulrich Han, [ca. 1469/70].
BMC 4:21–22 (IC.17263); Goff P-830.

In 1423, Giovanni Aurispa (ca. 1369–1459) returned to Italy from Constantinople with a collection of more than two hundred Greek manuscripts,
among which was Plutarch's *Parallel Lives.* That appears to be the earliest attestation of a Greek manuscript of Plutarch in the West, although the popularity of Plutarch increased rapidly, especially as a
result of Latin translations. In particular, the mor-
alistic writings, the *Parallel Lives* and the *Moralia,* had
a profound influence in the Renaissance, on, for
example, the writings of Hans Sachs (1494–1576),
Rabelais (1494?–1553), Montaigne (1533–92), and,
of course, Shakespeare (1564–1616).

Giovanni Antonio Campano (1429–77) edited
the first complete Latin translation of the *Parallel
Lives,* which was printed around 1470 at the press of
Ulrich Han (†1478), a native of Germany and the
second printer in Rome. This printing, however, is
marred by its many errors (Giustiniani 1979, 46).
Within a few months, Campano's edition was reprinted in Strasbourg by Adolf Rusch (fl. 1466–89).
Nicolas Jenson (ca. 1420–80) issued a third printing
of Campano's edition of the complete *Parallel Lives*
in 1478. The editio princeps of the original Greek
followed the Latin printings in 1517 at the Giunta
press in Florence.

References: Aulotte 1959; Giustiniani 1979.

Exhibition: Bridwell showing Venice: Nicolas Jenson, 2

January 1478 (06551); Harvard, WKR/10.2.5;

Union/*Columbia,* Inc/P-830.

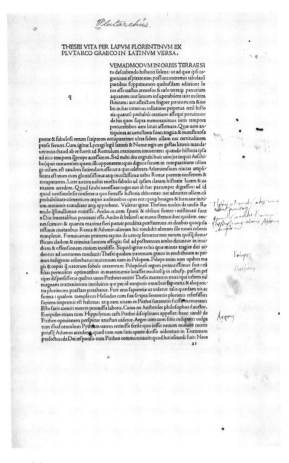

1.5, fol. a2ʳ.

By permission of the Houghton Library, Harvard University.

1.6, fol. D7ᵛ.

By permission of the Houghton Library, Harvard University.

1.6

Lascaris, Constantinos.

Erotemata cum interpretatione latina
[*Epitome*].

Venice: Aldus Manutius,
28 February 1494/5–8 March 1495.
BMC 5:552 (IA.24383); Goff L-68.

Sometime after the fall of Constantinople in 1453, Constantinos Lascaris (1434–1501) went to Italy, where he held a series of professorships. From 1468 until his death, he taught in Messina, where his most prominent student was Pietro Bembo (1470–1547).

Lascaris first published his Greek grammar in 1476 under the title *Epitome;* it was often printed subsequently under the title *Erotemata* (that is, "Questions"). He composed the work around 1465 as an introductory Greek grammar for Ippolita, the daughter of Francesco Sforza, duke of Milan. Early editions have a question-answer format similar to that used in Chrysoloras's *Erotemata* (written ca. 1397; first printed, in an adaption, ca. 1475–76). In several later editions, beginning with the second of 1480, a Latin translation appeared with the Greek text, and eventually the question-answer format was replaced by an organization according to grammatical category.

The 1495 edition of Lascaris's grammar holds a special place in the history of printing as the earliest dated book from the press of Aldus Manutius. It contains the Latin translation of Lascaris's grammar by Joannes Crastonus as well as the editio princeps of Aldus's *De litteris graecis et diphthongis.*

References: Bigliazzi et al. 1994, 1; Harlfinger 1989, 36–40; Renouard 1825, 1:1–18; Rosalia 1957/58.
Exhibition: Showing Ferrara: Joannes Maciochius Bondenus, 1510 at Bridwell (AFF9707) and Union/Columbia (Bridwell copy); Harvard, WKR/2.4.14.

INTEREA cū Roma gothoꝛ
irruptione agētium sub Rege
Alarico atꝗ ipem magnę cla-
dis euersa est: eius euersionem
deorū falsoꝛ mutorūꝗ culto-
res quos usitato noie paganos
uocamus: ín christianā religi-
onem referre conantes : solito
acerbius et amarius deū uerū
blasphemare coeperūt. Vnde
ego exardesces zelo domꝰ dei :
aduersus eorum blasphemias
uel errores: libros de ciuitate
dei scribere ístitui. Quod opus
per aliquot ános me tenuit. eo
ꝗ alia multa íntercurrebāt que differri
non oporteret. et me prius ad soluendū
occupabāt. Hoc aūt de ciuitate dei grāde
opus tandem. xxii. libris est termínatū.
quoꝛ quínꝗ primi eos refellunt qui res
humanas ita, psperari uolunt: ut ad hoc
multoꝛ deoꝛ cultū quos pagani colere
consueuerunt: necessariū esse arbitrenē.
et quia, phibēmr : mala ista exoriri atꝗ
abūdare contēdunt. Sequētes aūt qnꝗ:
aduersus eos loquimur qui fatentur hec
mala nec defuisse unquam nec defutura
mortalib9 : et ea nūc magna: nunc pua :
locis: tēporibus: personiꝗ uariari. Sed
deoꝛ multoꝛ cultū quo eis sacrificatur :
propter uitam post mortē futuram esse
utilem disputant. His ergo. x. libris due
istę uane opíniones christianę religioní
aduersarię refellunē. Sed ne quisꝗ nos
aliena tantū redarguisse : nō autē nostra
asseruisse reprehēderet : id agit ps altera
operis huius. quę. xii. libris continetur.
Quanꝗ ubi opus est: et ín porib9. x. quę
nra sunt asseram9 : et ín. xii. posteriorib9
redarguamus aduersa. Duodecim ergo
libroꝛ sequentiū primi quattuor cōtinet
exortū duarū ciuitatū. quarū est una

dei : altera huius mūdi. Secūdi quattuor
excursū earū seu ꝓcursum. Tercii uero
qui & postremi: debitos fines. Ita oīes
. xxii. libri cū sint de utraꝗ ciuitate con-
scripti: tínlū tamē a meliore acceperūt.
ut de ciuitate dei potius uocarentur . In
quoꝛ decio libro nō debuit ꝓ miraculo
poni: ín Abrae sacrificio flammā celitus
factā ínter diuisas uictimas cucurrisse .
qm hoc illi í uisíoe mōstratū est. In. xbii.
libro quod dictī est de Samuele nō erat
de filiis Aaron: dicendū potius fuit. non
erat filius sacerdotis . Filios qppe sacer-
dotum defunctis sacerdotibus succedere
magis legitimi moris fuit. Nam ín filiis
Aaron repīt pr Samuelis. sed sacerdos
nō fuit. nec ita ín filiis ut eū ípe genuerit
Aaron. sed sicut oēs illius populi dicūt
filii israel.

Loriosissimā
ciuitatem dei
siue ín hoc tē-
porū cursu cū
ínter impios
pegrinaē ex
fide niuens :
siue í illa sta-
bilitate sedis eterne quam nūc expectat
per pacientiam: quoadusꝗ iustitia con-
uertaē ín íudicii: deinceps adeptura per
excellētiā uictoria ultima & pace psca :
hoc ope ad te ínstituto & mea, pmissione
debito: defendere aduersus eos q cōdi-
tori eius deos suos pferunt fili carissime
Marcelíne suscepi. magnū opus & ar-
duū : sed deus adiutor noster est. Nam
scio qbus níribus opus sit: ut psuadeaē
suꝑbis quātā sit nírtus humilitatis. qua
fit ut oīa terrena cacumína temporali
mobilitate nurāria: non būano usurpata
fastu: sed diuína gratia donata celsitudo
transcendat. Rex ei et conditor ciuitatis

1.7, beginning of the *City of God*

I.7

Saint Augustine.

De civitate Dei.

[Subiaco: Conrad Sweynheym and Arnold
Pannartz], 12 June 1467.
Goff A-1230; *GW* 2874.

Conrad Sweynheym (†1477) and Arnold Pannartz
(†ca. 1476), both Germans, were the first printers in
Italy. In 1464, they established a press at the monastery of Subiaco, initiating the Italian trend of operat-
ing presses in monasteries, a natural development
from the scriptoria. There they printed the first edition of Augustine's *City of God* in 1467. Numerous
editions of this popular text followed, including, in
the next year, the edition of Johann Mentelin (ca.
1410–78), the first printed in Germany and the first
to provide medieval commentaries with the text.

Augustine's influence on Christian theology and
exegesis in the Middle Ages and Renaissance was
immense. In the sixteenth century, Catholics and
Reformers alike relied on his authority. Erasmus
edited his works (1528–29) and cited him frequently; Martin Luther (1483–1546) praised him in
Ein deutsch Theologia (1518), saying that the Bible and
St. Augustine had taught him more about the nature
of God and humankind than had any other sources;
and John Calvin (1509–64) found precedence for
the concept of predestination in Augustine, claim-
ing "plane nobiscum est Augustinus [Augustine is
clearly with us]" (*Institutes* III.iv.33).

References: Hall 1991, 30–55; Oberman 1975, 357–82;
Oberman and James 1991; Williams 1992, 111–12.
Exhibition: Bridwell, 06054; Harvard showing Strasbourg:
Johann Mentelin, 1468 (Inc/201); Union/*Columbia* showing
Venice: Nicolas Jenson, 1475 (A-1235); Yale, Beinecke/
Zi/+3289.

I.8

Boethius.

De consolatione philosophiae.

Strasbourg: Johann Grüninger, 25 August 1501.
VD16 B6404.

Boethius's writings on logic, philosophy, music,
mathematics, and theology were core texts in medieval schools. His *Consolation of Philosophy,* written
in prison shortly before his execution, has had
the most lasting influence. Boethius converses
with Philosophy personified as a woman, drawing
on Aristotle and Plato (in particular *Timaeus* and
Phaedo), as well as Cicero, Epicurus, Seneca, and
others, to develop an appealing form of Christian
stoicism.

A steady stream of editions and translations over
the past fifteen hundred years attests to the work's
popularity. The *Consolation* appears in most medieval library catalogs and still exists, according to
Chadwick, in about four hundred manuscripts.
With the invention of printing, it became a best-
seller, published more than seventy times in Latin
and vernacular translations during the fifteenth century (editio princeps 1471). It was translated into
English by a king (Alfred), a queen (Elizabeth I),
and a poet (Chaucer), and imitated by such authors
as Jean Gerson (1363–1429) and another doomed
man writing from his cell, Thomas More (1478–
1535). Dante (1265–1321) not only patterned his
famous conversations with a learned woman on
Boethius's work but also paid tribute to the author
by placing him in paradise.

The first illustrated edition appeared in 1501 at
the press of Johann Grüninger (†1532), an early
printer in Strasbourg known for his illustrated
books. A large woodcut at the beginning of the
second book depicts the passage in which Philosophy explains the mutability of Fortune, using the
image of the Wheel of Fortune.

1.8, fol. XXIII^v, the Wheel of Fortune

References: Chadwick 1981; Grafton 1981; Patch 1935,
46–123.
Exhibition: Bridwell, AFF5285; Harvard showing Cologne:
Heinrich Quentell, 1493 (Inc/1318); Union/*Columbia,*
B879/B632; Yale, YCBA/Leaf Coll. 1498 (three leaves).

1.9, Prothro B1, fol. [1ʳ],
illumination depicting St. Jerome

1.9

Biblia Latina.

France: thirteenth-century manuscript on vellum.

In the thirteenth century, France was a center for the production of small manuscript Bibles, which were probably designed for private reading and university study. The so-called Paris text of the Vulgate was established around 1220, perhaps on the initiative of Parisian stationers (Loewe in Lampe 1969, 2:147). The greatest success of the Paris text was in its canonical order and in its revision of chapter divisions (often attributed to Stephen Langton [†1228]). Moreover, the Paris text became the standard for printed Bible editions when Gutenberg, it seems, used it (see Schneider 1954). Gutenberg's text was followed with few emendations until critical editions began to appear in the sixteenth century.

This group of manuscripts is distinguished by a gothic script, known as Littera Parisiensis. Rubricated initials in red with blue penwork, or vice versa, commonly decorate the prologues, and biblical scenes are often depicted in initials at the beginning of books. Full of minute details, the scenes are confined to about one-half inch square. The pattern and composition of the scenes follow the same general scheme in numerous examples of Bible manuscripts from this place and period.

References: Branner 1977, 11–21; Denifle 1888, 278–83; Loewe in Lampe 1969; Schneider 1954.
Exhibition: Bridwell, Prothro B1; Harvard, MS Lat 261; *Union*/Columbia: Union, MS 48; Yale, Beinecke/MS 793.

I.IO

Biblia Latina.

[Mainz: Johann Gutenberg, 1454–55,
not after August 1456].
D&M 6076; Goff B-526; *GW* 4201.

The editio princeps of the Latin Bible is the first major work printed in Europe with movable metal type.

An early reference to the art of printing occurs in the *Cologne Chronicle* published by Johann Koelhoff the Younger (†after 1502) in 1499. The entry for 1450 reads: "Do was eyn gulden iair/ do began men zo drucken und was dat eyrste boich dat men druckde die Bybel zo latijn. [That was a golden (jubilee?) year. Then men began to print and the first book that was printed was the Bible in Latin.]" Citing the aging printer Ulrich Zell (†after August 1507) as the source, the anonymous chronicler identifies the inventor of the art as a "citizen of Mainz, born in Strasbourg, and named Junker Johann Gutenberg."

In fact, Gutenberg was born in Mainz (ca. 1397?–1468), although he worked in Strasbourg as a goldsmith from 1434 to 1444. Returning to Mainz in 1448, he set up a foundry and press, borrowing money for the venture from the banker Johann Fust (1400–1466). According to the court records of Mainz for 1455, when Fust demanded payments totaling 2,020 gulden, Gutenberg, who had probably just finished the Bible, was unable to comply with the terms of the loan and had to forfeit the press. Gutenberg's name does not appear in another document until 1465, and it is unclear where he went or what he did after losing the press. He died in Mainz on 3 February 1468.

The incipit of Jerome's letter to Ambrose is printed in red in some copies, but two-color printing does not occur throughout. Instead, chapter headings and capitals were left to be rubricated by hand, a practice common in early printed books.

The text is printed in double columns in gothic type. Estimations of the print run range from 70 to as many as 270 copies (Ing 1988, 69), with the majority printed on paper and up to 45 on vellum (Needham's high estimate).

References: Franz 1988, 31–36; Ing 1988; Needham 1985; Ruppel 1967.
Exhibition: Bridwell, 06117 (thirty-one leaves from the so-called Trier copy); Harvard, Inc/56; Union/*Columbia,* Inc/B-526 (Book of Revelation); Yale, YCBA/Folio/A/B/9 (four leaves from Epistles of Paul) and YCBA/Leaf Coll. 1 (one leaf from Book of Jeremiah).

Audite verbū dūi gētes: z annūciate
in insulis que ꝑcul sunt: z dicite. Qui
dispsit israhel cōgregabit eū: z custodi
et eum sicut pastoz gregē suū. Redimet
em̄ dūs iacob: z liberabit eū de ma
nu potētioris. Et veniet z laudabūt
in mōte syon: z cōfluent ad bona dūi
sup frumēto z vino z oleo z fetu pco
rum et armētoz: eritqz anima eoru qsi
ortus irriguus: et vltra non esurient.
Tūc letabit virgo in choro: iuuenes
et senes simul. Et cōuertā luctū eoz in
gaudiū: z cōsolabor eos: z letificabo
a dolore suo. Et inebriabo animā sa
cerdotū pinguedine: z ppls meus bonis
meis adimplebit ait dūs. Hec dicit
dūs. Vox in excelso audita est lamen
tatōnis luctus z fletus: rachel ploran
tis filios suos: z nolētis consolari su
per eis: quia non sunt. Hec dicit dūs.
Quiescat vox tua a ploratu et ocli tui
a lacrimis: quia est merces operi tuo
ait dūs. Et reuertent de terra inimici:
et est spes nouissimis tuis ait domin9:
et reuertent filij tui ad terminos suos.
Audiens audiui ephraim trāsmigrā
tem. Castigasti me dūe: et eruditus
sum qsi iuuenculus indomit9. Cōuer
te me z reuertar: quia tu dūs de9 meus.
Postqz em̄ cōuertisti me egi penitenti
am: z postqz ostendisti michi pcussi fe
mur meū. Cōfusus sum z erubui: quo
niam sustinui opprobrium adolescen
tie mee. Si filius honorabilis michi
ephraim: si puer delicat9: quia ex quo
locutus sum de eo adhuc recordabor
eius. Idcirco conturbata sunt viscera
mea sup eū: miserās miserebor eius
ait dūs. Statue tibi speculā: pone tibi
amaritudines. Dirige cor tuū in viā
rectā: in qua ambulasti. Reuertere vir
go isrl: reuere ad ciuitates tuas istas.

Vsqzquo delicijs dissolueris filia va
gas: Quia creauit dūs nouū sup terrā:
femina circūdabit virū. Hec dicit dūs
exercituū deus isrl. Adhuc dicent ver
bum istud in terra iuda et in vrbibus
ei9: cū cōuertero captiuitatem eoz. Be
nedicat tibi domin9 pulcritudo iusticie
mons sanctus. Et habitabunt in eo
iudas et omnes ciuitates ei9 simul agri
cole z minātes greges: quia inebriaui
animā lassam: z omnē animā esuri
entem saturaui. Ideo quasi de somno
suscitatus sum z vidi: et sompnus me9
dulcis michi. Ecce dies veniunt dicit
dūs: z seminabo domū iuda z domū
israhel semine hominis et semine iu
mentoru. Et sicut vigilaui sup eos ut
euellerem et demolirer et dissiparem et
dispderem et affligerem: sic vigilabo
sup eos ut edificem et plantem ait do
minus. In diebus illis non dicent ul
tra: patres comederut vuam acerbam
et dentes filioz obstupuerūt: sed unus
quisqz i iniquitate sua morietz. Omnis
homo qui comederit vuam acerbam:
obstupescent dentes eius. Ecce dies ve
niet dicit dūs: et feriam domui isrl et
domui iuda fedus nouū. Nō secūdū
pactū qd pepigi cū patribz eorū in die
qua apphendi manū eoz ut educerem
eos de terra egipti: pactū qd irritū fece
runt z ego dominat9 sum eoz dicit do
miu9: sed hoc erit pactū qd feriā cū do
mo israhel. Post dies illos dicit dūs
dabo legem meā in visceribz eoz: z in
corde eoz scribā eā: et ero eis in deū: et
ipi erūt michi i ppln. Et nō docebit ul
tra vir pximū suū: z vir fratrem suum
dicens: cognosce dūm. Omnes enī co
gnoscent me a minimo eoz usqz ad
maximū ait dūs: quia ꝓpiciabor ini
quitati eoz z peccati eoz nō ero memor

1.10, fol. 86, Jeremiah 31:10–34

I.11

Biblia Latina.

2 vols. Mainz: Johann Fust and Peter Schöffer,
14 August 1462.
D&M 6080; Goff B-529; *GW* 4204.

References: Ruppel 1937; Voulliéme 1922, 106–9.
Exhibition: Bridwell, 06119–20; Harvard, Inc/79 (fragment
with four leaves from Judges, Ruth, 1 + 2 Samuel);
Union/*Columbia,* Inc/B-529 (one leaf); Yale, YCBA/Leaf
Coll.5 (one leaf).

The 1462, or 48-line, Bible follows the text of Gutenberg's Bible, correcting some typographical errors but perpetuating many others. Like its model, the 1462 Bible is printed in double columns in the style of manuscript Bibles. The typeface, however, is new. The modified gothic font was probably designed by Fust's son-in-law and partner, Peter Schöffer (ca. 1425–1502), who may have worked as an illuminator and printer with Gutenberg before Fust took control of the press.

This is the first Bible with printed publication information. The colophons to both volumes include the Fust and Schöffer device — the first printer's device — of two shields hanging from a branch. The colophon to volume 2 also describes the novel method of production:

> Praesens hoc opusculum artificiosa adinuentione imprimendi seu caracterizandi absque calami exaratione in ciuitate Maguntina sic effigiatum et ad eusebiam dei industrie per Johannem Fust civem et Petrum Schoiffher de Gernsheym clericum diotesis eiusdem est consummatum, anno domini M.cccclxii, in vigilia Assumptionis Virginis Mariae.

[This little book was made in the city of Mainz by the artful invention of printing or character-making, without the labor of a pen, and it was completed for the glory of God, through the industry of Johann Fust, citizen, and Peter Schöffer of Gernsheim, clerk of the same diocese, in the year of our Lord 1462, on the eve of the Assumption of the Virgin Mary.]

israhel:reuertere ad ciuitates tuas istas. Ysq̅
q̅ deliciis dissolueris filia vaga? Quia crea
uit dominus nouum sup̅ terra̅: femina circun
dabit viru̅. Hec dicit dominus exercituum
deus israhel. Adhuc dicent verbu̅ istud in tra
iuda et in vrbibus eius: cu̅ conuertero captiuita
tes eor̅. Benedicat tibi dominus pulcritu
do iusticie mons sanctus. Et habitabu̅t in
eo iudas et omnes ciuitates eius simul agri
cole et minates greges: qz inebriaui animã
lassam: et omnez aiaz esuriente saturaui. Ideo
quasi de somnio suscitatus sum et vidi: et so
mnus meus dulcis michi. Ecce dies veniet
dicit dn̅s: et seminabo domui iuda et domum
israhel semine hominis et semine iumentor̅.
Et sicut vigilaui sup̅ eos ut euellere̅ et demo
lirer et dissipare̅ et disp̅ dere̅ et affligere:
sic vigilabo sup̅ eos vt edifice̅ et plante̅ ait
dominus. In diebus illis non dicet vltra. pa
tres comederu̅t vuam acerbam et dentes fili
oru̅ obstupuert: sed vnusquisqz in iniqtate
sua morietur. Omnis homo qui comederit vuã
acerba: obstupescent dentes eius. Ecce di
es veniet dicit dn̅s. et feriam domui israhel
et domui iuda fedus nouu̅. Non secundu̅
pactum quod pepegi cum p̅ribus eor̅ i die
qua app̅hendi manu̅ eor̅ vt educere̅ eos
de terra egipti: pactuz quod irritu̅ fecert et
ego dominatus su̅ eor̅ dicit dominus: sed
hoc erit pactu̅ quod feriaz cu̅ domo israhel.
Post dies illos dicit dominus dabo lege̅
meam in visceribus eor̅: et in corde eor̅ scri
bam eã: et ero eis in deu̅. et ipsi eru̅t michi in
p̅p̅l̅m̅. Et no̅ docebit vltra vir p̅ximu̅ suu̅. et
vir fratrem suu̅ dices: cognosce dn̅m. Oes
eni cognoscent me a minimo eor̅ usqz ad
maximu̅ ait dn̅s: qz p̅piciabor iniqtati eor̅
et peccator̅ non ero memor amplius. Hec
dicit dn̅s qui dat solem in lumie diei: ordi
ne lune et stellar̅ in lumine noctis: q̅ turbat
mare et sonant fluctus eius: dn̅s exercituu̅
nomen illi. Si defecerint leges iste coram
me dicit dn̅s: tu̅c et semen israhel deficiet vt
non sit gens coram me cuctis diebus. Hec
dicit dn̅s. Si mensurari poterint celi sursuz
et inuestigari fundameta tre deorsu̅: et ego
abiciam vniuersu̅ semen israhel p̅pter omia
q̅ fecerut dicit dn̅s. Ecce dies venient dicit

dominus: et edificabit ciuitas dn̅o a turre a
nanehel vsqz ad porta̅ a̅guli. Et exibit vltra
norma mensure in o̅sp̅ctu eius sup̅ colle̅ ga
reb: et circuibit goatha et ome̅m valle̅ cada
ueru̅ cineres et vniu̅sam regionem mortis.
vsqz ad torrente̅ cedron et vsqz ad anguli
porte equor̅ orie̅talis. Sctm dn̅i no̅ euelletur et
no̅ destruet̅ vltra i p̅petuu̅. **XXXII**
Uerbu̅ q̅d̅ factu̅ est ad iheremiã a dn̅o
in anno decimo sedechie regis iuda:
ipse est annus octauusdecimus nabuchodo
nosor. Tunc exercitus regis babilonis ob
sidebat iherusalem: et iheremias p̅pheta erat
clausus in atrio carceris qui erat in domo re
gis iuda. Clauserat enim eã sedechias rex
iuda dices. Quare vaticinaris dices hec dicit
dn̅s. ecce ego dabo ciuitatem istã in manu̅
regis babilois et capiet eu̅. et sedechias rex
iuda no̅ effugiet de manu̅ caldeoru̅ sz tradet̅
in manus regis babilonis. et loquetur os ei?
cum ore illius et oculi eius oculos illius vide
bu̅t. et in babilone̅ ducet sedechiã et ibi erit
donec visite̅ eum ait dn̅s: si aut dimicaueritis
aduersu̅ caldeos nichil p̅sperum habebitis e
Et dixit iheremias. Factu̅ est verbum domini
ad me dices. Ecce ananehel filius sellu̅ pa
truelis tuus veniet ad te dices. Eme tibi a
grum meu̅ qui est in anathot. Tibi enim co̅
petit ex p̅pinqtate vt emas. Et venit ad me
ananehel filius patrui mei secundu̅ verbum
dn̅i ad vestibulu̅ carceris: et ait ad me. Possi
de agru̅ meu̅ qui est i anathot in terra beiña
min: qz tibi o̅petit hereditas et tu p̅pinquus es
vt possideas. Intellexi aut q̅ verbu̅ domini
esset. Et emi agruz ab ananehel filio patrui
mei qui est i anathot. Et appendi ei argentu̅
septem stateres. et decee argeteos: et scripsi
in libro et signaui: et adhibui testes. Et appe
di argentu̅ i statera: et accepi libru̅ possessio
nis signatu̅ et stipulaco̅es et rata et signa fo
rinsecus. Et dedi libru̅ possessionis baruch
fillo neri filie maasie i oclis ananehel patru
elis mei i oculis testiuz qui scripti erant i li
bro emptionis: et i oculis omniu̅ iudeor̅ q̅
sedebant i atrio carceris. Et p̅cepi baruch
coram eis dices. Hec dicit dn̅s exercituum
deus israhel. Sume libros istos: libru̅ em
ptionis huc signatu̅ et librum huc et aptus

1.12

Biblia Latina.

[Rome: Conrad Sweynheym and Arnold Pannartz, 1471].

D&M 6081; Goff B-535; *GW* 4210.

In 1467, the printers Sweynheym and Pannartz moved from Subiaco to Rome and produced the first Bible printed in roman (as opposed to gothic) type — a font that is said to be based on the humanist minuscule. In addition, this Bible is the first and only one printed in Rome in the fifteenth century. Another innovation is the setting of the text across the full width of the page, instead of in columns.

This Bible includes the editio princeps of the *Letter of Aristeas* (in the Latin translation of Matthias Palmerius), supposedly by an Alexandrian Greek. According to "Aristeas," Demetrios of Phaleron, the third-century librarian at Alexandria, arranged for seventy-two Jewish translators to produce a Greek Pentateuch for the collection. Though separated, the translators arrived at identical versions. Their inspired translation, known as the Septuagint (the Seventy), became the text of the early church and Christian authorities. In the sixteenth century, however, most scholars held the Septuagint in relatively low esteem, preferring to return *ad fontes* to the Hebrew text, as Jerome had done for his Vulgate translation.

Cardinal Giovanni Andrea de' Bussi (1417–75), bishop of Aleria, edited this Vulgate text, using earlier printed versions, as well as manuscripts from the Vatican Library. The *Interpretationes Hebraicorum Nominum,* which is often found in manuscript Bibles, appears here for the first time in print. In his prefatory letter, however, the editor apologizes for the use of roman letters for the printing of Hebrew names, saying that this was unavoidable because Hebrew type was not yet available. De' Bussi dedicated the work to Pope Paul II.

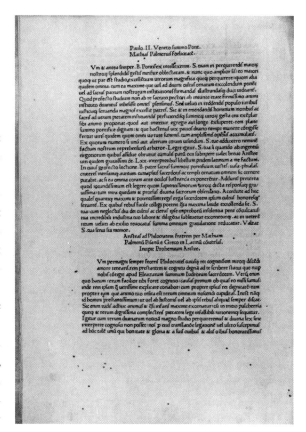

1.12, fol. 2ᵛ, beginning of the *Letter of Aristeas*

References: Feld 1982, 282–99; Feld 1985.
Exhibition: Bridwell only, AER0766.

1.13

Biblia.

Paris: Robert Estienne, 1528
(colophon: 28 November 1527).
D&M 6109.

References: Armstrong 1954, 11–12, 16, 72–78, 184, 204; Mortimer 1964, 1: no. 65; Renouard [1843] 1972, 27–28; Schreiber 1982, 37.
Exhibition: Bridwell, Prothro B300; Harvard, Typ/515/28.21OF; Union/Columbia, Prothro copy.

Through his scholarly editions and translations of the Bible, Robert Estienne, or Stephanus (1503–59), printer to Francis I, exerted enormous influence on the shaping of the Bible text in the sixteenth century. His first Bible, shown here, is often considered the first attempt at a critical edition of Jerome's Vulgate. In the preface, Estienne explains that, beginning in 1524, he collated several manuscripts and compared the text with printed editions, including the Complutensian Polyglot. Among his innovations is the placement of Acts directly after the Gospels. He also revised the *Index of Hebrew Names*.

Estienne continued to produce Latin, Greek, and Hebrew Bibles, often against the wishes of the Theological Faculty of the University of Paris, which had the right to censor books sold and published in the city. Beginning in 1546, the faculty of the Sorbonne tried to suppress most of the Estienne Bibles, declaring in one order of prohibition that the Bibles were "scattered with things that are erroneous, conducive to scandals, favoring Lutherans, and breathing heresies long ago condemned" (Armstrong 1954, 184). For the next four years, Estienne battled with the faculty before finally leaving for Geneva, where he became a Calvinist. In the next generation, however, church authorities returned to this text (in its revised version of 1538–40, by way of the Louvain Bible of 1547) and used it as the basis for the Sixtine Bible of 1590.

According to the "royal privilege," the text remained Estienne's property for five years and was not to be reprinted by others. His device of an olive tree and St. Paul with the motto "Noli altum sapere, sed time [Be not highminded, but fear]" (Rm 11:20) appears on the title page and on the first page of the appendix.

BIBLIA

NOLI ALTVM SAPERE,
SED TIME.

PARISIIS
Ex officina ROBERTI STEPHANI, eregione Scholæ Decretorum.
M. D. XXVIII.

CVM PRIVILEGIO REGIS.

1.13, title page

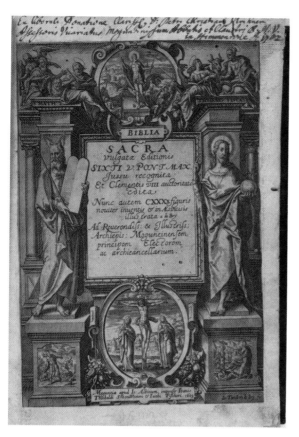

1.14, title page (1609 ed.)

1.14

Biblia Sacra.

Rome: Typographia Apostolica Vaticana, 1592.
D&M 6184.

However one judges its philological merits, the Sixtine Bible, the first attempt by the Catholic Church to issue a critical edition of the Vulgate, proved an embarrassment. Sixtus V (1520–90) had so irritated members of the College of Cardinals, especially Cardinal Bellarmine (1542–1621), that, after his death on 27 August 1590, many claimed that the text was too error-ridden for general use. This opposition was voiced despite the rigid endorsement of Sixtus's bull "Aeternus ille caelestium," printed as a preface to the Bible, that it was "true, legitimate, authentic, and infallible."

Clement VIII (1536–1605) formally withdrew the Sixtine Bible from circulation in 1592 and replaced it with the text established by a commission of scholars under the leadership of Cardinal Marco Antonio Colonna (†1597). Known as the Clementine, or Sixto-Clementine, Bible, it remained the officially sanctioned edition of the Roman Catholic Church until 1943, when Pius XII issued an encyclical encouraging new translations from the original languages.

The edition of 1609 is the first printing of the Clementine Bible in Germany. The engraved title page by the Flemish artist Johann Theodor de Bry (1561–1623?) depicts typologically related biblical events and figures, such as Moses and Christ, the sacrifice of Isaac and the crucifixion, and the prophets and evangelists. Johann Albin (fl. 1598–1620), distinguished as the official printer of the Holy Roman Empire, specialized in books supporting the Catholic Reformation, particularly the Jesuit missions.

References: Aland 1993; Benzing 1950; Kneller 1928; Le Bachelet 1911; Murphy 1983.

Exhibition: Showing Mainz: Johann Albin for Johann

Theobald Schonwetter and Jacob Fischer, 1609 at Bridwell (Prothro B290) and *Union*/Columbia (CB62/1609b); Harvard showing Lyons: Heirs of Guillaume Rouille, 1620 (And-Harv/R.B.R./BS75/1620); Yale, Beinecke/Mli105/+592.

1.15

Valla, Lorenzo.

De donatione Constantini.

[Strasbourg: Johann Grüninger], 1506.
VD16 V227.

The research of Lorenzo Valla (1405–57) on the Bible (especially his *Annotationes*) and on the *Donation of Constantine* exerted influence on both Reformation philology and polemic. The *Donation of Constantine,* a forgery probably from around the mid-eighth century, purportedly conveyed lands and jurisdiction in Italy and the East from Emperor Constantine the Great to Pope Sylvester I and the Catholic Church. In 1440, Valla composed his essay (which has at times the bitterness of a philippic) to impeach the validity of the *Donation* on philological and historical grounds and to criticize the papacy's history of asserting secular power. Though infrequently acknowledged, the first edition appeared at Strasbourg in 1506, probably at the press of Johann Grüninger (Setz 1976, 35–36).

Ulrich von Hutten (1488–1523), an ardent supporter of Luther, edited and published the second edition in 1518, just after the beginning of the Reformation. His edition established the work's important place as a source of humanist criticism of the papacy. Hutten also included works by Nicholas of Cusa (1401–64) and Antoninus of Florence (1389–1459) that questioned the authenticity of the *Donation.*

References: Bentley 1987, 108–22; Benzing 1956, 3, 118–19; Celenza 1994; Harvard College Library 1983, 8; Setz 1976.

1.15, fol. A2^r.
By permission of the Houghton Library, Harvard University.

Exhibition: Harvard, *IC/V2404/506db. Showing [Basel: Cratander, 1518?] at Bridwell (262.13 D677), *Union*/Columbia (UB 44.2/D67/1520), and Yale (Beinecke/Mz875/D6/1520).

1.16

Novvm instrumentum omne.

Edited, translated, and annotated by Erasmus of Rotterdam. 2 pts. Basel: Johann Froben, February 1516.
D&M 4591; *VD16* B4196.

The editio princeps of the Greek New Testament appeared in March 1516, along with Erasmus's Latin translation and *Annotationes*. It is often reported that the printer Johann Froben (†1527) asked Erasmus to work quickly so as to foil his Spanish rival, Cardinal Ximénez (1436?–1517), who was already printing a Greek New Testament. In fact, as early as 1514, Erasmus wrote that he had been working on his edition for two years (Allen 1906–58, no. 256, lines 152–58). It is true, however, that Froben printed the volume with remarkable speed, receiving it from Erasmus in September 1515 and printing it (more than a thousand pages) in only six months. Erasmus corrected the edition during the process, reworking it and adding commentary as it came off the press in proof stages.

Erasmus claimed in the preface to have consulted the oldest and best manuscripts, but none seems to date from before the twelfth century (Rummel 1986, 35–42). Only one text provided the basis for Revelation: a manuscript lent to Erasmus by Johannes Reuchlin, the *Codex Capnionis* (the Greek version of Reuchlin was "Capnion," meaning "little smoke"). It was slightly incomplete, a problem Erasmus resolved by translating six verses from the Vulgate into Greek. Such obstacles, along with the speed of production, resulted in an imperfect edition.

Erasmus's Latin translation is as noteworthy as his edition of the Greek text. The translation's departure from the Vulgate, as well as numerous textual emendations, prompted criticism from many quarters. In addition, his *Annotationes* went beyond Valla's criticism of the text and caused widespread controversy.

Although generally considered inferior to the Complutensian text, Erasmus's edition was far more influential among Reformers and humanists.

The woodcut borders are by Urs Graf (ca. 1485–ca. 1529); they were also used for the second edition (see page 4 for illustration).

References: Allen 1906–58; Bentley 1977; de Jonge 1983, 3–40; Rabil 1972, 88–93; Rummel 1986; Tarelli 1943. Exhibition: Bridwell, 06808; Harvard, *fNC5/Erl53B/1516/(A); *Union*/Columbia, CB37/1516e; Yale, Beinecke/Mlh691/+b516.

1.17

Novvm testamentvm omne.

Edited, translated, and annotated by Erasmus of Rotterdam. 2 pts. Basel: Johann Froben, March 1519.
D&M 4597; *VD16* B4197.

As early as three months after the *Novum instrumentum* had appeared, Erasmus began to acknowledge the need for a second edition. In a letter to Guillaume Budé (1468–1540), he described the ardors and the shortcomings of the process of publication, especially as regards the *Annotationes:*

> Edebatur simul et cudebatur opus, excudebatur singulis diebus ternio . . . delassatus iam ac pene fractus ad adnotationes perueni. Pro temporis modo proque valetudine praestiti quod potui. Nonnulla prudens etiam preterii, ad multa sciens conniuebam, in quibus mox ab aeditione a meipso dissensi. Proinde τὴν δευτέραν παρασκευάζω ἔκδοσιν. (Allen 1906–58, no. 421, lines 58–70)

[The work was being edited and printed at the same time; a ternion was being printed every day. . . . Exhausted and almost broken, I came to the *Annotationes.* I did what I could, considering the time limita-

1.17, title page

tion and my health. I discreetly passed over several things and at many places I knowingly closed my eyes, about which I disagreed with myself soon after publication. Therefore, I am preparing a second edition.]

In the second edition, Erasmus changed the title to *Novum Testamentum,* added a good deal of introductory material, corrected misprints, collated additional manuscripts, and enlarged on the annotations. He also provided a revised Latin translation,

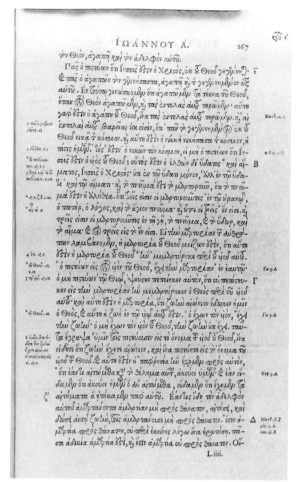

1.18, p. 167, 1 John 5:1 ff.

which departed even further from the Vulgate and provoked yet more attacks. Luther based his German translation on this edition.

Beginning with the third edition of 1522, Erasmus's text was slightly less controversial. The most important change was the addition of the "comma Johanneum" (that is, 1 Jn 5:7–8 in the Vulgate version, which was a proof text for the Trinity). Erasmus claimed that a Greek manuscript, which had been discovered in Dublin, contained the spurious passage.

References: Allen 1906–58; Rabil 1972, 88–95; Rummel 1986. Exhibition: Bridwell, Prothro B10; Harvard, *fNC5/ Erl53B/1519; *Union*/Columbia, CB37/1519e; Yale, YCBA/ Leaf Coll. 2153 (one leaf).

1.18

Τῆς καινῆς διαθήκης ἅπαντα.

Nouum Iesv Christi D. N. Testamentum.

2 pts. Paris: Robert Estienne, 15 June 1550. D&M 4622.

Robert Estienne's 1550 edition, his third edition of the New Testament in Greek, established the textus receptus for subsequent editors. His documentation of collations of fifteen manuscripts (including the *Codex Bezae*) resulted in the first critical apparatus for an edition of the Bible. The apparatus appears in the inner margin, with the collated manuscripts distinguished by Greek letters (β for *Codex Bezae,* etc.). This is the most influential of Estienne's scholarly works and also the edition of the Bible that he claimed most provoked the theology faculty at the Sorbonne and led to his departure from Paris (see Renouard [1843] 1972, 564–67). Oddly enough, there is no evidence that the 1550 New Testament was ever condemned, although other Estienne Bibles had been censured by the faculty (Armstrong 1954, 206). By 1550, the opposition in Paris became so unbearable, and perhaps unsafe, that Estienne left the city and set up shop in Geneva.

Known as the *Editio Regia,* the 1550 edition is printed in the Royal Greek type ("grecs du roi") designed for Estienne's first Greek New Testament (1546). The type was cut by Claude Garamond (†1561), who, it is said, based it on the hand of Angelo Vergecio, a calligrapher at the court of Francis I.

References: Armstrong 1954, 136–38, 206; Mortimer 1964, 1: no. 78; Renouard [1843] 1972, 564–67; Schreiber 1982, no. 105.

Exhibition: Bridwell, 00372 (Harrison Collection); Harvard, Bridwell copy; Union/*Columbia,* Book Arts Z232/Es86/ 1550/B47; Yale, Beinecke/Mlh691/+546ec.

1.19

Reuchlin, Johannes.

De rudimentis hebraicis.

Pforzheim: Thomas Anshelm, 27 March 1506. *VD16* R1252.

Johannes Reuchlin's *De rudimentis hebraicis* (1506) was the pioneering work for the humanist study of Hebrew grammar and lexicography. Reuchlin had learned Hebrew mainly from Jacob ben Jehiel Loans (†ca. 1506), and he based the *Rudimenta* on several works by Rabbi David Kimchi (ca. 1160–1235), and, according to Greive, also on a work by Moses Kimchi (†ca. 1190). Although he understood the incompatibilities between the grammatical systems of Hebrew and Latin and Greek, Reuchlin used Latin paradigms to describe Hebrew, showing, for example, Hebrew equivalents for the five noun cases of Latin. The pages of the *Rudimenta* turn left to right as in Hebrew books, even though the book is in Latin.

Because of his command of Hebrew, which at the time was a rare accomplishment for a Christian, Reuchlin was drawn into one of the greatest controversies of the period. When asked for a legal opinion

LIBER

prefertim cum noftrates Iudęi uel inuidia uel impericia ducti chriftia
num neminem in eorum lingua erudire uelint.idcȝ recufant cuiufdã
rabi Ami authoritate qui in Thalmud בוקיר ita dixit.

[Hebrew text]

verbum e uerbo fic.Non explanantur uerba legis cuiquam gentili eo
quod fcriptum eft.Qui adnunciat uerba fua Iacob.pręcepta fua et iu╸
dicia fua Ifrael.non fecit fimiliter omni genti.Nobis autem in ftatu
gracię aliter mandatur Matthęi decimo. Quod in aurem auditis pre
dicate fuper tecta quod et ego facio.Tecȝ imitari iubebo.& pro hoc
ergo memento mei deus et parce mihi fecundum multitudinem mife
rationum tuarum.amen.

Exegi monumentum ęre
perennius Nonis
Martijs Anno.
M.D.VI.

1.19, colophon

by the imperial court, he wrote a defense of Jewish writings against the efforts of Johannes Pfefferkorn (1469–ca. 1521) and others to confiscate all Hebrew books in the Holy Roman Empire. This controversy became the subject of a famous humanist satire, *The Letters of Obscure Men* (1515 and 1517). Reuchlin later published an improved study of Hebrew, *De accentibus et orthographia linguae hebraicae* (1518). He is also an important figure in the history of Renaissance literature as the author of *Henno* (first published 1498), the first successful humanist drama in Germany.

In perfect Christian-humanist fashion, Reuchlin concluded the *Rudimenta* with a statement of modesty from the New Testament and one of pride from Horace: "Let me make an end of teaching, but may you never make an end of learning. To us, however, in the state of grace, it is commanded by the tenth chapter of Matthew: what you hear in your ear and what I do, preach over the rooftops, and I will order you to imitate [all that] and for this reason, therefore, remember me, o God, and spare me according to the multitude of your mercies, amen. I have build a monument more lasting than bronze on the nones of March in the year 1506" (quoted from the colophon).

References: Brod 1965, 105–34; Geiger [1871] 1964, 110–45; Greive 1978; Harlfinger 1989, 311–22.
Exhibition: Bridwell, 31360; Harvard, And-Harv/R.B.R./605.2/R44.4r/1506; *Union*/Columbia showing *De accentibus et orthographia linguae hebraicae*. Hagenau: Thomas Anshelm, 1518 (RB); Yale, DIV/GR3/R317p.

1.20

Reuchlin, Johannes.

De arte cabalistica.

Hagenau: Thomas Anshelm, March 1517.
VD16 R1235.

Inspired by the work of Pico della Mirandola, Reuchlin became one of the founders of the Christian Kabbalah with the publication of *De verbo mirifico* (1494) and, more important, *De arte cabalistica* (1517). The latter work, which is dedicated to Leo X, is a Socratic-style dialogue set in Frankfurt. The interlocutors are Philolaus (a Pythagorean), Marranus (a Muslim), and Simon (a Jew). Simon, an exile of the 1492 Spanish expulsion, teaches the others at great length about the Kabbalah, with particular emphasis on numerology (and its compatibility with Pythagorean numerology) and the mysteries of the hidden meanings of Hebrew characters. Reuchlin, however, applies the mysteries to Christianity and, in fact, appropriates the Kabbalah as a source of Christian revelation. At a high point in the work, Philolaus concludes that "all our studies in both [that is, both Pythagoreanism and Kabbalah] lead back to the salvation of humankind [Omnia nanque studia nostra utrique reducunt ad humani generis salutem]" (fol. F3^v).

Scholem has identified Reuchlin's primary source, a medieval miscellany of Kabbalistic texts now in the collection of the Jewish Theological Seminary (Halberstamm 444).

References: Blau 1944, 41–64; Geiger [1871] 1964, 164–202; Jones 1983; Scholem 1987; Spitz 1963, 61–80; Zika 1977. Exhibition: Bridwell, AFJ1032; Harvard, *fGC5/R3174/517; *Union*/Columbia showing reprint in Pistorius's *Ars Cabalistica* (Basel: Sebastian Henricpetrus, 1587), RB:82A.

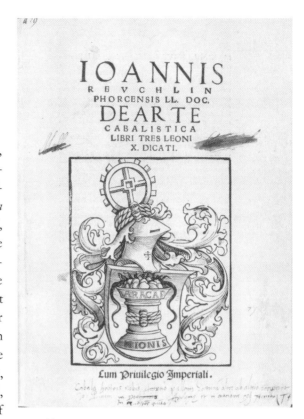

1.20, title page

I.21

Biblia Rabbinica.

4 vols. Venice: Daniel Bomberg, [1516–17?].
D&M 5083.

The Hebrew Bible had been printed several times before the New Testament was printed in Greek. The first complete Hebrew Bible was produced by the Soncino press as early as 1488.

In 1516–17?, under the editorship of Felix of Prato (†1539), Daniel Bomberg (1483–1553) produced the first printed Rabbinic Bible (that is, Hebrew Scripture with Targumim, traditional commentaries, and, in subsequent editions, the Massora). In his second edition of 1524–25, he produced a new text, prepared by Jacob ben Chayyim (ca. 1470–ca. 1538), whose version became the textus receptus, the standard form of the Massoretic text for subsequent scholarship by both Jews and Christians.

Bomberg moved from Antwerp to Venice around 1515 and established the first Hebrew press in that city. He became the most important printer of Hebrew, producing, in all, nearly two hundred Hebrew books.

References: Amram 1909; Bloch [1933] 1976, 68–78; Goshen-Gottstein 1972.

Exhibition: Bridwell showing Venice: Daniel Bomberg, 1546 (Prothro B320); Harvard showing Venice: [Daniel Bomberg], 1524–25 (Heb1650.524/F*); *Union*/Columbia, CB 24 1517a; Yale, Beinecke/Mld291/+517p.

I.22

Hebraica Biblia.

2 vols. Basel: Johann Bebel for Michael Isingrin and Heinrich Petri, 1534–35.
D&M 5087; *VD16* B2881.

The three great early Christian Hebraists were Reuchlin, Konrad Pellikan (1478–1556), and Sebastian Münster (1488–1552). Münster was a Franciscan priest and professor of Hebrew at Tübingen, Basel, and Heidelberg, as well as the author of numerous works on the Hebrew language. In the 1520s, he became a follower of Luther (translating some of Luther's works into German) and broke with the church formally in 1529. He later married the widow of a printer in Basel, and his stepson Heinrich Petri became his printer.

Münster's Hebrew Bible (with Latin translation) first appeared in a folio edition in 1534–35. The following year, Froben issued the Hebrew text separately in quarto without the Latin translation. The Hebrew text is derived from the first *Biblia Rabbinica* of Felix of Prato, rather than from that of Jacob ben Chayyim, which had appeared at the press of Daniel Bomberg in 1524–25 and which was generally considered to be more scholarly. Nonetheless, Münster's text served as the basis for many subsequent editions and translations.

References: Burmeister 1970; Harlfinger 1989, 325–27; Raupp in Bautz and Bautz 1975– , 6:316–26.

Exhibition: Showing Basel: Johann Froben and Nikolaus Episcopius, 1536 at Bridwell (Prothro B89) and Yale (1742/Yale Library/13.4.6); Harvard, *fGC5/M8895/534b; *Union*/Columbia showing Basel: Michael Isingrin and Heinrich Petri, 1546 (CB24/1546).

פלוגתא דסיפרא

בן אשר		בן נפתלי	בן אשר
טוב הרהב	בן נפתלי	טוב הרהב	בן אשר
ולא תיראון	בן נפתלי	ולא תיראון	בן אשר
ובלחתיבו	בן נפתלי	ובלחתיבו	בן אשר
ויהי כאשר	בן נפתלי	ויהי כאשר	בן אשר
ויכתן	בן נפתלי	ויכתן	בן אשר
אמר אצבר	בן נפתלי	אמר אצבר	בן אשר
ונחרס	בן נפתלי	ונחרס	בן אשר
אתן גרלך	בן נפתלי	אתן גרלך	בן אשר
כתעפך	בן נפתלי	כתעפך	בן אשר
כי לא תעבר	בן נפתלי	כי לא תעבר	בן אשר
את הרכרים	בן נפתלי	את הרכרים	בן אשר
אמר יכאת	בן נפתלי	אמר יכאת	בן אשר
והיה כי יבוזך	בן נפתלי	והיה כי יבוזך	בן אשר
וכסל גוים	בן נפתלי	וכסל גוים	בן אשר
הכרית וההסר	בן נפתלי	הכרית וההסר	בן אשר
והיה פיקב תמתג	בן נפתלי	והיה פיקב תמתג	בן אשר
בלבכך	בן נפתלי	בלבכך	בן אשר
כס נרול ורב	בן נפתלי	כס נרול ורב	בן אשר
אמר יכאת	בן נפתלי	אמר יכאת	בן אשר
ויכתב על	בן נפתלי	ויכתב על	בן אשר
תסתת תוס	בן נפתלי	תסתת תוס	בן אשר
ובלכתע כררך	בן נפתלי	ובלכתע כררך	בן אשר
ובכסכך	בן נפתלי	ובכסכך	בן אשר
את נכולך	בן נפתלי	את נכולך	בן אשר
לייראת את	בן נפתלי	לייראת את	בן אשר
תמלך	בן נפתלי	תמלך	בן אשר
בתתך לו	בן נפתלי	בתתך לו	בן אשר
אמר יכחרי	בן נפתלי	אמר יכחרי	בן אשר
על תמלכתנ	בן נפתלי	על תמלכתנ	בן אשר
הגוים האלה	בן נפתלי	הגוים האלה	בן אשר
אמר פרית	בן נפתלי	אמר פרית	בן אשר
ולס בכמרס	בן נפתלי	ולס בכמרס	בן אשר
והחזיק כה	בן נפתלי	והחזיק כה	בן אשר
אמר יכבל	בן נפתלי	אמר יכבל	בן אשר
לעמר	בן נפתלי	לעמר	בן אשר
את כל דברי	בן נפתלי	את כל דברי	בן אשר
למתן סוכים אותך	בן נפתלי	למתן סוכים אותך	בן אשר
ביום ההוא	בן נפתלי	ביום ההוא	בן אשר
אמר נסכבת	בן נפתלי	אמר נסכבת	בן אשר
את תריך	בן נפתלי	את תריך	בן אשר
זיכוכך	בן נפתלי	זיכוכך	בן אשר
יתכאהו בארץ	בן נפתלי	יתכאהו בארץ	בן אשר
אם סכותי ברכי	בן נפתלי	אם סכותי ברכי	בן אשר
רכבות אלפי	בן נפתלי	רכבות אלפי	בן אשר
ירעפו טל	בן נפתלי	ירעפו טל	בן אשר
ויתא ר33י עס	בן נפתלי		

ספר הטכיס סל סכריס · ספר כראסית · מבכרחל
הכולם עד סמת יוסף אלכ'יס וסלס נוחות
ותסע סניס · ספר סני · והוא ספר ואלה סמות
מסמת יוסף עד הסכ'ה הסכת לכ'אתם כני יסראל מ'ארן עד
מהוקס התסכן מאה וארכעיס סנה · ספר סלימי · ויקרא · והוא ספר תורת
כהניס · מסחיקס התסכן כאחר לחרם הראסון · ועד החרם הסני חרם ימים
כתוני כאחר לחרם הספי כסנה הסנית · ספר רביעי וידכר · והוא
ספר חומס הסקוריס · כאחר לחרם הסני כסנה הסנית · עד ארכעיס סנה
כעסתי עסר חרם · כאחר לחרם · סלמיס וסמנה סניס ותסעה וחמסים
ספר חתיסי ואלה הדברים וחוא ספר · מסנה תורה · מת אהרן הכהן · וחיה
מסה הככיר אחריו סכ'לס חרמים וסנכ'ה ימים · ויום סהיה תת החח
קרוס וכריך לכרכה · כתכוב כיום ההוא נקרא ב
תורת תמה · נקרא ספר מסה · התוורה נקרית עד סם מסה הנאמן כתכו זכרו לג'ה

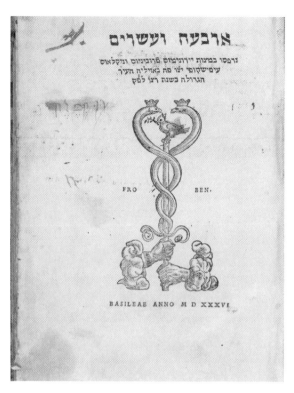

אורבעה ועשרים

נדפסו במצות יירונימוס פרובניוס ונקלאוס
עפישקוף ישו פת בצוילה העיר
חגרולה בשנת רצו לפק

FRO   BEN.

BASILEAE ANNO M D XXXVI

1.22, colophon of 2d ed. (Basel: Johann Froben, 1536)

1.23

Biblia.

3 pts. Lyons: Antoine du Ry, 1528
(colophon: 29 January 1527).
D&M 6109.

In 1528, after several decades of study, Santi Pagnini (1470–1541) published a Latin translation of the Bible, done from the original languages. It was the Renaissance's first complete Latin translation of the Bible and, despite many typographical errors, was widely used. The Old Testament, in particular, was valued for its extreme literalness, a quality that no doubt appealed to neophyte students of Hebrew. Pagnini felt that Latin should be accommodated to the structure of Hebrew because Hebrew had been God's original language (Guerra 1990, 195–96).

In a letter to Johannes Bugenhagen (1485–1558), Luther praised Pagnini's version as well as the one by Sebastian Münster, both of whom, he said, translated "fideliter." In the same letter, however, he criticized both for their reliance on Targumim and Rabbinic commentary (*WA Br* 8:175–79, no. 3205).

References: Guerra 1990; Schmitt in Bautz and Bautz 1975– , 6:1433–34.
Exhibition: Bridwell, 00004 (Harrison Collection); Harvard, Bridwell copy; *Union*/Columbia, Bridwell copy.

1.24

Vetus Testamentum iuxta Septuaginta.

Rome: Francisco Zanetti, 1586 (1587).
D&M 4647.

Spurred on by humanist (and often "Protestant") efforts at producing authentic editions, the Council of Trent ordered the preparation of not only a new Vulgate text but also editions of Hebrew and Greek Bible texts. Under the patronage of Pius V, Gregory XIII, and Sixtus V, Cardinal Antonio Carafa (1538–91), who served as chief editor, relied mainly on the codex *Vatican B* (Vaticanus graecus 1209) to produce the Sixtine, or Vatican, edition of the Septuagint, which became the basis for most subsequent editions until the nineteenth century and is still admired for its accuracy and scholarship. The text of this edition was reprinted in the London Polyglot.

According to Darlow and Moule, the title-page date of the first edition (printed as "M.D.LXXXVI") has been changed by hand in almost every copy (see illustration). Based on the bookseller's license, dated 9 May 1587, they conclude that the later publication date is correct.

References: Hall in Greenslade 1963, 57–58; Pani 1990, 413–28.

Exhibition: Bridwell, Prothro B219; Harvard, Prothro copy; *Union*/Columbia, CB34/1587.

1.25

Biblia Polyglotta.

6 vols. Edited by Diego López de Zuñiga et al., under the patronage and at the expense of Cardinal Francisco Ximénez de Cisneros. Alcalá: Arnao Guillén de Brocar, 1514–17 (papal privilege printed after 22 March 1520). D&M 1412.

Begun in 1502, this polyglot contains the first printed edition of the Greek New Testament (colophon dated 10 January 1514) and the editio princeps of the Septuagint. Cardinal Francisco Ximénez de Cisneros, founder of the trilingual university in Alcalá (Complutum), supported the work of Hebrew and Greek scholars under the leadership of Diego López de Zuñiga (†1531). The editors consulted manuscripts the cardinal had borrowed from Venice and the Vatican (though not the codex *Vatican B*) or purchased. According to Geanakoplos, Demetrios Ducas was the primary editor of the Greek New Testament. Norton cataloged four states (noting the possibility of a fifth one) for the

1.24, title page

1.25, vol. 2: fol. B1ᵛ, Psalm 22

New Testament volume and speculated that state C may have circulated before Ximénez's death in 1517.

In the prefatory letter (composed in 1517), Ximénez diplomatically asserted that the "meaning of heavenly wisdom [coelestis sapientiae sensus]" can emerge from any language. Nonetheless, after translation, Scripture remains full of meanings "which are not able to be understood in any way other than from the very fount of the original language [quae nequeant aliunde quam ex ipso archetypae linguae fonte cognosci]" (vol. 1: fol. ❖3ʳ).

There are four volumes of the Old Testament, with Jerome's Vulgate in the center of the page between the Hebrew text (with roots printed in the margin) and the Septuagint (with an interlinear Latin translation); the *Targum Onkelos* is printed for the Pentateuch along with a Latin translation. Volume 5 is the New Testament in Greek, and volume 6 includes various indices and study aids, including a Hebrew and Aramaic dictionary, a Hebrew grammar, and interpretations of Greek, Aramaic, and Hebrew names. Ximénez's death and the difficulty in obtaining papal approval delayed official publication of the work until 1521/22, even though all six volumes had been printed by 1517.

The Greek type for the New Testament, based perhaps on medieval Greek uncials, is upright and free of ligatures. These characteristics may be appealing to the modern reader, but the Aldine Greek type became the preferred style throughout the sixteenth century.

References: de Jonge 1983, 14–17; Geanakoplos 1962, 231–46; Hefele [1851] 1968, 113–47; Norton 1978, 11–15; Olin 1990, 61–64; Woody 1971.

Exhibition: Bridwell, 24780; Harvard, And-Harv/Safe folio 303/1514; Union/*Columbia,* Book Arts Z232/B78/1514/B47; Yale, Beinecke/Mlh191/+514.

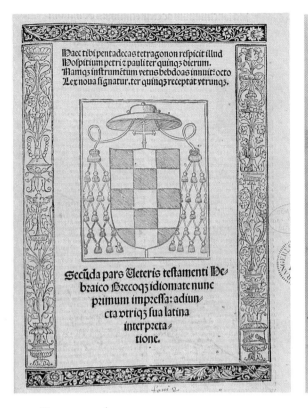

1.25, title page to vol. 2

1.25, vol. 5: fol. A3r, Gospel of John

1.26

Psalterium Hebraeum, Graecum, Arabicum, et
Chaldaeum, cum tribus latinis interpretationibus
et glossis.

Genoa: Pietro Paolo Porro, 16 November [1516].
D&M 1411.

With the exception of one proof page from a triglot
Old Testament project apparently begun and aban-
doned by Aldus Manutius, the earliest example of
polyglot printing is probably Erasmus's appendix to
volume 8 of his edition of Jerome, published by
Amerbach in 1516. (The preface to the appendix is
dated August 25.) It includes, in four parallel columns on facing pages, the Psalms in Greek of the
Septuagint, Jerome's Latin translation of them, Jerome's Latin translation of the Hebrew Psalms, and

Psalterium, Hebręum, Gręcũ,
Arabicũ, & Chaldęũ, cũ tribus
latinis ĩterp̃tarõ ibus & glossis.

1.26, title page

the Psalms in Hebrew. Konrad Pellikan assisted with the Hebrew text (see fol. A1ᵛ).

The Psalter printed later in the same year by Porro (colophon dated "mense .VIIIIbri," that is, November) was more ambitious. Its text appears in eight columns: Hebrew; Vulgate translation of the Hebrew; Vulgate translation of Greek; the Greek Septuagint; Arabic (it is the second example of Arabic printing); Aramaic; Latin translation of the Aramaic; and Latin notes in the eighth column and in the margin. Agostino Giustiniano (1470–1536), bishop of Nebbio, was the editor. His preface announces plans to publish the entire Bible in this form (fol. A2ʳ), but it never appeared.

The pride of the Genoans for a native son is apparent in the gloss to Psalm 19:4 (fol. c6ᵛ–c7ʳ), "et in fines mundi verba eorum." The lengthy note gives an account of the life and discoveries of Christopher Columbus (1451–1506), in part as an explanation of the new meaning of the "ends of the world." The long passage is commonly considered the first printed biography of the explorer.

The title page and colophon are printed in each of the five languages.

References: Berkowitz 1968, 173; Gistelinck and Sabbe 1994, 104–8, 258–59; Norton 1958, 38.

Exhibition: Bridwell, Prothro B48; Harvard, Typ/525/16.210F; Union/*Columbia,* B893.1/BI/B16; Yale, Beinecke/Mla400/+516g.

I.27

Biblia Sacra Polyglotta.

6 vols. Edited by Brian Walton. London: Thomas Roycroft, [1654]–57.
D&M 1446.

Called the London Polyglot, this is generally considered the most accurate of the so-called four great polyglots. (The other three are the Complutensian [Item 1.25], Plantin [1569–72], and Paris [1629–45, also called La Jay's Polyglot].) The chief editor, Brian Walton (1600–1661), who was made bishop of

1.27, frontispiece engraving, depicting Brian Walton

Chester (1660–61) after the Restoration, began work on the project in 1647, after having studied Oriental languages at Oxford. Eventually, many scholars collaborated on the project, including John Lightfoot (1602–75) and James Ussher (1581–1656). Among the prefatory materials are charts on biblical weights and measures, descriptions of the second temple, and a "Sacred Chronology," which computes the dates of major historical and biblical events "ab orbe condito." The text appears in nine languages: Hebrew, Samaritan, Aramaic, Greek, Arabic, Syriac, Ethiopic, Persian, and Latin.

References: Berkowitz 1968, 182; Copinger 1897, 49–50; Mathieson 1985, no. 23.

Exhibition: Bridwell, AFH9300/1–6; Harvard, And-Harv/folio/Codman/B582; Union/*Columbia,* B220.5/C57; Yale, DIV/939089.

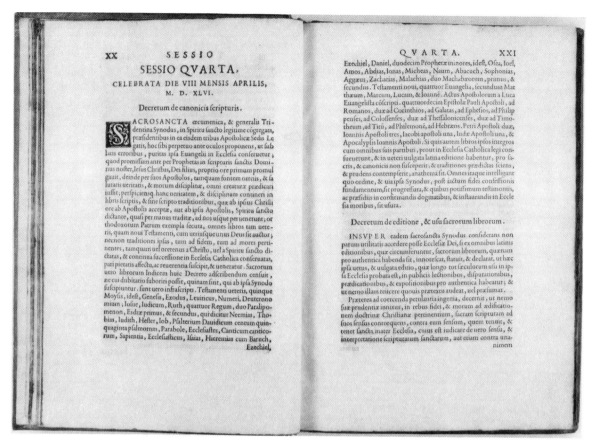

1.28, pp. XX–XXI, "Decretum de canonicis scripturis"

1.28

Council of Trent (1545–63).

Canones, et decreta sacrosancti oecvmenici, et generalis Concilii Tridentini.

Rome: Paulus Manutius, 1564.
Adams C-2797.

The Council of Trent established the canonical books of the Bible, decreed that the church alone was authorized to interpret Scripture, and pronounced that tradition and biblical precedents (not sola Scriptura) were the basis for belief and authority in the church.

Pope Paul III (1468–1549) convened the council in 1545 in the northern Italian city of Trent. The council met during three extended periods over the next eighteen years (and under three different popes) and addressed many of the issues that had provoked the Reform movement. Recognizing problems of ecclesiastical corruption, the participants passed canons and directives to raise moral standards among the clergy. In general, however, they held to tradition, reaffirming the seven sacraments and other matters of Catholic dogma, including transubstantiation, veneration of the Virgin, celibate priesthood, and justification by good works, as well as by faith.

Paulus Manutius (1512–74), son of Aldus, became the official printer to the pope in 1561 and was commissioned by Pius IV to publish the canons and decrees of the Council of Trent in 1564. During that year, he and his son Aldus the Younger printed the work at least eleven times in three editions. This edition, the first in folio, is extremely rare and remarkable for the large number of errors in the text, which have been corrected in a contemporary hand in most extant copies (Renouard 1825, 2:36).

References: Jedin 1961, vol. 2; Kuttner 1979; Renouard 1825, 2:35–43.

Exhibition: Bridwell, 19461; Harvard, *fCC/T723/1564; *Union*/Columbia showing Lyons: Guillaume Rouille, 1566 (KJ51/1566); Yale showing second Aldine folio of 1564 (Beinecke/Mnj31/+1564b).

1.29

Church of England. *Articles.*

London: Richard Jugge and John Cawood, 1571. *STC* (2d ed.) 10039.

The *Thirty-Nine Articles,* drawn up by the Church of England in 1562 and first published in English in 1571, outline the basic beliefs of the Anglican communion. Matthew Parker (1504–75) and other bishops revised the forty-two articles put forth by Thomas Cranmer (1489–1556) during the reign of Edward VI. Although they do exclude Catholic and Anabaptist views, the *Articles* otherwise define issues of doctrine in rather broad terms, with brief directives on such tenets of the Anglican faith as belief in the Trinity (Article 1), the nature of Christ (Article 2), the sacraments of baptism and the eucharist (Article 15), and the ancillary nature of good works (Articles 12 and 14). The concept of sola Scriptura is addressed in Article 6, and the importance of the vernacular in worship is stated succinctly in Article 24: "It is a thing playnely repugnant to the worde of God, and the custome of the primitive Churche, to have publique prayer in the Churche, or to minister the Sacramentes in a tongue not understanded of the people."

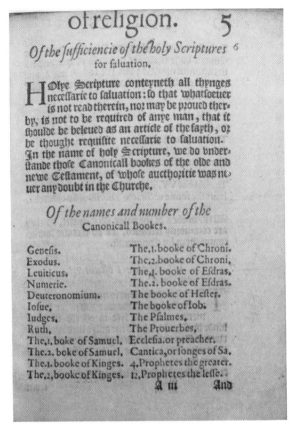

1.29, fol. A3r, Article 6.
By permission of Union Theological Seminary.

Article 6, the opening shown here, establishes the canon of the Bible and declares that Scripture contains all that is necessary for salvation.

Reference: Bicknell 1947.
Exhibition: Bridwell, Union copy; Harvard, STC/10039.5; *Union*/Columbia, McAlpin 1571/A79; Yale, Beinecke/ Mnm37/1571.

2.1

Biblia Latina, with the *Glossa ordinaria.*

4 vols. [Strasbourg: Adolf Rusch for Anton Koberger, after 23 September 1481?].
See D&M 6083, note; Goff B-607; *GW* 4282.

The first Latin Bible printed with glosses, this edition contains the *Glossa ordinaria* and an interlinear gloss. These commentaries, which are compilations of patristic interpretations, were attributed to Walafrid Strabo (†849) and to Anselm of Laon (†1117), respectively, but are actually the work of several generations of biblical scholars. The printer adapted the page layout from manuscript practice, placing the *Ordinary Gloss* around the text and interlinear commentary — a format quickly adopted by other printers.

Something of the printing history is known from a letter that Adolf Rusch wrote to the printer Johann Amerbach (1444–1514) in Basel. Rusch, son-in-law of the Strasbourg printer Johann Mentelin, printed this Bible for Anton Koberger (ca. 1440–1513) with type borrowed from Amerbach. In the letter, however, Rusch admits that he held back at least a hundred copies for himself — unbeknown to his publisher — and he asks Amerbach not to republish the work until he has liquidated his own stock.

The collation of this work is complex, and the number of volumes differs according to the ordering of the signatures (Walsh 1991–94, 1:63).

References: de Hamel 1984, 1–27; Geldner 1982, 684–88; Smalley [1952] 1964, 56–66; Walsh 1991–94, 1:62–64.
Exhibition: Bridwell, 06150–52 (Harrison Collection); Harvard, Inc/299; *Union*/Columbia, CB62/1480r; Yale, YCBA/Leaf Coll. 279 (two leaves).

tu es petrus· et super hanc pe-
tram edificabo ecclesiam meam.
Et porte inferi non preualebut
aduersus eam. Et tibi dabo cla-
ues regni celoꝝ. Et quodcunꝗ
ligaueris super terram erit liga-
tum z in celis: z quodcuꝗ solue-
ris super terrã: erit solutũ z in cel
Tunc precepit discipulis suis vt
nemini dicerent qz ipse esset Jhesus chꝛist. Erinde cepit Jhesus
ondere discipulis suis qz oporte
ret eum ire bierosolimã· z multa
pati a senioribꝰ et scribis et prin
cipibus sacerdotũ z occidi z ter
cia die resurgere· Et assumens
eum petrus cepit increpare illuz
dicens: Absit a te dñe·non erit ti

vade post me sathana· scandaluz
es michi·qz nõ sapis ea quç dei
sunt: sed ea quç sunt bominum·
Tunc Jhesus dixit discipul suis
Si quis vult post me venire ab
neget semetipsum z tollat cruce
suam z sequatur me. Qui eni vo
luerit animam suam saluam face
re perdet eam. Qui autem perdit
clerit animam suam ipropter me:
inuenet eam. Quid enim pꝛo
dest bomini si mundum vniuer
sum lucretur: anime vero suç de
trimentũ paniatur. Aut quã da
bit homo· commutationem pꝛo
anima sua· Filius enim hominis
veturus est in glozia patris sui

2.1, vol. 3: fol. CXVI, "Tu es Petrus"

2.2

Thomas Aquinas.

Catena aurea super quattuor evangelistas.

2 vols. Rome: Conrad Sweynheym and
Arnold Pannartz, 7 December 1470.
BMC 4:12 (IC.17159); Goff T-225.

Medieval biblical commentary often took the form
of a compilation of quotations from patristic sources
to explicate passages. This genre, known as the
catena patrum ("chain of the fathers"), reached its
apex in a work by Thomas Aquinas (1225?–74),
respectfully called the *Golden Chain* by later readers.
In it, Aquinas concatenates selections from eighty
Greek and Latin authors to form a commentary on
the four Gospels. The work became the model for
subsequent *catenae* and an important source for medieval and Renaissance exegetes. In addition to
offering authoritative commentary, Aquinas preserved fragments of some works that are no longer
extant. The work was popular; it was copied hundreds of times in manuscripts and published often
in the fifteenth and sixteenth centuries.

The editio princeps appeared in 1470 at the press
of Sweynheym and Pannartz (on exhibition at Harvard). It was edited by Cardinal Giovanni Andrea
de' Bussi.

References: Newman 1841–45, 1:i–xii; Weisheipl 1974,
171–73.
Exhibition: Showing Venice: Bonetus Locatellus for
Octavianus Scotus, 4 June 1493 at Bridwell (06672) and Yale
(Beinecke/Zi/+5043); Harvard, Inc/3314; *Union*/Columbia
showing [Basel: Michael Wenssler], 1476 (RB:85A).

2.3

Nicholas of Lyra.

Postilla super totam Bibliam.

5 vols. Rome: Conrad Sweynheym and Arnold
Pannartz, 18 November 1471–26 May 1472.
BMC 4:14 (IC.17180–84); Goff N-131.

Because of his deep knowledge of Hebrew and rabbinic learning, Nicholas of Lyra (ca. 1270–1349) was
often said to have been Jewish by birth. However
that may be (and it seems unlikely), it is known that
he entered the Franciscan Order as a young man
and became a Doctor of Theology at Paris. He was
one of the few Christians with a command of
Hebrew, which made his commentary of the Hebrew Scripture extraordinarily valuable to early humanists. There exist about seven hundred manuscripts of Lyra's *Postilla* from 1350 to 1450, and
more than one hundred editions from the first century of printing.

Lyra practiced the traditional fourfold approach
to biblical interpretation, but his preference for
"natural exegesis," by which he seems to refer to
analysis based on literal meanings, made him a particular favorite of Luther. Indeed, Luther often
praised his exegetical skills, once macaronically:
"Lira ist sehr gut, praesertim in conciliandis locis
scripturae, qui videntur pugnare. Do ist er wun-
derlich. Sine Lyra non intelligeremus nec novum
nec vetus testamentum [Lyra is very good, especially
in reconciling places in scripture which seem to be at
odds. He's marvelous at that. Without Lyra we
would understand neither the New nor the Old Tes-
tament]" (*WA* 48:691, no. 7118).

The editio princeps of Lyra's commentary was
printed by Sweynheym and Pannartz in a style similar to their edition of Augustine's *City of God*. It is
first in a long line of incunabular editions of Lyra
and, more commonly, the Bible surrounded by
Lyra's commentary.

Primus prologus Nicolai de Lyra de
commendatione sacre scripture in generali.

Ec omnia liber uite Ecc. xxiiii. Secundum q̃ dicit beatus Grego.
homelia. xxxv. Euangeliorum temporalis uita eterne uite comparata
mors est potius dicenda q̃ uita. Scientie uere a philosophis tradite
ordinantur ad finem consequendum in presenti uita quia scientie
practice ab eis tradite ordinantur ad felicitatem politica loquendo
de policia presentis uite. Similiter scientie speculatiue ordinatur
ad felicitatem contemplatiuam loquendo de contemplatione que
potest haberi in uita presenti & per uiam nature que dependet ex phātasmate. Vnde
dicit. iii. de anima. Quod intelligentibus nobis aliqd necesse e simul phātasma speculari.
Et de tali speculatione dicit ibidem q̃ intelligere corrumpit in nobis quodam interius cor/
rupto. Sacra aut scriptura ordiat ad felicitatem future uite quam philosophi nesciuerut.
Secdm q̃ dicit beatus Hieronymus in epistola ad Paulinum de omnibus sacre scripture
libris hoc doctus Plato nesciuit. hoc Demosthenes eloquens ignorauit. Ex qbus con/
cluditur q̃ libri a philosophis descripti continentes scientias ordinatas ad finem in hac
temporali uita tantumodo & modo naturali consequendum: si comparentur ad libros
sacre scripture que ordinatur ad finem uite eterne magis dicendi sut libri mortis q̃ uite.
Sed liber continens sacram scripturam que licet in multis libris partialibus diuidatur:
sub uno tamen libro continetur: qui nomine generali Biblia dicitur liber uite proprie
nominatur: secdm q̃ dicit in uerbo passumpto. Hec omnia etce. In qua sacra scriptura
quadrupliciter describitur secdm quattuor excellentias quibus omnem scripturam aliam
excellit. Primo enim describitur ut singularis eminentie q̃ notat pronomen singulare
· cum dicit hec. Secudo describitur ut generalis continentie q̃ ostedit signu uniuersale:
cum dicitur: Omnia. Tertio ut specularis intelligentie q̃ notat codicio libri cu dicit.
liber. Quarto ut salutaris efficacie q̃ ostendit consecutio finis intenti: cum dicit uite.
Circa primum sciendum q̃ una scientia eminentior est altera seu honorabilior duplici
decausa ut habetur primo de anima. Vna est quia est de nobiliori subiecto. alia qa
procedit certiori modo. & propter utraqi sacra scriptura que pprie dicit theologia:
cum ipsa sola sit textus huius scientie: omnes scientias alias antecellit. Primo quia habet
deum pro subiecto qui est in summo totius nobilitatis propter q̃ nominat theologia
quasi sermo de deo. Secundo quia procedit modo certiori alie eni scientie humanitus
reperte procedunt per inuestigationem rationis humane in quo quidem processu licet
non sit error quantum ad cognitionem primorum principiorum que sunt per se nota:
secudu q̃ dicit. ii. Metaphisice. In foribus qs delinquet: tn in deductione conclusionu
ex principiis potest esse error: maxime quantum ad conclusiones a primis principiis
longinquas: Vnde & in tali pcessu omnes philosophi innitentes humane inuestigatioi
inueniuntur in aliquibus errasse. Et ideo de singulari eminentia huius scientie dicitur.
Deutro. iiii. Hec est sapientia uestra & intellectus coram populis. Sapietia eni pprie
dicitur illa scientia que considerat altissimas causas ut habet primo Metaphisice. Sacra
uero scriptura habet deum pro subiecto: ut dictum est: q est prima causa simpliciter
omnium. Et ideo pprie dicit sapientia sed conuenienter addit uestra. ad distinguendu
sapientiam sanctoru seu Catholicoru que e i ipsa sacra scriptura a sapietia philosophor
& hoc potissime in duobus uidelicet i pprietatibus de deo cognitis. & i fine cognitiois
licet enim philosophi habuerint cognitionem de deo. Hoc tamen solum fuit quantu

This work has great significance for the history of books and printing because the fifth volume (fol. 2$^{\mathrm{r-v}}$) includes a list of twenty-eight volumes previously published by Sweynheym and Pannartz, with the size of each print run indicated.

References: Bunte 1994, 11–26; Merrill 1975.
Exhibition: Bridwell, 06489–93; Harvard showing Nuremberg: Anton Koberger, 12 April 1493 (And-Harv/R.B.R./f307/Lat/1493); Union/*Columbia* showing Venice: [Bonetus Locatellus] for Octavianus Scotus, 9 August 1488 (Inc/N-132); Yale showing Strasbourg: Johann Mentelin, ca. 1472 (YCBA/Leaf Coll. 71 [one leaf]).

2.4

Luther, Martin.

Enarrationes epistolarvm et evangeliorvm, qvas postillas vocant.

Wittenberg: Johann Rhau-Grunenberg, 7 March 1521.
B 848; *VD16* L4548.

In the preface to the first edition of his *Postils* in 1521, Luther explains that he is publishing these commentaries, or postils, at the encouragement of Frederick (1463–1525), Elector of Saxony, who asked him to turn to exegesis and away from controversial writings. Luther says that his goal is to combat centuries of inept commentaries with the "purest and simplest sense of the Gospel [purissimo et simplicissimo Euangelii sensu]" (fol. A4^{r}). Not surprisingly, he uses this forum to criticize bishops and "papists."

The term *postilla,* which was also used to describe Lyra's commentaries, probably comes from "post illa verba" (after these words), in reference to the line-by-line explanation of scriptural passages.

The work was printed six times in 1521, first at the press of Johann Rhau-Grunenberg (fl. 1508–25). A German translation appeared in the following year with a woodcut by Hans Baldung Grien (1484/5–1545) depicting Luther as a monk inspired by the Holy Spirit (see illustration on p. 22). Baldung's woodcut first appeared in *Acta et res gestae* (1521), a description of Luther's actions at the Diet of Worms.

References: *The Illustrated Bartsch,* 12:39 (313) for Baldung's woodcut; *WA* 7:459–62.
Exhibition: Bridwell, AER9123; Harvard, *GC5/L9774/B521e; Union/Columbia showing Strasbourg: Georg Ulricher, 1530 (GT4/P2/A/1530).

2.5

Luther, Martin.

Epistel Sanct Petri gepredigt vnd ausgelegt.

Wittenberg: Nickel Schyrlentz, 1523.
B 1726; *VD16* L4593.

This work is based on a series of sermons on 1 Peter
delivered by Luther in Wittenberg in late 1522 or
early 1523 after his return from the Wartburg. In the
preface, he calls Peter's letter one of the noblest
books in the New Testament and reminds the
reader that all the apostles teach the same thing:
"vnd ist nit recht/ das man vier Euangelisten vnd
vier Euangelia zelet/ denn es ist alles/ was die
Apostel geschrieben haben/ eyn Euangelion [it is
not correct to count four evangelists and four Gospels, for everything that the apostles have written is
one Gospel]" (fol. A1ᵛ). Further, Luther says that
the right of interpretation belongs to all Christians,
"not to the pope or councils" (fol. A2ᵛ).

Reference: *WA* 12:249–399.
Exhibition: Bridwell, AES0295; Harvard, *GC5/L9774/523e;
Union/Columbia, L Pam B-1726; Yale showing [Augsburg:
Silvan Otmar], 1523 (Beinecke/Me45/L973/A3/v.2).

2.5, title page

Der Prophet Jona /ausgelegt durch Mart. Luth.

2.6, title page (second printing, 1526)

2.6

Luther, Martin. *Der Prophet Jona.*

Wittenberg: Michael Lotter, 1526.
B 2268; *VD16* B3913.

Jonah was the first of the prophetic books Luther translated. Others appeared separately over the next few years, before a complete translation of the Prophets was issued in 1532. In the preface, which was not printed in every 1526 edition, Luther accounts for the lull in his Bible translating since the appearance of the New Testament and Pentateuch. He was preoccupied, he says, with his efforts against the "Schwärmer [enthusiasts]," but now it is time to leave that to others and take up biblical studies again.

He chose the Book of Jonah for explication over the Gospels, he explains, not only because he had been lecturing on the minor prophets at the University of Wittenberg in 1525 but also because the victors of the recently concluded Peasants' War are wary of the New Testament and the radical ideas that they believe it spawned. Jonah, however, "is well suited for the present time" because it teaches trust in God and reminds readers of Christ's death and resurrection (fol. A2ᵛ–A3ʳ). Jonah, which, Luther says, means "dove" in Hebrew, represents the Holy Spirit and, consequently, the triumph of the Gospel it inspired (fol. L1ᵛ).

In 1526 alone, Luther's *Der Prophet Jona* was printed sixteen times (thirteen in German, three in Latin). The first two printings appeared at the press of Michael Lotter (fl. 1523–46), brother of the printer Melchior Lotter the Younger (ca. 1470–1549). The brothers used the same presses and often collaborated on the printing of Lutheran tracts.

References: Benzing 1982, 498; Raeder 1983, 256–73; *WA DB* 2:393, no. 22.
Exhibition: Bridwell, AFE7444 (second printing, 1526; B2269); Harvard, *GC5/L9774/526p; *Union*/Columbia showing Augsburg: Johannes Knobloch, 1526 (L-Pam B-2270).

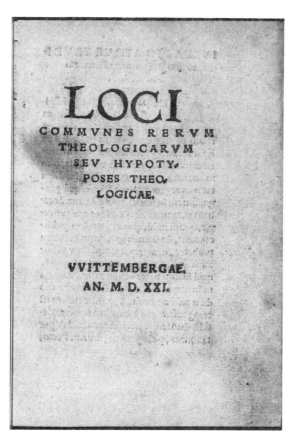

2.7, title page.

By permission of the Houghton Library, Harvard University.

2.7

Melanchthon, Philipp.

Loci commvnes rervm theologicarvm.

Wittenberg: [Melchior Lotter the Younger], 1521.
VD16 M3584

The *Loci communes* are considered the first systematic theology of the Reformation. Philipp Melanchthon (1497–1560) based the *Loci* on the Bible, especially on the topics raised by Paul in Romans. As one might expect from the basis in Paul, the most important *loci* are the law, sin, and grace. The polemical tone, especially the opposition to scholasticism, is occasionally reminiscent of Erasmus, even of his *Praise of Folly*. Interestingly, Erasmus complimented the *Loci communes* in a letter of 6 September 1524 (Allen 1906–58, no. 1496). Nonetheless, he says that he disagrees with many things and that he wishes he had been able to discuss them with Melanchthon before the work had been printed.

An unauthorized publication of lecture notes on Romans, the *Lucubratiuncula* (1520), compelled Melanchthon to complete the *Loci communes* swiftly. Luther called the work unsurpassed ("invictum libellum") and worthy of inclusion in the canon; he also worked on a German translation of it, although nothing resulted from those efforts. Melanchthon undertook revisions throughout his career; the last printing during his lifetime, the *Loci praecipui theologici* (1559), was some four times the size of the first.

References: *CR,* vol. 21; Engelland in Melanchthon 1951–75, 2/1:1–3; Harvard College Library 1983, 35–36.
Exhibition: Bridwell, AFL7461; Harvard, GC5/ M4807L/1521; *Union*/Columbia showing German translation by Georg Spalatin, [Augsburg: Sigmund Grimm and Marx Wirsung, 1522] (GT91/LGS/1521); Yale showing Wittenberg: V. Creutzer, 1544 (Beinecke/Zg16/M48/544).

2.8

Melanchthon, Philipp.

Annotationes Philippi Melanchthonis in Epistolas Pauli ad Rhomanos et Corinthios.

Nuremberg: Johann Stuchs, 1522.
VD16 M2447.

Luther published the first edition of Melanchthon's *Annotations on Paul's Letters to the Romans and Corinthians* at Nuremberg in 1522 without the author's permission. He admits his "sin" in the preface but chastises Melanchthon for not thinking highly enough of the commentary to publish it himself. "You say scripture alone must be read in place of commentaries" (fol. a2ʳ⁻ᵛ). But Luther does not consider the *Annotations* a commentary; they are "at most an index for reading scriptures and for knowing Christ." To Melanchthon's contention that his notes are not polished enough for publication, Luther replies that this should not be troubling because it means that Paul, not Melanchthon, will get the glory.

The first printing was so riddled with typographic errors, however, that Luther regretted his deed (see *WA* 12:56). The *Annotations* were published eleven times in Latin and German over the next three years.

References: Beutenmüller 1960, 149; *WA* 10/2:305; Wengert 1987, 32–33.
Exhibition: Bridwell, ADB1347; Harvard showing
Strasbourg: Johannes Herwagen, 1523 (And-Harv/ R.B.R./608.2/M51.4anm/1523/no. 3); Union/Columbia, Bridwell copy; Yale, Beinecke/Mlz755/523Mb.

2.8, fol. A2ʳ, Luther's introduction

2.9

Cajetan, Tommaso de Vio.

Jentacula novi testamenti.

Rome: Marcello Silber for Jacopo' Giunta, 1525.

Tommaso de Vio Cajetan (1469–1534), best known as the cardinal who first confronted Martin Luther at the Diet of Augsburg in 1518, wrote this commentary on sixty-four passages of the New Testament in order to help priests prepare sermons. It was his first published exegetical work.

A professor of philosophy and theology at Padua, Pavia, Brescia, and Rome, Cajetan was the author of an important commentary on Aquinas's *Summa theologica.* Although he was assigned to be Luther's initial challenger, Cajetan himself had advocated reform of the monastic orders and the cardinalate. Moreover, he shared the humanists' doubts about the text of the Vulgate and often consulted Erasmus's Greek New Testament as well as Hebrew texts (with the help of assistants) for his own research. In his scriptural interpretations, he sought the *sensus literalis,* or literal sense, often drawing criticism from more conservative forces within the church.

Apparently, his meeting with Luther at Augsburg was cordial, albeit unsuccessful. Although Luther would not disavow his beliefs and wrote critically of Cajetan, in later years he came to appreciate Cajetan's reasoned and tolerant views. According to the *Tischreden* (*WA TR* 2:596, no. 2668), he joked that Cajetan had become a Lutheran ("Porro ille Sylvester Caietanus postremo factus est Lutheranus").

References: Hallersleben 1984; Wicks 1983.

Exhibition: Bridwell, ACX1962; Harvard showing Lyons: Jacopo Giunta, 1537 (Typ/515.37/870); Union/*Columbia* showing Salamanca: Matthias Gastius, 1571 (BX1757/V5/1571).

2.10

Calvin, John.

In librvm Psalmorum, Iohannis Caluini commentarius.

[Geneva]: Robert Estienne, 15 July 1557.
Adams C-286; *IA* 129.933.

The *Commentary on Psalms* is one of Calvin's several important works on Hebrew Scripture. The commentary for each psalm includes three elements: a paraphrasing *argumentum,* a literal Latin translation of the Hebrew, and an extensive commentary on the text.

Calvin probably devoted more attention to the Psalms than to any other book of the Hebrew Bible. He directed efforts to compose a Psalter for congregational use (see Item 4.16); wrote lengthy lectures on the Psalms (1552–55/56); focused on the Psalms in his lectures for the "Congrégation" (1555–59); delivered Sunday sermons on the Psalms (otherwise, he gave sermons on Hebrew Scripture during the week only); and published this detailed *Commentary on Psalms,* first in Latin (1557) and then in French (1558).

Calvin does not completely eschew christological analogies, but a distinctive element of his commentary is its historical focus, a concern that he developed through the research of Martin Bucer (as acknowledged by Calvin in the preface) and which is not unrelated to Nicholas of Lyra's "double literal sense." According to Calvin, the "historical David" that emerges from the commentary is useful as a source of instruction for the sixteenth-century church. Calvin's interest in edification is apparent in his use of the Ciceronian mirror metaphor: "I am accustomed to calling this book, not inappropriately, an anatomy of every part of the soul (ἀνατομὴν omnium animae partium), for no one could discover an emotion in himself, of which an image does not reflect in this mirror" (fol. ¶2ʳ).

The depiction of David (Calvin, of course, recognized that David was not the sole author of the Psalms) as a kind of Christian mirror for personal edification may also have inspired the famous autobiographical preface, in which Calvin reflects on the history of his own calling.

References: Pitkin 1993; Renouard [1843] 1972, 87.

Exhibition: Bridwell, AFD4014; Harvard, *fFC5/C1394/557i; Union/Columbia, Bridwell copy; Yale showing Geneva: Nicolaus Barbirius and Thomas Courteau, 1564 (Beinecke/1977/174).

2.11

Calvin, John.

Harmonia ex tribus Euangelistis composita, Matthaeo, Marco et Luca: adiuncto seorsum Iohanne, quod pauca cum aliis communia habeat. Cum Iohannis Calvini commentariis.

2 pts. [Geneva]: Robert Estienne, 1560.
Adams C-348; *IA* 129.970.

Calvin wrote commentaries on every book of the New Testament except 2 and 3 John and Revelation. After completing his commentary on the Gospel of John in 1553, he turned to the synoptics, arranging them in the medieval style of a Gospel harmony because, as he says in the introduction, "it is not possible to comment skillfully and intelligently on one Gospel without comparing the other two" (fol. ¶8ᵛ). For the Latin text, he consulted Erasmus's first and second editions and the Vulgate (probably one of Estienne's editions) but composed his own version for the passages quoted and explicated.

References: Parker 1971, 159–67; Schellong 1969.
Exhibition: Bridwell, AEQ3262; Harvard showing [Geneva]: Anchora Crispiniana, 1572 (*FC5/C1394/B572c); *Union/Columbia*, CB68.6/1560.

2.11, p. 259, Matthew 16, Mark 8, and Luke 9

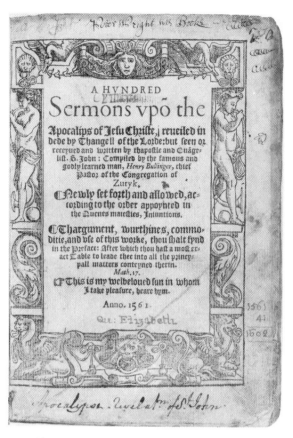

2.12, title page

2.12

Bullinger, Heinrich.

A Hvndred Sermons vpon the Apocalips of Jesu Christe.

London: John Day, 1561.
IA 127.375.

The sermons on Revelation by Heinrich Bullinger (1504–75) were first published in 1557 in Latin. Over the next ten years, they appeared seventeen times in five different languages. This is the first English edition. His interpretation conforms to the general practice among Protestant exegetes to read the text as a condemnation of the Roman Church, as, for example, in the interpretation of the harlot of Babylon as the papacy.

Bullinger was the son of a Swiss priest (who later married Bullinger's mother when the Reformation was introduced to Switzerland). Before his break with the Catholic Church, he taught in the Cistercian monastery of Kappel, where he even lectured on Melanchthon's *Loci* in the early 1520s. Bullinger was instrumental in the Swiss Reform movement, becoming Zwingli's successor in Zurich after the Reformer's death at the battle of Kappel. His relations with many exiled English Protestants resulted in the formation of close ties with the Reform movement there after the reign of Mary Tudor. His sermons were popular in England, and he corresponded with most major English Reformers during his long tenure in Zurich.

References: Blanke and Leuschner 1990; Staedtke 1972, 1:355.
Exhibition: Bridwell, 00542; Harvard, STC/4061; Union/Columbia, Bridwell copy; Yale, DIV/790611.

2.13

Testamentum novvm with *Annotationes.*

Edited and translated by Théodore de Bèze. 2 pts. [Geneva: Henri Estienne], 1589.
D&M 4651.

Henri Estienne (1528–98) printed numerous editions of the Greek New Testament of Théodore de Bèze (1519–1605), including the editio princeps of 1565. Bèze edited the Greek text and provided his own Latin translation as well as the traditional Vulgate version. These are printed in three parallel columns on each page. His *Annotations,* which had been printed with his Latin translation earlier by Henri's father, Robert, and which he continued to expand on in each succeeding edition, usually appear at the bottom of the page in small type. The 1589 edition includes the explication of "search the Scriptures" discussed on p. 37.

Born in Vézelay in 1519, Bèze was raised by an uncle in Paris until 1528. Later, as a young man in Bourges he met Calvin and other Parisian exiles. After an education in the law, he settled in Paris, where he became known as a humanist and Latin poet. Many of his French psalm poems were incorporated into the Geneva and Huguenot Psalters. In 1549, he resolved to follow the Reformers to Geneva, where he eventually served as rector of the Academy that Calvin had founded in 1559. In 1564, he became Calvin's successor.

Reference: Geisendorf 1949.
Exhibition: Bridwell, 00026; Harvard, Bridwell copy; Union/*Columbia* showing [Geneva]: Henri Estienne, 1565 (B225.48/B65); Yale showing [Geneva]: Henri Estienne, 1588 (Beinecke/Mlh691/+565bf).

2.14

Flacius Illyricus, Matthias.

Clavis scripturae sacrae, seu de sermone sacrarum literarum.

2 vols. Basel: Heirs of Sebastian Henricpetri, 1628.

Matthias Flacius (1520–75) wrote the first important explanation of Reformation hermeneutics in this work entitled *Key to the Sacred Scripture* (first published in 1567). It consists of a biblical-theological dictionary (part 1) and an outline of the rules of exegesis (part 2). His success in this effort led him to publish a reworking of Erasmus's Greek New Testament in 1571, complete with revised annotations reflecting Lutheran theology.

Flacius studied at Basel, Tübingen, and Wittenberg and was befriended by Melanchthon and Luther early in his career. He later became a staunch Lutheran and a professor of Hebrew at the University of Wittenberg. After Luther's death, he led the so-called Gnesiolutherans, who were critical of the Augsburg Interim and the adiaphorist movement of Melanchthon (the so-called Philippists). He also published the first church history from a Lutheran point of view, the *Magdeburg Centuries* (1559–74), in which he claims to show how the moral authority of the papacy has declined through the centuries, citing the female pope, among others, as evidence of the degeneration of St. Peter's line.

References: Hagen 1990, 186–95; Kraus 1969, 28–29; Matešíc 1993; Mirković 1980; Olson 1990.
Exhibition: Bridwell, AFK6086, gift of the curator, Jaroslav Pelikan; Harvard showing Leipzig: Johannes Justus Erythropilus and Christian Goezius 1695 (And-Harv/R.B.R./BS440/.F53/1695); Union/Columbia showing Basel: Sebastian Henricpetri, 1609 (CD14.1/F47/1609); Yale showing Basel: Sebastian Henricpetri, 1617 (Sterling/Me45/F593/+C5/1617).

in dem haus des herren. Aber die sibenzig haben ge=
tulmetzsch vor der zükunfte xpi vnd das das sy nie
gewise haben das haben sp aufgesprochen mit zwp=
feltigen fremdē synnen: aber wir schreiben nach vn
sers herrē martter vnd nach seiner auffersteeung
nicht allein die propheceyen der zükunftigen ding
sunder auch die hystorien das ist das aussprechen der
ding die geschehen sein wann anders werden auf=
gesprochen die ding die man hörte· vnd anders die
ding die man suchte. Was wir bas vernemen das
müg wir bas aussprechen· Darumb höre du seind:
vnd hab ein erforschen du nach claffer. Ich verdam
nit auch strauffe ich nie die·lxx·tulmetzen sunder
ich vorsetz vnd aussprech sicherlich die·xij·botten
für die alle·lxx· Cristus der lautet mir durch iren
mund vnd die selben sese ich das sp sein gesetze für
die propheten in den geistlichen gaben die do gibt der
heilig geist: in den gar nachent die tulmetzschen ha
ben den letzsten grad. Du seind was lasen dich peini
gen den neyd vnd den hass: was reitzseu wider mich
die gemüte der vngelerten. An welicher stat dich
dunket das ich geirret hab in der auslegung frag
die hebreischen habent meister in vil steeten. Was
die haben von xpo das habent nie dein pücher. Es
ist ein ander ding ist das sp bewert haben widersich
hernach die gezeugt gezeucknis von den·xij·lumen
die lateinischen pücher sint bas geleutert wann di
kriechischen: vnd die kriechischen bas wann die he
breischen· Vnd also hab ich dise ding geredt wiz
die neidischen. Nu bit ich dich du aller liebster desi
derp: wann du mich geheissen hast das ich mich vnd
wunden han eins sölichen wercks· das sich an hebet
von dem puch der schöpffung· das du mir geholff
sepest in deinem gebette· das ich müg aufgespreche
dise pücher in lateinische sprach mit dem selbē geist
mit dem die selben pücher sein geschriben. Amen

Incipit liber Genesis. capi [ornate initial] n dem anegang geschieff got
den himel vnd die erde. wann
die erde was eytel vnd lere :
vnd vinster waren auff dem
antlütze des abgrundes· vnd
der geist gotz ward getragen
auff die wasser. Vnd got der
sprach· liecht werde gemacht
Vnd das liecht ward gemacht· vnd got der sache dz
liecht das es ward güt: vnd er teilet das liecht von ō
vinster· vnd das liecht hieß er den tag vnd die vinz
ster die nacht. Vnd es wart gemacht abent vnd der
morgen ein tag. Vnd got der sprach· Vestenkeit
werd gemacht in mitz der wasser: vnd teilt die was
ser vō den wassern. Vnd got macht die vestenkeit
vnd teilte die wasser die do waren vnder der vesten
keit von den die do waren ob der vestenkeit· vnd es
ward getan also· Vnd got der rieff die vestenkeit dē
himel: vnd es ward gemacht abent vnd der morgē
der ander tage. Wann gott der sprach· Die wasser
die do sint vnder dem himel die werdnt gesamet an
ein stat vñ die dürre derschein. Vnd es ward getan
also· Vnd gott der rieff die dürre die erde: vnd die
samenung des wassers hieß er das mere· Vnd got

der sach das es was güt vnd sprach· Die erde keim
grüns kraut vnd mache samen: vnd das ōphelbau
min holtze mach wücher nach sein geschlecht ·des
same sey in jm selbs auf der erde· Vnd es ward ge
tan also· Vnd die fürbracht grüns kraut vnd
bringt den samē nach irem geschlecht: vñ das holtz
mache den wücher vñ ein pglichs het samen nach
seinem bilde· Vnd got der sach das es was güt: vñ
es ward gemacht abent vnd der morgen der dritte:
tag· Wañ got der sprach· Liecht werdent gemacht
in der vestenkeit des himels· vnd teilent den tag vñ
die nachte: vnd sind in zeichene vnd in zeite vnd in
iare· das sy leichtent in ō vestenkeit des himels· vñ
entleichten die erde· Vnd es wart getan also· Vñ
got der mach zwey michel liecht: das merer zü leich
ten das es vor were dem tage· vnd das mynner zü
leichten das es vor were der nacht vnd steernen· vnd
saezte sy in die vestenkeit des himels das sy leichtent
auff die erde: vnd vorwere dem tag vnd der nacht
vnd teiltē das liecht vnd die vinster· Vnd got der
sach das es was güt: vñ es ward gemacht abent vñ
der morgen der vierde tag· Joch got ō sprach· Die
wasser für furent kriechende dinge einer lebendige
sele vnd gefügel auff der erde· vnder der vestenkeit
des himels· Vnd got geschüff groß walvisch· vnd
vnd ein geleiche lebendige sele· vnd sein beweglich
die die wasser für fürē in iren bilden· vnd ein ieg
lichs gefügel nach seinem geschlechte· Vnd gotte ō
sach dz es was güt· vñ gesegent in sagent· Wachse
vnd werd gemanigueltigt· vnd erfüllet die wasser
des meres· vnd die vogel werdent gemanigueltigt
auff der erde. Vnd es ward gemacht abent vnd der
morgen der fünfte· Vnd gotte der sprach· Die erde
für füre ein lebendige sele in irem geschlechte· die
viche vnd die kriechenden ding· vnd die tier der er=
dē nach iren bilden· Vnd es ward getan also· Vñ
got der macht die tier der erde nach iren bilden· vñ
die viche vnd ein iglichs kriechendes ding der erden
in seinem geschlecht· Vnd got der sach das es was
Vñ sprach· Wir machen einen menschen zü vn
serm bild vnd zü vnser gleichsam· vnd er wirt vō
sein den vischen des meres· vnd den vogeln des hi=
mels· vnd den tieren der erden· vnd einer igklichen
geschöpfft vnd allen kriechendē dingen das do wirt
bewegt auff ō erde. Vnd got der beschüff dē mensch
en zü seinem bilde vnd zü seiner gleichsam· zü dem
bilde gottes beschüff er in· vnd er beschüff sy menn:
lichs vnd weiplichs· Vnd got der gesegent sp· vñ:
sprach· Wachse vnd werd gemaniguelagkt vnd er
füllent die erde· vnd vnderlegt sy· vnd ir werd her:
schen den visch des meres· vnd den vogel des himels
vnd alle selige ding die do werdent bewegt auff der
erden· vnd got der sprach· Sehe ich hab euch gegebē
alles kraut bringet den samen auf der erde· vnd alle
die holzer die do habent den samen ires geschlechtes
in jn selber· das sp euch sind zü einem essen vnd allē
seligen der erde vnd eim pglichen vogel des himels
vnd allen den dingen die do werdent bewegt auff ō
erde· vnd in den do ist die lebendig sele· das sie sp ha
ben zeessen. Vnd es ward getan also· Vnd got der
sach alle ding die er het gemacht· das sp waren gar

3. BIBLES FOR THE PEOPLE

3.1

Biblia Germanica.

[Strasbourg: Johann Mentelin, before
27 June 1466].
D&M 4176; Goff B-624; *GW* 4295.

Johann Mentelin printed the editio princeps of the
Bible in German, which is also the first Bible printed
in any vernacular language.

The translation is based on what is known as the
Spanish recension of the Vulgate, and it is generally
accepted that Mentelin's source was a fourteenth-
century translation from the Nuremberg vicinity.
Despite the archaic language and the frequent awk-
wardness, the text was highly successful, influenc-
ing, either directly or indirectly, the thirteen subsequent High German translations before Luther's
Septembertestament (see Reinitzer 1987, 6:1276–80).

Mentelin used a small, rounded gothic typeface,
which enabled him to print the entire German Bible
in one volume. In addition to important Bibles
(both the Latin Vulgate and this German translation), Mentelin printed the editio princeps of Wolfram von Eschenbach's *Parzival* (1477), the masterpiece of the German Middle Ages.

References: Kurrelmeyer 1904–15; Reinitzer 1983, 65–66;
Reinitzer 1987; Schorbach 1932.
Exhibition: Bridwell, 06164; Harvard, Bridwell copy; Union/
Columbia, on loan from the Grolier Club; Yale, YCBA/Leaf
Coll. 8 (fragment).

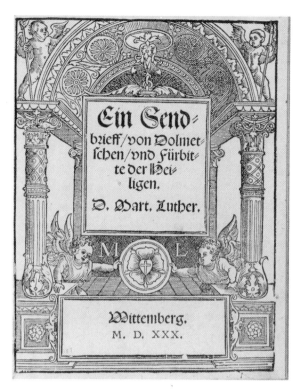

3.2, title page (second printing, 1530)

3.2

Luther, Martin.

Ein sendbrieff von Dolmetzschen vnd Fürbit der heiligenn.

[Nuremberg: Johann Petreius for Georg Rottmaier], 1530.
B 2840; *VD16* L5949.

In 1530, Luther wrote *Ein Sendbrief von Dolmetschen,* a treatise explaining his theory and methods of translation. One should not approach the text rigidly, he says, but rather translate word-for-word in some cases and sense-for-sense in others. He also defends his German Bible, in particular, his rendering of Rm 3:28 — "allein durch den Glauben [through faith alone]" — against the Catholics, who objected to the insertion of "allein" (see pp. 43–44).

Luther describes the foundation of his German style in a memorable formulation. To translate into clear and understandable German, "man mus die mutter ihm hause/ die kinder auff der gassen/ den gemeinen man auff dem marckt drumb fragen/ . . . vnd darnach dolmetschen [one must ask the mother at home, the children in the alley, and the common man in the market place about it, and translate accordingly]" (fol. B3ʳ).

The title-page border of the second edition of 1530, shown here, is attributed to the workshop of Lucas Cranach (1472–1553). It had appeared in the first edition of Luther's work on Christian education (*An die Ratsherren aller Städte deutschen Lands, daß sie christliche Schulen aufrichten und halten sollen* [1524]; B 1875). Its distinctive motifs are Luther's initials and his sigil, a heart and cross in the center of a white rose. In a letter to Lazarus Spengler (1479–1534), he described the symbol as "an emblem of my theology" (*WA Br* 5:1628), explaining that the rose represents the peace and joy that heartfelt belief and contemplation of Christ's sacrifice bring to the faithful. The border was often used for works by

Luther as a sign that he had authorized the publication.

References: Stolt 1983, 242–48; *WA* 30/2:627–46.
Exhibition: Bridwell showing Wittenberg: Georg Rhau, 1530 (second printing, 1530; B2841) (AER9417); Harvard *GC5/ L9774/530S3; Union/Columbia, Bridwell copy; Yale, Beinecke/Me45/L977/Se29/530.

3.3

Luther, Martin.

Euangelium Von den tzehen auszsetzigen.

Wittenberg: [Melchior Lotter the Younger, 1521]. B 985; *VD16* L4714.

Luther had been translating the Bible in his exegetical and homiletical works for several years before his New Testament was published. This translation of Luke 17:11–19 (the parable of the ten lepers) from 1521 appears in the context of a discussion of the sacrament of penance. In the preface, he acknowledges his contentious relations with the church, particularly over the matter of indulgences: "Ich armer bruder hab aber einn new fewr antzundt/ und ein groß loch in der Papisten taschen gebissen/ das ich die beicht hab angriffen [I, poor monk, have sparked a new fire and bitten a big hole in the pocket of the papists because I have attacked confession]" (fol. A2ʳ). He goes on to claim that the cardinals would like to see him dead ("tod/ tod/ tod") and that he expects to be burned as a heretic. The story of the ten lepers, according to Luther's interpretation, illustrates that forgiveness and purification come from belief in God's mercy, without the church's mediation.

References: Reinitzer 1983, 108; *WA* 8:336–97.
Exhibition: Bridwell, AER9177; Harvard, Bridwell copy; Union/Columbia, Bridwell copy; Yale, Beinecke/Me45/ L973/A3/v.3 and YCBA/Leaf Coll. 2268 (title page).

3.3, title page

3.4, fol. dd4ʳ, Lucas Cranach, *Harlot of Babylon*. By permission of Johns Hopkins University.

3.4

Das Newe Testament Deûtzsch.

Translated by Martin Luther. 3 pts. Wittenberg: [Melchior Lotter the Younger for Lucas Cranach and Christian Döring, September 1522]. D&M 4188; *VD16* B4318.

Luther's translation of the Bible, though by no means the first one in German, played a major role in the success of the Reformation. During his protective custody at the Wartburg (May 1521 to March 1522) — a moment of mythic proportions in German history — he decided to translate the Bible.

When he returned to Wittenberg in the spring of 1522, he brought a completed draft and entrusted it to Melanchthon for correction. The New Testament was then printed by Melchior Lotter the Younger in September 1522 and ever since has been called the *Septembertestament*. Although it was printed in a large run of about three thousand copies, the demand for it was so great that another, revised translation appeared in December 1522 (known as the *Dezembertestament*). The twenty-one woodcuts by Lucas Cranach, Luther's friend and follower, illustrate only Revelation and are clearly influenced by Dürer's *Apocalypse* series.

Martin Luther's German Bible stands as a philological monument and a literary masterpiece. The shoemaker-poet Hans Sachs gave Luther the sobriquet "die Wittenbergische Nachtigal" (the Wittenberg nightingale), not only as a description of his role as a harbinger of new ideas but also in recognition of his eloquence.

References: Reinitzer 1983, 130–34; Schmidt 1962, 93–112. Exhibition: Bridwell, on loan from the John Work Garrett Library, The Johns Hopkins University; *Union*/Columbia showing Wittenberg: Melchior Lotter, 1524 (CB77/1524); Yale, YCBA/Leaf Coll. 2303 (six leaves).

3.5, inserted after fol. XIII, Lucas Cranach, *Sacrifice of Isaac*

3.5

Das Allte Testament deutsch.

Translated by Martin Luther. 3 vols. Wittenberg: [Melchior Lotter the Younger for Lucas Cranach and Christian Döring], 1523–24.
D&M 4189; *VD16* B2894.

In 1523, only a year after the New Testament appeared, Luther's translation of the Pentateuch was published as the first volume of *Das Allte Testament*. Luther consulted several Hebrew scholars, both Christian and Jewish, in the course of preparing the text, most important of whom were Melanchthon and Matthias Aurogallus (ca. 1490–1543). There were several editions of the Old Testament available in print by this time, and Luther also consulted the commentaries of Nicholas of Lyra and the *De rudimentis hebraicis* of Johannes Reuchlin. Nonetheless, in his preface he criticizes the state of Hebrew studies ("denn die Ebreische sprache ligt leyder zu gar darnidder;" fol. A6ʳ) and admits that he found the task daunting. His confidence, however, far outweighs his modesty:

> Ich aber/ wie wol ich mich nicht rhumen kan/ das ich alles erlanget habe/ thar ich doch das sagen/ das disse deutsche Bibel/ liechter und gewisser ist an vielen ortten denn die latinische/ das es war ist/ wo die drucker sie mit yhrem vnvleys (wie sie pflegen) nicht verderben/ hat gewisslich hie die deutsche sprach eyn bessere Bibel denn die latinische sprache/ des beruff ich mich auff die leser. (fol. A6ʳ)

[While I cannot boast that I have gotten everything right, nevertheless I dare to say that this German Bible is clearer and more correct in many places than is the Latin. I call on the reader to give witness that this is true; provided that the printers do not (as is their custom) spoil it with their carelessness, the German language has here a better Bible than the Latin.]

References: Reinitzer 1983, 109–29, 142–44; Schmidt 1962, 137–43; *WA DB* 2:272–75.

Exhibition: Bridwell, Prothro B21; Harvard, Typ/520.23/211F; *Union*/Columbia, CB74/1523; Yale, Beinecke/1977/+168 and YCBA/Leaf Col. 2710 (title page).

3.6

Biblia/ das ist/ die gantze Heilige Schrifft Deudsch.

Translated by Martin Luther. 6 pts. Wittenberg: Hans Lufft, 1534.
D&M 4199; *VD16* B2694.

The first complete edition of Luther's Bible in High German appeared in 1534 and was quickly reissued in 1535, 1536, and 1541. Luther had revised the text, in particular the Pentateuch, and Justus Jonas (1493–1555) and Melanchthon completed the translations of the apocryphal Books of Judith, Tobit, Baruch, 2 Maccabees, and parts of the Book of Esther, all of which appear here for the first time. It should be noted, however, that an edition of Luther's Bible in Low German, complete with translations of the Apocrypha, had appeared the year before at the press of Ludwig Dietz (†1559) in Lübeck. The origins of this version are not known, though Luther's follower Johannes Bugenhagen, who was active in Northern Germany and Denmark, has been suspected as the conduit (if not the adapter) of the text.

Throughout his life, during which 430 complete or partial editions of his translation appeared in print (Reinitzer 1983, 111), Luther continued to revise and refine his work. The last edition of 1545 was authorized by the Elector of Saxony in 1581 and remained unaltered and largely unquestioned until the late nineteenth century.

The 1534 Bible appeared at the press of Hans Lufft of Wittenberg (fl. 1523–59), a prolific printer of Reformation works. It contains 117 woodcuts, some of which are signed by the MS master, who was probably active in the workshop of Lucas Cranach. The image of the Harlot of Babylon is again depicted, as in the *Septembertestament,* with the papal tiara.

References: Reinitzer 1983, 170–74; *WA DB* 2:545–53.

Exhibition: Harvard, *fGC5/L9774B/1534; showing Wittenberg: Hans Lufft, 1535 at Bridwell (Prothro B234) and *Union*/Columbia (CB72/1535); Yale, YCBA/Leaf Coll. 3211 (six leaves).

Gottes wort
bleibt ewig.

Biblia/das ist/ die
gantze Heilige Sch-
rifft Deudsch.

Mart.   Luth.

Wittemberg.

Begnadet mit Kür-
fürstlicher zu Sachsen
freiheit.
Gedruckt durch Hans Lufft.

M. D. XXXIIII.

3.6, title page. By permission of the Houghton Library, Harvard University.

3.7

Das naw testament.

Translated by Hieronymus Emser. Dresden: Wolfgang Stöckel, [1527].
D&M 4191; *VD16* B4374.

The phenomenal success of Luther's German Bible prompted a Catholic response in 1527, when Hieronymus Emser (1478–1527) published a German translation of the New Testament that mimicked the style and format of the *Septembertestament.* At the urging of Duke George of Saxony (1471–1539), who had forbidden the use of Luther's Bible in his realm, Emser translated the Vulgate (consulting the Greek in places) into German. Naturally, his version reflected Catholic interpretation of Scripture. He also included polemical annotations directly attacking Luther's views.

It is clear from the afterword, however, that Emser was not entirely comfortable with the project. He has translated the holy text, he says, "Wiewol ich der sach bey mir selber noch nicht eyns byn/ ob es gut odder bös sey das man die Bibel verdewtschet/ vnd dem gemeynen vngelarten man fürlegt [although I am not really sure myself if it is good or bad to translate the Bible into German and put it before the common and uneducated]" (fol. 195ᵛ).

Emser's Bible is illustrated, surprisingly enough, with Cranach's woodcuts from the *Dezembertestament.* In the effort to undermine Luther's version, perhaps, the Dresden printer Wolfgang Stöckel (†1541) acquired all but two of the Cranach woodcuts of the Apocalypse. Additional woodcuts of the evangelists and other scenes by Georg Lemberger (ca. 1495–ca. 1540) were, apparently as the Cranach illustrations had been, also obtained from Luther's printer, Melchior Lotter.

References: Reinitzer 1983, 196–98; Smolinsky 1984; Strand 1982, 5–8.
Exhibition: Bridwell, 31461; Harvard, Bridwell copy; *Union/ Columbia,* CB77/1527; Yale showing Freiburg: Johann Faber, 1529 (Beinecke/Mln44/y529e).

3.7, fol. CLXXXIXʳ, Lucas Cranach, *Harlot of Babylon* (original block modified)

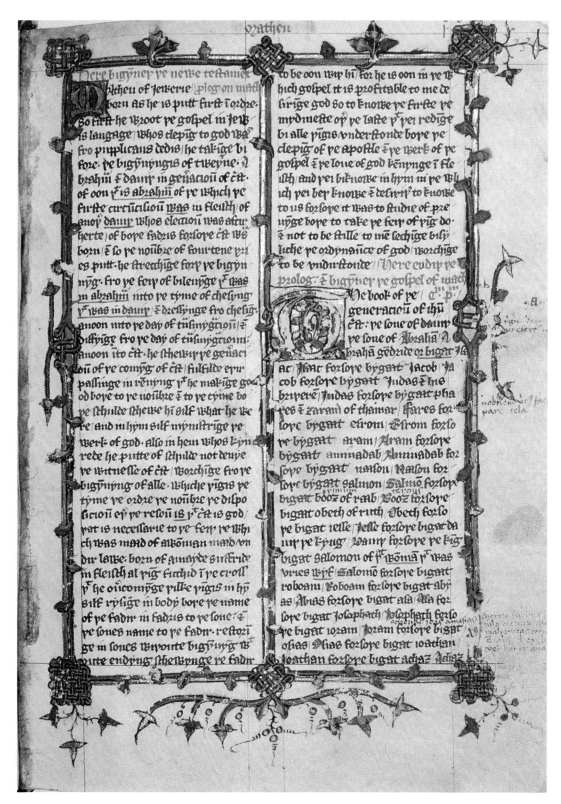

3.8, Prothro B281, fol. 1ʳ, prologue and beginning of Matthew

3.8

New Testament in English.

Translated by John Wycliffe et al. England: fifteenth-century manuscript.

John Wycliffe (†1384), often heralded as a proto-Reformer, represents the widespread anticlerical movement of the fourteenth century. A critic of ecclesiastical corruption, he wrote extensively on the need to reform the church by returning to the authority of Scripture. To combat what he viewed as superstitious practices of the clergy, he translated the Vulgate into English. Partial translations of the Bible into English had existed since the Anglo-Saxon period, of course. With the assistance of Nicholas of Hereford (fl. 1390), however, Wycliffe produced the first complete Bible in English. Because their chief concern was the authority of the text, Wycliffe and Hereford were careful to use a literal, word-for-word approach. Around 1395, John Purvey (1353?–1428?) revised the Wycliffite version into a more felicitous English.

The "Constitutions of Oxford," promulgated by English church authorities in 1408, outlawed the translation and reading of Scripture in the vernacular. Nonetheless, the Lollards, who were inspired by Wycliffe, produced hundreds of copies of the Wycliffite Bible in manuscript. Almost two hundred manuscript copies of the Wycliffe Bible (some of which are handsomely decorated) still survive, attesting to its popularity, despite the danger of owning it.

References: Fristedt 1953–73; Hargreaves 1979, 171–74.
Exhibition: Bridwell, Prothro B281; Harvard, MS Richardson 3; Union/*Columbia,* Plimpton MS Add.3; Yale, Beinecke/ MS 125.

foz the Philistines saying / come bp yet thys once / foz he hath shewed me all his herte.

Then the Lozdes of the Philistines came and bzought the money in their handes . And she made him slepe bpon her lappe / and sent foz a man / and cut of the seuē lockes of hys heed & begāne to vere him. But his strenght was gone from him . And she sayde the Philistines be bpō the Samson. And he awooke out of hys slepe and thought to go out as at other tymes before & shake him selfe / & wist not that the Lozde was departed from hym. But ý Philistines toke him and put out hys eyes / and bzought hym doune to Gaza / and bounde him with fetters . And he was made to grinde in the pzeson house / how be it the hearre of his heed beganne to growe agayne after that he was shozne.

Then ý Lozd of ý Philistines geathered thē to geather foz to offer a solempne offring bnto Dagon their God / & to reioyse: foz they sayde / oure God hathe delyuered Samson oure enemye into oure handes. And whē the people sawe him / they pzaysed their God: foz they sayd oure God hath delyuered into oure handes oure enemye / ý destroyed oure contreye and slue manye of bs. And when their hertz were merye they sayd: sende foz Samson & lett him playe before bs. And they fette Samson out of ý pzesonhouse / & he played before thē / & they set him betwene ý pillers.

And Samson sayde bnto the ladd that leed him by the hāde: sett me that J maye touche the pyllers that the house stande bpō / & that J maye leane to thē . And the house was full of men & wemen. And there was all ý lozd of the Philistines. And there were bpon the roufe a thze thousand men & wemen / that beholde how Samson played.

And Samson called bnto the Lozde / and sayde: my Lozde Jehouah thynke bpon me / & strengthen me / at this tyme onlye O God / that J maye be auenged of the Philistines foz my two eyes . And Samson caught the two myddell pyllers on which ý house stode and on which it was bozne bp / the one in his ryght hande / & the other in his lefte / & sayde: my soule dye with the Philistines / & bowed them with might. And the house fell bpon ý

lozdes and bpō All the people ý were therin. And so the deed which he slewe at hys deeth / were moo then they which he slewe in hys lyfe. And then his bzethzen and all the house of his father came downe and toke hym bp / and bzought hym and buryed hym betwene Zarah and Esthaol / in the burying place of Manoah hys father . And he iudged Israell twentye yere.

¶ Of Micah whose mother made him an Jdoll of syluer. Of the young pzeast of the lynage of Leui of Bethlehem.

¶ The .rbii. Chapter.

Here was a mā in moūt Ephzaim / named Micah whych sayde bnto his mother: the leuē hūdzed syluer- lynges ý were takē frō the / aboute which thou cursedst & saydest in myne eares: Beholde the syluer is wyth me foz I toke it awaye. Then sayd his mother / blessed be thou my sonne / in the Lozd. And so he restozed the leuen hundzed syluerlynges to hys mother agayne. And his mother sayde: J vowed the syluer bnto the Lozde of myne hande foz my sonne : to make a grauē ymage & an ymage of metall. Now therfoze I geue it ý agayne. And he restozed the moneye agayne bnto his mother. Then his mother toke two hundzed syluerlynges & put them to a goldsmyth / to make therof a grauē ymage and a ymage of metall / which remayned in the house of Mi- cah. And ý mā Micah had a chapell of Gods / and made an Ephod and ymages / & fylled the hand of one of his sonnes which became hys pzeast. Foz in those dayes there was no kyng in Israel / but euery man dyd what thought hym best.

And there was a younge mā out of Beth- lehem Juda / & out of the kynredes of Juda: which young man was a Leuite and soiour- ned there. And the mā departed out of ý citie of Bethlehem Juda / to go dwell where he coulde fynde a* place. And he came to mount Ephzaim / & to ý house of Micah as he iour- neyed. And Micah sayde bnto hym / whence comest thou: and the Leuite answered him: J am of Bethlehem Juda / & go to dwell where J maye fynde a place. And Micah sayde bn- to him: dwell with me / and be bnto me a fa- ther and a pzeast. And I wyll geue ý ten syl- uerlynges by yere and raymēt of all sortes / and thy meate and dzynke.

And the Leuite went & beganne to dwell with the man / and was bnto hym as dere as one of his awne sonnes. And Micah fylled ý hande of the Leuite / and the young man be- came his pzeaste / and cōtynued in the house of Micah . Then sayde Micah / now J am sure ý the Lozde wsllbe good bnto me seing I haue a Leuite to my pzeast.

* bnderstande / where he myght get moare pzofett oz auauntage.

n. iiij. ¶ The

3.9

The Bybble, which is all the holy Scripture:
In whych are contayned the Olde and Newe
Testament truly and purely translated into
Englysh.

Translated by William Tyndale. 4 pts. [Antwerp?:
Matthew Crom for Richard Grafton and Edward
Whitchurch of London], 1537.
D&M 17.

William Tyndale (ca. 1494–1536) translated the first
printed edition of the New Testament in English.
Prohibited in England, it had to be printed on the
Continent, although even there a first attempt to
publish the work at Cologne in 1525 was thwarted by
the authorities. The first complete printed edition appeared at Worms in 1526. Two copies of the Worms
edition survive, and only a single exemplar of the
interrupted Cologne printing (through Matthew 22).

Tyndale also translated the Pentateuch and, most
likely, the historical books from Joshua to 2 Chronicles. He had not completed the project, however,
before he was burned at the stake as a heretic in
October 1536. The following year, under the name
Thomas Matthew, Tyndale's friend John Rogers
(1500–1555) published a complete Bible, compiling
lightly edited versions of Tyndale's translations and
filling in with Coverdale's renditions of the books of
the Hebrew Bible not done by Tyndale. The so-
called Matthew's Bible appeared in 1537, the second
complete edition of the English Bible and the version most influential for subsequent English translations.

Although he claims Erasmus's Greek New Testament as the basis for his English version, Tyndale
clearly used Luther's work as well, even rendering
some of Luther's German prefaces into English.
Defending his English translations against critics,
chief among whom was Thomas More, Tyndale ar-
gued that "Saint Jerome . . . translated the Bible
into his mother tongue. Why may not we also?"

3.9, fol. Hh5r, beginning of Song of Songs

(from *The Obedience of a Christian Man,* quoted from
Daniell 1994, 229).

The impact of Tyndale's Bible on the English
language should not be underestimated. His words
and cadences echo not only in the Geneva and King
James versions but also in modern English expressions that derive from the Bible, such as "fruit of the
vine," "give up the ghost," and "filthy lucre."

References: Bruce 1978, 24–53, 64–66; Daniell 1994, 333–57.
Exhibition: Bridwell, Prothro B169; Harvard showing
London: J. Daye and W. Seres, 1549 (*50R–574);
Union/*Columbia* showing London: Thomas Raynalde
and William Hyll, 1549 (Plimpton/220.52/1549F);
Yale, DIV/939080.

3.10

Biblia. The Bible/ that is, the holy Scripture of the Olde and New Testament, faithfully and truly translated out of Douche and Latyn in to Englyshe.

Translated by Miles Coverdale. 6 pts. [Marburg: Eucharius Cervicornus and Johannes Soter?], 1535. D&M 7.

In 1535, Miles Coverdale (1488–1568) saw to press the editio princeps of the complete English Bible. He does not claim to translate from the original languages. Instead, he used Luther's German Bible, Pagnini's Latin translation, the Zurich Bible, and the Vulgate as his source texts; he probably also relied on Tyndale's New Testament. Coverdale's Bible is the first English Bible to appear with royal approval.

Like Luther, Coverdale had been an Augustinian monk. He criticized ecclesiastical corruption from the pulpit and finally left the order in 1528. According to John Foxe's account, he went to the Continent, where he assisted Tyndale in the translation of the Pentateuch. It seems that Coverdale survived the shifting fortunes of the Reformation in England through frequent stays abroad. He returned to his country when Thomas Cromwell was in power, and with his support Coverdale produced the Great Bible (1539) and its 1540 revision, known as Cranmer's Bible. He left once again for the Continent when Cromwell fell in 1540, returned under Edward VI, left when Mary came to power, and returned again to live out his days under Elizabeth I. One of the few political misjudgments he made is in the 1535 Bible, which he dedicates to Henry VIII, commending himself to Henry's "dearest iust wyfe, and most vertuous Prynces, Quene Anne" (fol. ✠2ʳ) only months before Anne Boleyn's execution. The Bible was printed on the Continent, perhaps in Marburg, with a title page border attributed to Hans Holbein. All copies with title pages save one (British Library), however, contain a slightly altered version printed by James Nicholson of Southwark in London (also in 1535; see page 40). For the 1538 edition of the New Testament (on exhibition at Harvard), Coverdale had his English version printed next to the Vulgate text to demonstrate their general agreement.

References: Mozley 1953, 65–124; Sheppard 1935. Exhibition: Bridwell, Prothro B92; Harvard showing Southwark: James Nicholson, 1538 (*Bi56.538); Union/ Columbia, on loan from General Theological Seminary; Yale, Beinecke/1971/+159.

3.11

a. *The Byble in Englyshe.*

5 pts. [London]: Edward Whytchurche, 1540. D&M 30.

b. *The. holie. Bible.*

5 pts. London: Richard Jugge, [1568]. D&M 89.

The so-called Great Bible (1539) was a revision of Matthew's Bible by Miles Coverdale and others. For the second edition of 1540, Archbishop Thomas Cranmer (1489–1556) wrote a preface on the importance of English Bible translation. His introduction was reprinted later in the first edition of the so-called Bishops' Bible (1568), a revised version of the Great Bible by another Archbishop of Canterbury, Matthew Parker.

Cranmer cited John Chrysostom, who, he says, exhorts "that every man shoulde reade by him selfe at home in the meane dayes and time, betweene sermon and sermon" (fol. ★4ʳ). Expanding on Tyndale's desire to "bring the ploughboy to the New Testament," Cranmer says that the Bible is for the

3.11a, fol. IVʳ, beginning of Cranmer's prologue

people: "Here may all maner of persons, men, women, young, olde, learned, vnlearned, riche, poore, priestes, lay men, lordes, ladyes, officers, tenauntes, and meane men, virgins, wiues, widdowes, lawyars, marchauntes, artifiers, husbandmen and all maner of persons . . . learne all things what they ought to beleve" (fol. ★5ʳ).

References: Berkowitz 1968, 121–22; Mozley 1953, 201–305. Exhibition: (a) Bridwell, Prothro B61; Harvard showing London: Richard Grafton, 1540 (*71–483F); Yale, DIV/939085; (b) Bridwell, Prothro B38; Union/Columbia, Bridwell 00017 (Harrison Collection); Yale, Beinecke/1977/Folio/118.

3.11b, fol. A2ʳ,
illustration to Genesis 2:22

The defcription of the holie land and of the places mencioned in the foure Euangeliftes.

3.12, inserted after p. 1

3.12

Bible.

2 pts. Geneva: Rouland Hall, 1560.
D&M 77.

During the reign of Queen Mary (July 1553–November 1558) works by Tyndale and Coverdale, including the Bible translations, were burned throughout England. The restrictions on Bible study and translation as well as other, more life-threatening, consequences of counter-Reformation efforts under Mary's rule caused many Protestants to flee to Geneva. John Knox (1505–72) served as their pastor until 1557, succeeded in this task by William Whittingham (1524?–1579). It was Whittingham, along with at least one other Marian exile, Anthony Gilby (†1585) — and perhaps assisted by Knox and Coverdale — who produced the Geneva edition. It was first published in Geneva in 1560. The translators based their text on Tyndale's New Testament and Coverdale's Great Bible, which they compared with the translations of Luther, Pagnini, Leo Juda (1482–1542), Münster, and the 1555 revision of Olivétan. They also consulted the Complutensian, Estienne's Greek New Testament, and Estienne's Latin translation of 1556, with annotations by Bèze.

Apparently hindered by the unwillingness of Archbishop Matthew Parker to authorize it, the Geneva Bible was not printed in England until 1575, even though Elizabeth I supported the use of English Bibles as early as 1559. After 1575, however, it became the most popular English version, printed twenty times over the next decade. Most of Shakespeare's biblical quotations come from the Geneva version. It is also sometimes called the Pilgrims' Bible because the early Puritan settlers of America preferred it to the King James Version.

References: Hall 1995; Stout 1982, 19–29; Shaheen 1984, 156–58.

3.13

The Nevv Testament.

Translated by Gregory Martin. Reims:
John Fogny, 1582.
D&M 134.

Gregory Martin (†1582) is generally credited as the translator of the first Catholic Bible in English, often designated as the Reims-Douai, or the Douai, version. He taught Hebrew and Bible at the English College in Douai, a center for disaffected Catholics during Elizabeth's reign. With the assistance of William Allen (founder of the college), Richard Bristow, and others, he began work on the translation around 1578. As of 1578, the college was relocated temporarily to Reims, where the New Testament was printed in the year of Martin's death. As indicated on the title page, the translation is based on the Vulgate, although Martin also used the Greek New Testament: "translated faithfvlly into English, out of the authentical Latin . . . diligently conferred vvith the Greeke and other editions in diuers languages." Martin's translation of the Old Testament was probably edited by scholars at the Douai College; it was finally published, with the New Testament, at Douai in 1609/10.

Although Martin agreed to translate the New Testament into English, he cautions against widespread access to the text. Using language that echoes yet contradicts that of Cranmer in the preface to the Great Bible, he says: "We must not imagin that in the primitiue Church . . . translated Bibles into the vulgar tonges were in the handes of euery husbandman, artificer, prentice, boies, girles, mistresse, maide, man . . . tinker, tauerner, rimer, minstrel . . . and for euery prophane person and companie. No,

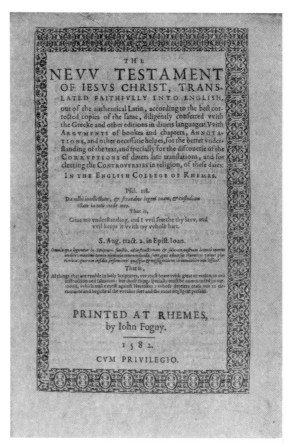

3.13, title page

in those better times men were neither so ill, nor so curious of them selves, so to abuse the blessed booke of Christ; neither was there any such easy meanes before printing was inuented, to disperse the copies into the handes of euery man, as there now is" (fol. a3ʳ).

References: Bruce 1978, 113–26; Carleton 1902.

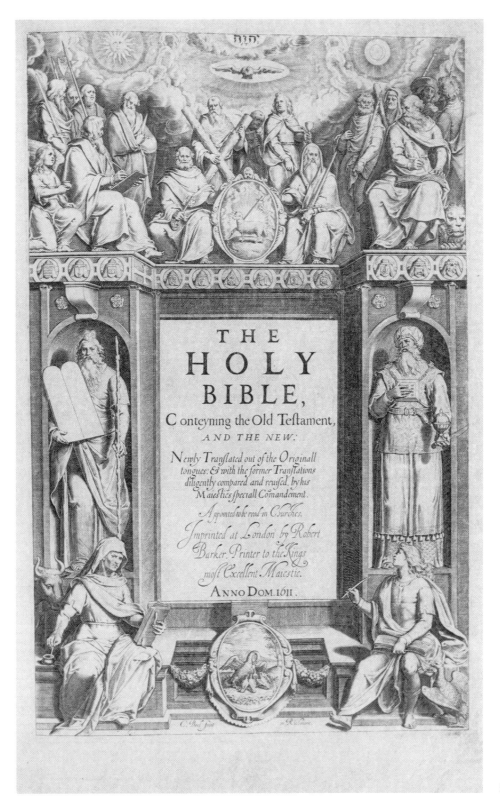

3.14

*The Holy Bible, Conteyning the Old Testament,
and the New: Newly Translated out of the
Originall tongues: & with the former
Translations diligently compared and reuised,
by his Maiesties speciall Commandement.*

2 pts. London: Robert Barker, 1611.
D&M 240.

References: Hind 1955, 2:315 (on the title-page engraving);
Morgan 1990; Newman 1981.
Exhibitions: Bridwell, 10601/A; Harvard, Bi65.611; *Union/
Columbia*, CB92/1611; Yale, Beinecke/MMlm143/611.

The King James Version or the Authorized Version of the English Bible was made by a team of translators appointed by James I. The desire for a uniform translation was expressed by James as early as 1604, but work seems to have begun in earnest around 1609. It was first published in this edition of 1611 and remained the standard English Bible until the nineteenth century, when the Revised Version was published (although many idiomatic biblical phrases in English are still quoted in the language of the King James Version). Using the Bishops' Bible as a basis, about forty-seven translators worked in six groups: two at Westminster under the direction of Lancelot Andrews (1555–1626); two at Cambridge under Edward Lively (1545?–1605); and two at Oxford under John Harding (fl. 1620). The translators also consulted Tyndale, Coverdale, and the Geneva version, as well as the Greek and Latin texts.

Two impressions of this first edition appeared in 1611: one renders Ruth 3:15 as "*She* went into the citie" (emphasis added), whereas the other, and probably earlier, impression reads "*He*." Each spawned a separate series of editions between 1611 and 1614, which are commonly referred to as She and He Bibles.

The title-page engraving is signed by Cornelius Boel (†after 1616). A close copy was made of the title page, which is often erroneously called a second state. The Bridwell copy on exhibition has both the original engraving and the copy (which is tipped in). The illustration shown here is of the original.

يسوع لاتلمسيني لاني لم اصعد بعد الى ابي امضي الى اخوتي

Iesus, Ne tangas me, quia non ascendi adhuc ad patrem meum : uade ad fratres meos,

وقولي لهم اني صاعد الى ابي وابيكم والهي والهكم جآآت

& dic eis, qa ascēdēs sū ad patrē meū & patrē uestrū, & Deū meū & Deū uestrū. Venit

مريم المجدلية فبشرت التلاميذ انها رآت الرب وانه قال

Maria Magdalene, & nuntiauit discipulis, Quia uidit dominum, & quia dixit

لها هـــــــذا ۰

ei hoc.

الفصل الرابع والاربعون

Sectio quadragesima quarta.

فلما كان عشية ذلك اليوم الذي هو احد السبوت

Cùm ergo esset sero illius diei, qui erat una sabbathorum,

والابواب مغلقة في الموضع الذي كان التلاميذ

& fores erant clausę in loco, in quo erant discipuli

مجتمعين فيه من اجل خوف اليهود جآء يسوع ووقف

congregati propter metum Iudęorum : uenit Iesus & stetit

(Arabic and Latin edition),
"Noli me tangere"

3.15

Evangelium sanctvm domini nostri Iesu Christi

[Gospels in Arabic].

Rome: Typographia Medicea, 1591.

D&M 1636 and 1637.

The editio princeps of the Gospels in Arabic was edited by Giovanni Battista Raimondi (1540–1630), a scholar of Oriental languages and the first director of the Typographia Medicea. It is the first book from this press, which was established by Cardinal Ferdinando de' Medici (1549–1609) for printing works in non-Western languages with the goal of spreading Christianity to the East. The text was issued simultaneously in Arabic solely and in Arabic with interlinear Latin translation. The title page of the Arabic-only edition is dated 1590, although the colophons of both editions have 1591.

The Gospels are illustrated with 149 woodcuts (from 67 blocks), some signed with the initials A. T. (Antonio Tempesta, 1555–1630), others with L. P. (the cutter Leonardo Parasole, according to Mortimer), and a few are signed T. E.

References: Aspland 1873, 1–13; Mortimer 1974, 1: no. 64. Exhibitions: Bridwell, Prothro B12; Harvard, Typ/ 525.91.210F; Union/*Columbia*, B893/1BM/B90; Yale, YCBA/Leaf Coll. 3822 (two leaves).

3.16

a. *Biblii Cžeská.*

Venice: Petrus Liechtenstein, 5 December 1506. D&M 2180.

b. *Bibli Cžeské.*

6 vols. [Kralice: Zacharias Solín], 1579–93/94. D&M 2186.

A Czech (or "Bohemian") Bible translation existed long before the printing press or the Reformation. Ascribed most often to Cyril and Methodius (fl. 860) but also attributed to St. Jerome (a countryman, according to some Slavonic accounts), it was revised by Jan Hus (1372–1415), who promoted the vernacular version among his followers. In his version (first printed in 1475), Hus also established the orthographic and syntactic rules of modern Czech, including the system of diacritics. A 1506 revised edition reflected "Utraquist" or Calixtine beliefs that were popular in Prague. The Bible is lavishly illustrated with original woodcuts, including a xylographic title by an unidentified artist and many designs by Lucantonio degli Uberti (fl. 1495–1520). Uberti's elaborately framed preface of Jerome (see illustration) depicts Ambrose and Paulinus.

The most important Czech Reformation Bible is the so-called Kralice Bible, which informed the literary language in much the same way that Luther's translation had influenced German. Its beginnings go back to the translation of the New Testament into Czech by the humanist Jan Blahoslav (1523–71), which appeared in 1564. Members of the Unitas Fratrum continued Blahoslav's work on the estate of Jan ze Žerotína in the village of Kralice (near Brno), where the movement had a secret press.

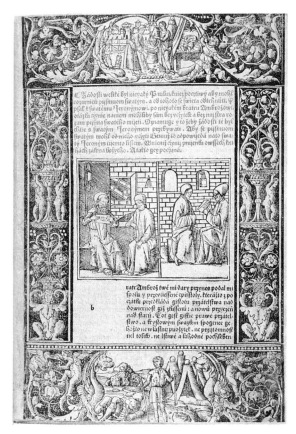

3.16a, [prefatory fol. 2r], beginning of Jerome's preface

3.16b, vol. 2, title page.

By permission of Union Theological Seminary.

Over the course of fifteen years, they produced a six-volume commentated Czech Bible. Although they claim to have returned *ad fontes* to the original languages, it is clear that earlier Czech versions were also consulted.

References: Bohatcová 1992; Malin 1881; Pelikan 1946; Strachen 1957, 38–41.

Exhibition: (a) Bridwell, 31462; Yale, Beinecke/Mln13/+506; (b) Harvard, *Bible/G.579; *Union*/Columbia, CB56/B6/1579.

3.17

Biblia / Det er den gantske Hellige Scrifft.

5 pts. Copenhagen: Ludwig Dietz, 1550.
D&M 3155.

Known as the Bible of Christian III, this is the first
printed translation of the whole Bible in Danish.
When Christian became king in 1536 (crowned by
the German Reformer Johann Bugenhagen), he declared that all his subjects were to become Lutherans. Soon afterward, he ordered the theological
faculty of the University of Copenhagen to produce
a Danish Bible based on Luther's German version.
The result, however, is by no means a slavish translation. It probably relies on a 1543 translation by
Christiern Pedersen (before 1480–1554). Pedersen,
best known as the editor of Saxo Grammaticus's
Gesta Danorum (now preserved only through his edition of 1515), was an important Danish humanist
and printer. He had translated parts of the Bible into
Danish as early as 1514 and the complete New Testament in 1529.

Christian III invited the printer Ludwig Dietz
from Lübeck to Copenhagen to produce the work.
To cover the costs of printing, the king required
every church in Denmark to purchase a copy of the
Bible.

Reference: Skarsten 1985, 43–44.
Exhibition: Bridwell, Prothro B192; Harvard,
Typ/540.50.210F; Union/Columbia, Prothro copy.

3.17, verso of title page, Christian III

3.18, title page

3.18

Dat niewe Testament.

Delft: Cornelis Heynrick z. Lettersnyder,
November 1524
D&M 3278.

The earliest printed Dutch Bible — a translation of
the Old Testament without the Psalms — appeared
in 1477 at Delft. The first edition of the New Testament, however, was not published until the second
decade of the sixteenth century. Three Dutch New
Testaments were published in quick succession,
each based on different source texts: the editio
princeps in Dutch was a translation from the Latin
Vulgate published in 1522 by Jacob van Liesveldt
of Antwerp; a Dutch translation of Luther's German Bible appeared in 1523, perhaps by the Franciscan Johan Pelt, who had translated Matthew from
Erasmus's Latin the year before; and the 1524 edition (shown here) is an anonymous translation of
Erasmus's Greek text. In all, twenty-five editions of
the complete New Testament in Dutch were published from 1522 to 1530.

References: Bruin 1937, 170–74; Duke 1990, 52–53.
Exhibition: Bridwell, Prothro B260; Harvard and
Union/Columbia, Prothro copy.

3.19

La Bible Qui est toute la Saincte escripture.

Translated by Pierre-Robert Olivétan. 4 pts.
Neuchâtel: Pierre de Wingle, June 1535.
D&M 3710.

Pierre-Robert Olivétan (ca. 1506–38) published the first French translation of the Bible from the original languages. The first edition, published in Neuchâtel in 1535, became the basis for French Protestant Bibles, including Calvin's revisions of Olivétan of 1543, 1546, and 1551, and the so-called French Geneva version of 1588.

Although compilations and commentaries such as the *Bible abrégée* and the *Bible historiale* were often printed in the fifteenth century, it was not until 1523 that the complete New Testament appeared in French in a translation by the humanist Jacques Lefèvre d'Etaples (†1536). Olivétan seems to have made some use of Lefèvre's version, especially for the Apocrypha, but his work, unlike Lefèvre's, is based on Hebrew and Greek texts.

Calvin contributed three prefaces to the first edition. In the first, he praises the idea of a vernacular Bible, although, in typical humanist fashion, he does so in Latin. The second is an appeal to Jews to convert to Christianity, and the third, which provides an introduction to the New Testament, is generally considered the precursor to his *Institutes*.

References: Chambers 1983, 88–92; Engammare 1991.
Exhibition: Bridwell, 31464; Harvard, And-Harv/Safe/
folio/307/FR/1535; Union/Columbia, Bridwell copy.

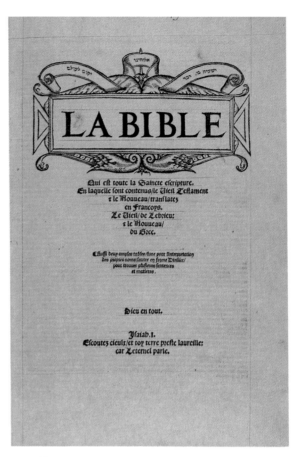

3.19, title page

3.20

La Bibbia.

Translated by Giovanni Diodati. 3 pts.
[Geneva: Johann Tornesius?], 1607.
D&M 5598.

Giovanni Diodati (1576–1649) translated the Bible into Italian (1607) and into French (1644). A native of Geneva and child of religious exiles from Lucca, he was known for his eloquence in both languages, as well as his mastery of the original Greek and Hebrew texts. His Italian translation has been praised for its elegance but faulted for its tendency to paraphrase. The introductions and notes reflect Calvinist theology, with special emphasis on typological interpretations of the Old Testament. Though not the first Italian translation of the Bible (the editio princeps of the Bible in Italian appeared in 1471), Diodati's version became the standard Protestant Bible in Italy. His metrical translations of the Psalms first appeared in the second edition of 1641.

Reference: McComish 1989, 167–208.
Exhibition: Bridwell, 00030 (Harrison Collection); Harvard showing second edition (with metrical Psalms) Geneva: Pietro Chovët, 1641 (And-Harv/S.C.R./folio/307/Ital); Union/*Columbia,* B220.55/D; Yale, Beinecke/Mln59/607db.

3.21

The Holy Bible: Containing the Old Testament and the New translated into the Indian language.

2 vols. Cambridge, Mass.: Samuel Green and Marmaduke Johnson, 1661–63.
D&M 6737.

The first complete Bible printed in America was a missionary Bible in the Natick-Algonquin language called Massachusetts. Working with interpreters, John Eliot (1604–90) transcribed an oral translation into the roman alphabet. He was encouraged in his work by Henry Dunster (ca. 1612–59), the first president of Harvard and the owner of the earliest known printing press in America (used by John Daye to produce the *Bay Psalm Book* in 1640), on which the first complete Bible was printed by Daye's successor Samuel Green in 1661 (New Testament) and 1663 (Old Testament). Words unknown to Native Americans, such as *Amen* and *God,* were inserted in English. Eliot, who was one of the translators of the *Bay Psalm Book,* also rendered the Psalms metrically in Massachusetts.

Cotton Mather (1663–1728) praised the undertaking: "Behold, ye Americans, the greatest honor that ever you were partakers of. The Bible was printed here at our Cambridge, and is the only Bible that ever was printed in all America, from the very foundation of the world" (Wright 1894, 11–12).

As Eliot became more fluent in the language, he began to improve on his translation. He published a revised New Testament in 1680 and a revised Old Testament in 1685. Within a few decades, however, the preference of missionaries for English and the encroachments of European Americans on native culture left only a few who could understand Eliot's Bible.

References: Ronda 1982; Tooker 1897; Wright 1894, 1–23.
Exhibition: Bridwell showing second edition, Cambridge: Samuel Green, 1685 (Prothro B64); Harvard, *AC6/El452.663ma; Union/*Columbia,* B220.598/C63; Yale, Beinecke/Pequot B473.

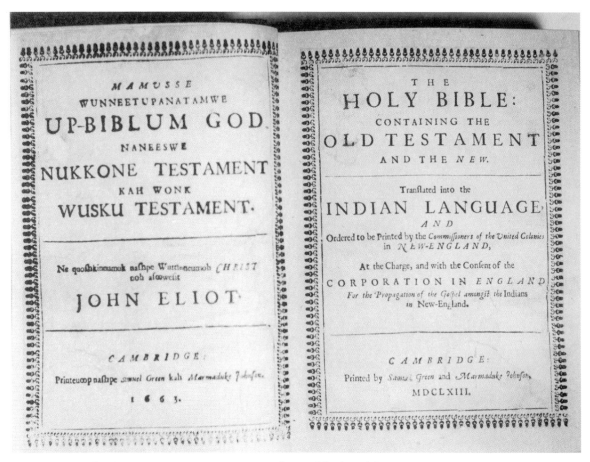

3.21, title pages of Old Testament (1663). By permission of Union Theological Seminary.

3.22

O Novo Testamento.

Translated by João Ferreira d'Almeida. Batavia [now Djakarta]: João de Vries, 1693.
D&M 7466.

The editio princeps of New Testament in Portuguese appeared in Amsterdam in 1681, the work of João Ferreira d'Almeida (1628–91), a pastor who served European colonists, especially Portuguese, in Java, Ceylon, and South India. His translation, which was completed in first draft and circulated in manuscript form as early as 1654, is based on Bèze's Latin text and unspecified Spanish, French, and Italian versions. In his later years, d'Almeida learned Greek in order to make revisions based on the original. He also translated the Pentateuch, though it did not appear in print until the mid-eighteenth century. His translations were later revised by missionaries for use in the Portuguese communities of the East Indies.

Reference: Swellengrebel 1972.

Exhibition: Bridwell only, Prothro B111.

LA BIBLIA,
QVE ES, LOS SA-
CROS LIBROS DEL
VIEIO Y NVEVO TE-
STAMENTO.

Trasladada en Español.

רבר אלהינו יקומ לעולם

La Palabra del Dios nuestro permanece para siempre. Isa. 40.

M. D. LXIX.

3.23

La Biblia.

Translated by Cassiodoro de Reina. 3 pts.
[Basel: Samuel Apiarius for Thomas Guarin],
September 1569.
D&M 8472; *VD16* B2868.

The earliest complete edition of the Bible in Spanish was translated by the Spanish Reformer Cassiodoro de Reina (ca. 1520–94) and printed for the first time in 1569. Reina had been a priest in Spain but went to Geneva in order to join the Calvinists. He spent some time in England, fleeing when charged with homosexuality and heresy, though returning later. In the 1580s he changed allegiances once again and became a Lutheran.

His translation is known as the Bear Bible because of the illustration on the title page, the device of the printer Apiarius (who, however, wished to emphasize the bees, because of his name, and not the bear). Reina's work was revised by Cyprian de Valera (1532–1602) and remains the Bible of Spanish Protestants.

The title page of the Bridwell copy (see illustration) represents variant A, as described by Darlow and Moule.

References: Hauben 1967, 85–107; Kinder 1975, 38–56.
Exhibition: Bridwell, AEX3674; Harvard, B1105–69*; *Union/Columbia*, CB87/1569; Yale, Beinecke/Mln87/569r.

3.24

Biblia Sacra.

Edited by Michael Servetus. Lyon: Gaspar Trechsel for Hughes de la Porte, 1542.
D&M 6120.

Roland Bainton poignantly wrote that "Michael Servetus has the singular distinction of having been burned by the Catholics in effigy and by the Protestants in actuality." Servetus (1509/11–53) was a man of broad learning, educated first as a lawyer in his native Spain, then as a medical doctor in France. He is chiefly remembered, however, for his radical theological views and dramatic death. Servetus favored adult baptism by immersion and expressed antitrinitarian sentiments, which caused quondam supporters like Martin Bucer (1491–1551) and Johannes Oecolampadius (1482–1531) to renounce him.

His edition of the Santi Pagnini Bible in 1542 (published under the pseudonym Michel de Villeneuve) contained no radical translations of passages dealing with baptism or the Trinity, although he tended to deemphasize typological and allegorical interpretations in his marginal notes. He also neglected to use allegorical headings normally assigned to the the Song of Songs, an interpretative gesture that probably irked Calvin in particular. These minor editorial preferences, though criticized, pale in comparison with his own inflammatory writings. In 1531, he published a tract *On the Errors of the Trinity,* and later he not only attacked Calvin's *Institutes* in his *Christianismi Restitutio* but also sent a "corrected" copy of the *Institutes* to the author.

With few friends among the Protestants or Catholics, Servetus lived incognito for several years before he was discovered and brought before the Catholic inquisition in Lyons in 1553 and condemned for his beliefs. He managed to escape before his execution, brashly appearing in Calvin's church in Geneva within a few months. Calvin promptly had him arrested. He was tried and convicted as a heretic, and burned at the stake. The case outraged many Reformers, including Luther, who said, "Heretics must not be suppressed or held down by physical force, but only combatted by the word of God" (Zweig 1951, 138).

References: Bainton 1960, 3, 95–100; Williams 1992, 924–34, 1243; Zweig 1951, 115–42.
Exhibition: Bridwell, Prothro B36; Harvard and Union/Columbia, Prothro copy.

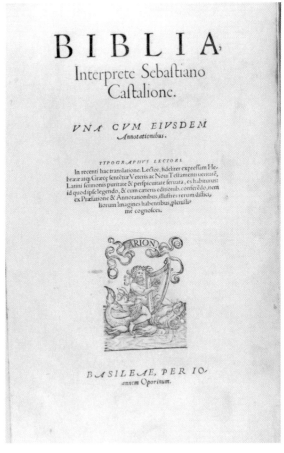

3.25, title page

3.25

Biblia.

Translated by Sebastian Castellio. 4 pts. Basel: Jacob Parcus for Johann Oporinus, March 1551. D&M 6131; *VD16* B2626.

Sebastian Castellio (†1563), a native of Savoy, became a follower and friend of Calvin in the 1540s, and served as head of the Latin school in Geneva. Later, the two clashed over Castellio's description of the Song of Songs as a love poem, and, more seriously, over the Servetus execution, which Castellio publicly decried. At the school in Geneva, Castellio had prepared a series of Latin conversations, published as *Dialogi sacri* (1541), in which biblical characters are presented in dialogues written in Classical Latin. The popularity of the work, which offered both religious and Latin instruction, encouraged Castellio to take this approach one step further by translating the Bible into Classical Latin. His effort was attacked, especially by the Geneva Reformers, who claimed that his Latin translation was blasphemous because it put Christian truth into pagan idiom. Catholics were also critical, placing it on the Index in 1554.

The translation is dedicated to Edward VI of England.

References: Guggisberg 1992; Williams 1992, 959–62.

Exhibition: Bridwell, Prothro, B59; Harvard, Bi35.51/F*; *Union*/Columbia, CB62/1551c; Yale, Beinecke/1977/+72.

4. THE BIBLE AND THE ARTS

4.1

Luther, Martin.

Widder die hymelischen propheten.

Wittenberg: [Lucas Cranach and
Christian Döring, 1525].
B 2086; *VD16* L7470.

The iconoclastic movement of the Reformation was
fomented in Wittenberg by Andreas Bodenstein
von Carlstadt, a professor of theology and a colleague of Luther. During the winter of 1521–22,
when Luther was sequestered at the Wartburg, Carlstadt and the "Zwickau Prophets" incited citizens
of Wittenberg to overturn altars and smash or burn
statues and paintings, creating the first major epi-
sode of iconoclasm in the Protestant Reformation.
The disturbances induced Luther to return to the
city to help calm the people. He preached a series of
sermons denouncing the violent removal of images.

By 1525, when *Against the Heavenly Prophets* appeared, Luther had begun to scorn Carlstadt's
works openly. He called him "unser ergester feynd"
(fol. A2ʳ) and, on the crucial issue of the Ten Commandments, claims to have shown "wie D. Carlstad
Mosen gar nicht verstehe [how Dr. Carlstadt does
not understand Moses at all]" (fol. E1ʳ).

Luther occasionally expressed reservations concerning the value of visual arts in worship, but he
never called for the destruction or removal of images. As Christensen has noted, Luther "moved
from an originally critical, even somewhat negative,
evaluation of church art to an ultimately rather posi-
tive one — finally providing an endorsement that
laid the theological foundation for the creation of
an important tradition of Protestant religious art"
(Christensen 1979, 42).

References: Christensen 1979, 42–65; *WA* 18:37–214;
Wandel 1995.

Exhibition: Bridwell, AER9370; showing Wittenberg:
[Cranach and Döring], 1525 (B 2087) at Harvard (*GC5/
L9774/525wb) and Yale (Beinecke/Me45/L973/A2/1525a);
Union/Columbia, L-Pam B-2086.

entwenung. Vñ do sara het geschē dē sun agar
der egiptierin spiled mit ysaac ire sun. sy sprach
zu abrahā. Würff auß dise dirn. vñ irē sun. wañ
der sun der dirnē wirt nit ein erb mit ysaac mey
nem sun. Abrahā nam das schwerlich auf. vmb
seinē sun. Got sprach zu im. Es soll dir nit heit
geschē werdē. vo des kinds vñ seiner dirne we
gen. Alse ding die dir sara sagt höre ir stymme.
wann in ysaac wirt dir geruffet oder genennet
dē same. vñ auch dē sun der dirne. mache ich in
ein groß volck. wañ er ist dein same. Darumb a=
braham stund auff frü. vñ nam das brot vñ eyn
krug mit wasser. vñ satzt in auff ir achselen vñ
antwurt ir dz kind vñ ließ sy. So sy was abgegā
gen. sy irret in der einöde bersabee. Vñ so das
wasser wz verzeret in dē krug. sy warff dz kind
vnder ein baum der daselbs wz. vñ gieng hyn=
weg. vñ sah verr als ei boge mocht geschiessen.
Wañ sy sprach. ich wil nit sehe dz sterbend kind
Es saß ir entgegē vñ hube auff seyn stymme
vñ waynt. Vñ got der herre hört dye stym des
kindes. Vñ der engel des herrē rüfft agar von
hymel sagend. Agar was thustu. Du solt dir nit
fürchtē. Wañ got hat erhöret die stym des kin
des an der stat in der es ist. Stee auff nym das
kind vñ halt sein hand. wann ich mach es in ein
groß volck. Vñ got tet auf ire augē. Sy sahe ei
bruñe des wassers. sy gieng hyn vnd füllte den
krug vñ gab dē kind zetrincken. vñ was bey im.
Es wuchß vñ wonet in der eynöde. vñ ward ein
iünger schütz. vñ wonet i der wüste pharan. vñ

sein muter nā im eyn weyb von dē landē egipti.
In der selbē zeyt sprach abimelech zu abrahā
vñ phicol. der fürst seins heres. Got der ist mit
dir in alle dinge. die du tust. Darumb so schwe
re mir bey got daz du mir nit schadest vñ meinē
nachkummen vñ meinē geschlecht. aber thu mir
nach der erbarmūg dye ich dir tet. Thu mir vñ
dē land. in dē du hast gewandest als ei fremder
Abraham der sprach. Ich wil schwerē vñ kam
an abimelech vmb dē bruñe des wassers den
sei knecht het genomē mit gewalt. vñ abimelech
der antwurt. Ich hab nit gewißt wer das ding
hat gethan vnnd auch du hast mirs nit kunt
than. vnd ich hab es nit gehört on heut. Dar=
umb abraham nam schaff vñ ochssen vñ gab
sy abimelech. Vñ sy schlugen beyd eyn gelübd.
Vñ abraham der stalt besunder siben lemmer
der hertt. Abimelech sprach zu im. Was wollen
im dise siben lemmer. Dz du hast heyssen steen
besunder. Vñ er sprach. Dise siben lemmer ent
phahe von meyner hand das sye mir seyn in ge
zeugnuß. daz ich grub disen bruñe. Darüb die
stat ward genennet Bersabee. wann do schwur
yetweder. vñ gienge ein gelübd vmb dē bruñe
des eyds. vñ abimelech stund auf. vñ achaphat
seyn eyden. vnnd phycol der fürst seyner ritter=
schafft vñ kerten wider in das land der palesty
ner. Aber abrahā pflantzt dē walt bersabee vñ
rüffet an da dē namē des herrē des ewige got
tes. vnd er was eyn pawer des lands der pale=
styner manig tag.

4.2, fol. XIIII^r, *Sacrifice of Isaac*

4.2

Biblia Germanica.

Nuremberg: Anton Koberger, 17 February 1483.
D&M 4184; Goff B-632; *GW* 4303.

The ninth printed German Bible (eleventh, if one counts the two Cologne Bibles in Low German) was Anton Koberger's imprint of 1483. Its 109 woodcuts are the same used in the Quentell Cologne Bible of 1478/79 (which Koberger may have helped finance), and their appearance here influenced subsequent Bible illustration, in particular the Malermi Bible (1490) and the Lübeck Bible (1494). Despite vast differences, the illustrations for Revelation from the Koberger edition undoubtedly influenced Dürer's designs for his *Apocalypse* (Price 1994, 691).

Koberger (ca. 1445–1513), initially a goldsmith, became one of the most important printers in fifteenth-century Germany. He may have operated as many as twenty-four presses and produced approximately 250 works between ca. 1471 and 1504.

In the colophon, the language of the Bible is said to be "pure, clear, correct, and in common German." In fact, the German of the Koberger Bible is significantly more modern and fluent than that of the Mentelin (see Item 3.1).

References: Eichenberger and Wendland 1977, 91–96; Price 1994; Reinitzer 1983, 69–70.
Exhibition: Bridwell, 06171–2; Harvard, Typ/Inc/2028; *Union*/Columbia: Thompson CB72/1483; Yale, YCBA/Leaf Coll. 350 (four leaves).

4.3

Dürer, Albrecht, and

Benedictus Chelidonius.

Passio domini nostri Jesu.

Nuremberg: [Hieronymus Höltzel for] Albrecht Dürer, 1511. Commonly known as the *Large Passion.*
VD16 S4587.

The *Large Passion* is a set of twelve woodcuts by Dürer, accompanied by Benedictus Chelidonius's centos. Dürer began the series around 1496/97, during the same time that he worked on the *Apocalypse* (published as a book in 1498). It is often said that the engraved *Passion* by Martin Schongauer (ca. 1450–91) influenced Dürer, although the differences between the series are far greater than the similarities. For example, Schongauer did not include the Last Supper in his *Passion.*

In the *Last Supper,* Dürer depicts Christ's announcement of the betrayal and the reaction of the disciples. Judas is seated in the front of the table on the right, clutching a purse and contorting his head to the right. The figure on the left pouring wine is the innkeeper mentioned by Luke (22:10). As the first in the series (after the title-page woodcut of *Man of Sorrows*), it may serve as a visual introduction to Dürer's theme of the viewer's (and humankind's) complicity in the perpetual suffering of Christ. The title-page poem conveys this idea directly: (Christ speaking) "I bear these harsh wounds for you, humankind, and I cure your diseases with my blood. . . . And you, ungrateful to me, often pierce my wounds with your desires; I am often beaten by your sin."

References: *The Illustrated Bartsch* (1978–   ), 10:.205 (*Last Supper*); Panofsky 1955, 138–39; Unterlinden 1991, 370–93.
Exhibition: Bridwell, 11011; Harvard and Union/Columbia, Bridwell copy; Yale, YUAG/1976.102.10/B-L (Gift of Ralph Kirkpatrick) and YCBA/Leaf Coll. 1763 (title page).

4.3, Albrecht Dürer, *Last Supper,* from the *Large Passion*

4.4

Dürer, Albrecht, and

Benedictus Chelidonius.

Passio Christi.

Nuremberg: [Hieronymus Höltzel for] Albrecht
Dürer, 1511. Commonly known as the *Small
Passion.*
VD16 S4588.

Dürer's *Small Passion,* with thirty-seven woodcuts, is
the most extensive series he designed and published. (Dürer is named as the publisher on the
colophon: "Impressum Nurnberge per Albertum
Durer Pictorem"; Höltzel, who served as printer, is
not named.) It appeared as a book in 1511, the same
year in which he issued the *Large Passion* and the *Life
of the Virgin,* and in which he reissued, in Latin, the
Apocalypse (originally published both in Latin and
German versions in 1498).

Although it is rarely interpreted as such, the *Small
Passion* is a book that exemplifies Christian humanism in Germany. Each image illustrates a religious
poem by the Franciscan schoolteacher Benedictus
Chelidonius. Chelidonius's thirty-seven poems, all
of which were, according to *VD16,* first published in
1506, are prayers as well as reflections on the religious meaning of the scenes; they are cast, in a
display of humanist virtuosity, in no fewer than
twenty different meters.

Christ at Emmaus (image 33, counting the title-
page woodcut) depicts the astonishment of the disciples as a visual echo of their confused amazement
in the *Last Supper* (image 8) of the series. Moreover,
the presence of the sacrament is much more pronounced in this image than in the *Last Supper.*
Chelidonius also focuses on the sacrament in his
poem; it ends by assigning Christ a humanist epi-
thet, "panis olympicus" (Olympian bread).

4.4, Albrecht Dürer, *Christ at Emmaus,* from the *Small Passion*

References: *The Illustrated Bartsch* (1978–), 10:.248 (*Christ at
Emmaus*); Panofsky 1955, 139–45.
Exhibition: Bridwell, 11012; Yale, YCBA/Leaf Coll. 1764
(eight leaves).

4.5, Albrecht Dürer, *Last Supper* (1523). By permission of the New York Public Library.

4.5

Dürer, Albrecht.

Last Supper.

Single-sheet woodcut, 1523.

Based on a set of drawings by Dürer from 1520 to 1523, Panofsky postulated that the artist was planning an *Oblong Passion,* a woodcut series in an innovative horizontal format. The *Last Supper* of 1523 would be, then, the only completed design that was used for a woodcut. Panofsky's suggestion, despite its almost universal acceptance, is not entirely convincing. The oblong *Last Supper* drawing of 1523 (Winkler 889) is, indeed, compatible with the iconography of Dürer's Passion series. Like the compositions in the *Large Passion* and the *Small Passion*

(Dürer's *Engraved Passion* did not include the Last Supper), it depicts Christ's announcement of the betrayal. The betrayal by Judas was considered one of the greatest sufferings of Christ and, consequently, occurs in Passion series.

The woodcut of 1523, however, depicts the New Commandment, recorded by John, "Love one another, as I have loved you" (Jn 15:12). One might go so far as to suggest that the representation of Christ speaking the new commandment gives the composition an especially strong evangelical quality. It is difficult, however, to assign such a composition to a Passion series, because it does not depict a moment of Christ's suffering.

This woodcut is often cited as evidence of Dürer's adherence to Lutheran views, in this case an endorsement of utraquism. Interestingly, Carlstadt had dedicated a utraquist tract of 1521 to Dürer. The city of Nuremberg, moreover, had endorsed utraquist masses since Holy Week of 1523. This might be the context for the prominent display of the chalice in the image. Panofsky also noted that the empty charger in the foreground may have been intended to express disapproval of the Catholic understanding of the mass as a sacrifice.

References: *The Illustrated Bartsch* (1978–   ), 10:.253; Panofsky 1955, 218–23; Seebaß 1971 (on Dürer and the Reformation). Exhibition: Bridwell only, on loan from New York Public Library.

4.6

a. Holbein, Hans, and Nicolas Bourbon.

Historiarum ueteris instrvmenti icones ad uiuum expressae.

Lyons: Melchior and Gaspar Trechsel [for Jean and François Frellon], 1538.

b. Holbein, Hans, Nicolas Bourbon, and Gilles Corrozet.

Icones historiarvm veteris testamenti.

Lyons: Jean Frellon, 1547.

This series by Hans Holbein (1497–1543) of ninety-two woodcuts of Old Testament scenes, accompanied by a Latin text by Nicolas Bourbon (1503–ca. 1550), appeared in 1538, the same year as his *Dance of Death* (which uses four of the same woodcuts). The Holbein blocks, some of which were probably cut by Hans Lützelburger, were reused in later Frellon editions (1539, 1543, 1547 [two editions], 1549) and widely imitated in similar works, including Pierre Regnault's 1538 and 1544 editions (in which more than half of the images are reversed) and a pirated edition published by Joannes Steelsius in Antwerp (1540). French verses by Gilles Corrozet were added in the 1539 edition, and Spanish and

DAVID Saulis armis reiectis, ac solius Dei potentia confisus, lapide funda iacto Goliath interficit. Philisthæos in fugam vertit.

I. REGVM XVII.

Dauid occit Goliath d'une pierre,
Sans estre armé, en Dieu se confiant.
Par un enfant le geant mis par terre,
Des Philistins l'ost retourne fuyant.

4.6b, fol. f2ᵛ, Hans Holbein, *David and Goliath*

English texts appeared in 1543 and 1549, respectively.

The verses often reflect typological interpretations, as in the text that accompanies the image of the sacrifice of Isaac: "Abrahae fides tentatur. Filium suum Isaac immolare iubetur. Saluator omnium CHRISTUS promittitur. [The faith of Abraham is tested. He is ordered to sacrifice his son Isaac. Christ is foreshadowed, savior of all]" (1538 ed., fol. B3ʳ).

References: Mortimer 1964, 1: no. 276 and 281; Van der Coelen 1994.

Exhibition: (a) Harvard, Typ/515/47.454/(A); (b) Bridwell, 10226; Union/*Columbia,* Book Arts/NC251/H69/1547/H69; Yale, YCBA/Leaf Coll. 3410 (twelve leaves).

4.7, title page by Lucas Cranach

4.7, fol. B4ᵛ, Lucas Cranach, *St. Paul*

4·7

Pollicarius, Johannes, and Lucas Cranach.

Der heiligen XII. Aposteln ankunfft/ beruff/ glauben/ lere/ leben vnd seliges absterben.

Wittenberg: Heirs of Georg Rhau, 1549.
VD16 P4031.

Johannes Pollicarius, a Lutheran pastor in Weissenfels, published several devotional, musical, and polemical works, the most successful of which was this devotional tract on the Apostles' Creed. *VD16* records eight editions of it, in both German and Low German, between 1549 and 1599. This edition of 1549 typifies Georg Rhau's practice (here perpetuated by his heirs) of creatively reusing older (even pre-Reformational) woodblocks to produce beautiful but affordable devotional tracts for domestic use. The images of the apostles with the instruments of their martyrdom were originally designed and used by Lucas Cranach the Elder for a series depicting the martyrdoms of the apostles (ca. 1512). Rhau, it seems, first used the blocks in his 1539 edition of the Apostles' Creed (*Das Symbolum oder gemeine Bekenntnis der zwelff Aposteln,* a work that, as of 1547/48, was frequently reissued with the *Hortulus animae*).

Pollicarius acknowledges the visual program, to a degree, with his quaint statement that the articles of the Apostles can be comprehended only with the "eyes of faith [allein mit den augen des glaubens]" (fol. A3ʳ). A 1562 edition of Valentin Boltz's *Illuminierbuch* reprints Pollicarius's tract "für die so lust haben diese Figuren . . . zu illuminieren [for those who wish to illuminate the figures]" (quoted from the title page).

References: *The Illustrated Bartsch* (1978–   ), 11:92 (*St. Paul*); Koepplin and Falk 1974–76, 1:395–98, 2:556–57.
Exhibition: Bridwell, 31359; Harvard, Typ/520.49.706F; Union/Columbia, Bridwell copy.

4.8

Amman, Jost.

Künstliche Vnd wolgerissene figuren, der fürnembsten Evangelien, durchs gantze Jar sampt den Passion vnd zwölff Aposteln.

Frankfurt: Peter Fabricius for Siegmund Feyerabend, 1579.
IA 104.814; *VD16* A2297.

4.8, fol. L1^r, Jost Amman, *John 1*

Amman (1539–91), one of the most successful graphic artists of the late Renaissance, specialized in serial illustrations, many of which were based on the Bible. He is often considered the artistic successor to Virgil Solis (1514–62), and, like him, resided in Nuremberg and undertook several projects for Siegmund Feyerabend (1528–90) of Frankfurt. His first lengthy work was the woodcut illustrations for the Feyerabend Bible of 1564. *Künstliche Vnd wolgerissene figuren* (first published in 1579) was one of Amman's most elegant works. Each of the images from the Bible, Passion of Christ, and martyrdom of the Apostles has two Latin elegiac couplets in superscript and German couplets in subscript, all of which are interpretations of Bible passages.

Feyerabend's introduction to this work makes the usual statement that biblical pictures benefit common or young people. He adds, however, that these images are intended for those interested in art, a claim that he also makes on the title page: "Allen vnd jeden der Kunst liebhabenden zu besonderm nutz vnd wolgefallen."

References: Andresen [1864] 1973, 186; Hampe 1907–50, 1:410–13; *The Illustrated Bartsch* (1978–   ), 20/1:2.75.
Exhibition: Showing Frankfurt: Johann Feyerabend for Siegmund Feyerabend, 1587 at Bridwell (Prothro B308), Harvard (Typ/520.88.140), and Union/Columbia (Prothro copy); Yale, Beinecke/Z82/1K.

4.9, fol. C3^r, Matthäus Merian, *Daniel 3* (The Fiery Furnace). By permission of Union Theological Seminary.

4.9

Merian, Matthäus, and

Johann Ludwig Gottlieb.

Icones Biblicae.

4 pts. Pt. 1: Frankfurt: Theodor de Bry, [1625];
Pt.2: [n.p., 1626]; Pt. 3: Frankfurt: Erasmus
Kempffer, 1627; Pt. 4: Frankfurt: Matthäus
Merian, 1627.

Matthäus Merian (1593–1650), well known as a to-
pographical and architectural engraver, is also the
publisher and artist of an influential "picture Bible"
of the seventeenth century. In his preface, Merian
says that his purpose was to make "ein recht hiero-

glyphisch Werck nicht allein zur belustigung und
ergetzung/ sondern auch und zwar fürnemlich zu
auffmunterung der Gemüter [a truly hieroglyphic
(that is, emblematic) work, not only to amuse and
delight, but also, and primarily, to encourage the
spirit]." Latin, German, and French verses by Johann Ludwig Gottlieb accompany copperplate engravings of important scenes from the Bible.

Though now rare, the *Icones Biblicae* were extremely popular in the seventeenth century and inspired several imitators. In 1659, for example,
the Dutch publisher Danckertz produced an unauthorized copy of the work with newly done etch-
ings after Merian's engravings by Peter Holsteyn
and added Dutch translations in verse and prose by

the poet Reiner Anslo (on exhibition at Bridwell). Merian received no credit in this version for being the source of the designs and verses.

Merian was born in Basel and later worked in Frankfurt, where he married the daughter of the engraver Johann Theodor de Bry. Their children, Matthäus, Kaspar, and Maria Sibylla, all became important artists.

References: Reinitzer 1983, 254–57; Schmidt 1962, 304–29; Zülch 1907–50, 24:413–14.

Exhibition: Bridwell showing the copy by Peter Holsteyn, Amsterdam: Dancker Danckertz, 1659 (Prothro B19); Harvard, H620–29; *Union*/Columbia showing Strasbourg: Heirs of Lazarus Zetzner (Thompson YF67/M56/1629).

4.10

Hessus, Helius Eobanus.

Psalterivm vniversvm.

Marburg: Eucharius Cervicornus, 1537.
VD16 B3162.

Eobanus Hessus (1488–1540) was professor of history at Marburg when he published his poetic paraphrases of the entire Psalter in 1537. He had previously made a name for himself as a Latin poet and as a professor of Latin and poetics at the Ägidiengymnasium in Nuremberg and at the University of Erfurt. He was widely regarded as one of the best Latin poets in Germany, especially after the publication of his *Christian Heroides* (*Heroidum christianarum epistolae*) in 1514. Just before his death, he published the first complete Latin poetic translation of the *Iliad* (1540).

With the onset of the Reformation, he became a staunch supporter of Luther and turned increasingly to biblical themes for his poetry. His Psalter, cast in elegiac couplets, is notable for being the first humanist poetic rendering of the Psalms from a Lutheran perspective. He composed his first elegiac psalms in 1527. In 1529, Luther wrote to him with a request for a poetic translation of Psalm 118, usually

considered Luther's favorite. Hessus responded by publishing a poetic version of it along with versions of sixteen other psalms in 1530. Thereafter, the Wittenberg Reformers urged him repeatedly to render the entire Psalter in elegiac couplets, which he finally accomplished with the 1537 publication. Subsequent editions, beginning with the second in 1538, added introductory couplets for each psalm as well as congratulatory letters from Luther and Melanchthon. In his letter, Luther wrote that he "read, reads, and shall always read [these psalms] with great pleasure [. . . et summa uoluntate legi, lego, legamque semper]" (*WA Br* 8:107, no. 3167). Melanchthon admired the musicality of Hessus's renderings and endorsed music as a great force on the emotions.

Although Hessus's psalm renderings enjoyed great popularity in schools throughout the sixteenth century, many other writers, perhaps most importantly George Buchanan (first edition in 1566), paraphrased the Psalms in Classical meters.

Reference: Krause 1879, 2:97–98, 204–7.

Exhibition: Showing Strasbourg: Crato Mylius, 1544 at Bridwell (ADB0884) and Union/Columbia (Bridwell copy); Harvard, And-Harv/R.B.R./453.2/Lat 1537.

4.11

Bèze, Théodore de.

Abraham Sacrifiant.

In *Poemata*, 185–229. [Geneva: Henri Estienne, 1576].
IA 118.709.

The Reformation provided strong impetus for the development of biblical drama, which became, perhaps, the most widely and frequently cultivated theatrical genre of the sixteenth and seventeenth centuries in Northern Europe. Luther himself encouraged biblical drama with his contention, expressed in the forewords to both Judith and Tobit (in the Bible of 1534), that parts of the Bible were ancient Jewish dramas. "Denn Judith gibt eine gute, ernste, dapffere Tragedien, So gibt Tobias eine feine liebliche, Gottselige Comedien [For Judith provides a good, serious, courageous tragedy; Tobit also provides a fine, charming, pious comedy]" ("Vorrhede auffs Buch Tobia," *WA DB* 12:108). Luther even claims that the Septuagint version of Tobit, which unlike the Vulgate is cast in the first person at the beginning, resembles a drama: "Vnd das Griechische exemplar sihet fast also, das es [that is, Tobit] ein spiel gewest sey." Paul Rebhun (ca. 1500–1546), one of the earliest Lutheran biblical dramatists, printed Luther's prefaces to Judith and Tobit in the afterword to his play *Susanna* (first published 1536), as justification for his genre.

Many Catholics, of course, number among the important writers of biblical drama. The Jesuits in particular frequently used biblical themes (in addition to such other sources as saints' lives) for the thousands of dramas they produced at their schools.

Bèze was professor of Greek at the Lausanne Academy when he composed *Abraham Sacrifiant* in 1550. The epigraph on the title page indicates the Reformational tenor of his interpretation: "Abraham a creu à Dieu, il luy a esté reputé à iustice" (Rm 4:3), a point further stressed in the prologue: "Vous le [that is, Abraham] verrez par foy iustifié." The work is occasionally said to be the first tragedy written in French, although Bèze apologized for the untragic quality of the plot in a prefatory letter "aux lecteurs." He also pointed out that his choral odes (which he calls "cantiques") do not have a Classical organization. *Abraham Sacrifiant* enjoyed considerable popularity in the sixteenth century. Frankish noted eleven editions between 1550 and 1598, with the possibility of an additional printing from 1595.

The *Poemata* of 1598 includes the Latin translation of the play. Bèze contributed an introduction to this translation, in which he explains the genesis of the play at the Lausanne Academy.

References: Cameron, Hall, and Higman 1967; Frankish 1969; Soulié 1989, 642–43; Street 1983, 21–29.

Exhibition: Showing *Poemata* [Geneva: Henri Estienne and Jacques Stoer, 1598] (*Abraham Sacrifiant* on pages 283–345) at Bridwell (Harvard copy) and Harvard (*FC5/B4694/548pg); Yale, Beinecke/Haq15/B469.

4.12

Acciaiuoli, Maddalena Salvetti.

Il David Persegvitato O Vero Fuggitivo.

Poema Eroico.

Florence: G. A. Caneo, 1611

Maddelena Salvetti Acciaiuoli (†1610), a Florentine noblewoman, wrote numerous sonnets and canzoni, many of which were published in her *Rime Toscane* (1590) and later anthologized in collections of vernacular verse. Her epic poem about David, incomplete at her death and published posthumously by her husband, recounts the life of David, drawing on the biblical account and the Psalms themselves. In a subplot, she tells the love story of the Amazon queen Pethesilea and Italo, son of King Tarracone, from whom, it is asserted, the house of Medici descends. This is the first edition of the poem and includes other religious poems as well as a history of the Acciaiuoli family. An engraved portrait of the poet is on the title page.

Exhibition: Bridwell, AER4418; Harvard, *IC5/Ac252/590r; Union/Columbia, Bridwell copy.

4.12, title page

4.13

a. Milton, John.

Paradise Lost. A Poem. Written in ten books.

London: Peter Parker, Robert Boulter, and
Matthias Walker, 1667.
STC (Wing) M2136.

b.————.

Paradise Regain'd. A Poem In IV Books. To

which is added Samson Agonistes.

London: J. M. for John Starkey, 1671.
STC (Wing) M2152.

Milton's epics represent the poetic culmination of hundreds of years of typological interpretation of

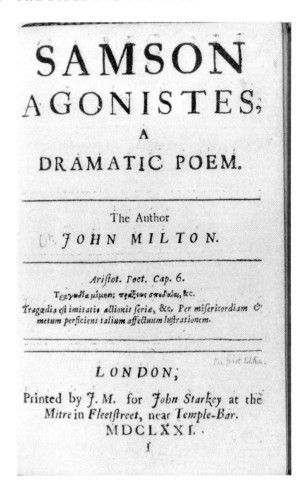

4.13b, title page of *Samson Agonistes*

the Bible. Searching the Hebrew Scripture for symbolic antecedents of the New Testament had been a common exegetical method in the Middle Ages, and although Reformers preferred literal interpretation, they did not necessarily reject typological views — as evidenced in this exhibition by Luther's exegesis of the Book of Jonah (Item 2.6) and the verses accompanying Holbein's Old Testament images (Item 4.6).

There are thousands of Bible quotations in Milton, and, even in the absence of direct quotation, Scripture suffuses virtually every line. In *Paradise Lost* (first issued in 1667), Adam and Eve represent humankind, of course, but also prefigure the Second Adam:

> Of man's first disobedience, and the fruit
> Of that forbidden tree, whose mortal taste
> Brought death into the world, and all our woe,
> With loss of Eden, till one greater Man
> Restore us, and regain the blissful Seat,
> Sing, Heav'nly Muses. . . . (ll. 1–6)

Paradise Regain'd (first published in 1671 with the first edition of *Samson Agonistes*) provides the happy ending intimated in the opening of *Paradise Lost*:

> . . . now thou hast aveng'd
> Supplanted Adam, and by vanquishing
> Temptation, hast regain'd lost Paradise. (ll. 606–8)

In *Samson Agonistes,* Milton perpetuates the patristic interpretation of Samson as Christ, dying to save his people, but also hints at Samson's kinship to Adam as one who tragically succumbed to temptation.

References: Galden 1975, 72–99; Hill 1993; Sims 1962, 259–78.
Exhibition: (a) Harvard, *EC65/M6427p/1667; Yale, Beinecke/Ij/M642/667Ab; (b) Bridwell, 01799; Harvard, Smyth/4572.5; Union/*Columbia*, B823M64/U55/1671; Yale, Beinecke/1977/2532.

4.14, no. 24, "Ein feste Burg." By permission of Niedersächsische Staats- und Universitätsbibliothek, Göttingen.

4.14

Luther, Martin.

Geystliche Lieder.

Leipzig: Valentin Bapst, 1545.
B 3593; *VD16* G851.

Luther was an accomplished musician — he played the lute and flute and had a fine tenor voice — and, more important, was a remarkably creative composer. Like many of his generation, he endorsed Augustine's view that music was a gift from God. One of the *Tischreden* records his statement "Ich gebe nach der Theologia der Musica den nähesten Locum und höchste Ehre [I give music the next place after theology and accord it the highest honor]" (*WA TR* 6:348, no. 7034).

His first known composition was "Ein newes lied wir heben an" (1523), a deeply moving balladesque account (in AAB bar form) of the execution of two Augustinian monks in Brussels, the first "martyrs" of the Reformation. His subsequent compositions and adaptations were intended for liturgical use, an issue he began addressing in 1523 with the publication of *Formula missae*. The first Lutheran hymnal was probably the so-called *Achtliederbuch* (1524), although expanded hymnals appeared quickly and often. The Wittenberg *Chorgesangbuch* of 1524 has settings in four voices by Johann Walter (1496–1570), Luther's most significant musical collaborator. The Wittenberg *Gemeindegesangbuch* of 1529, of which no copy survives, was the first hymnal published for general congregational use. The last hymnal Luther was to see through press was the *Geystliche Lieder,* published by Valentin Bapst in 1545, with a new introduction by Luther.

In the nineteenth century, scholars gave Luther little, if any, credit for the melodies for his hymns. That has changed dramatically in recent decades. Markus Jenny, a leading authority on Luther's music, attributes twenty-two original melodies to him with certainty; eleven additional melodies are probably by Luther, and two further melodies are possibly by him. Jenny also credits Luther as the originator of the "Psalmlied," which was to become one of the most successful forms of church music in the sixteenth and seventeenth centuries.

Luther's poetic achievements in the hymns have always been recognized. In the pioneering work on German poetry *Das Buch von der deutschen Poeterey* (1624), Martin Opitz (1597–1639) praised his metrical sensibility, in particular as illustrated by "Erhalt uns Herr bei deinem Wort." It is also interesting that the original literary Faust, the Dr. Johann Faust of the 1587 chapbook, uttered a desperate lamentation, before being taken to hell, with a quotation from Luther's most famous work: "Wo ist meine feste Burg?" (chap. 94: "Doctor Fausti Weheklag").

References: Blankenburg 1962, 1344–46; Jenny 1983a, 303–21; Jenny 1983b, 170–74; Jenny 1985, 36–51.

Exhibition: Bridwell, on loan from Niedersächsische Staats- und Universitätsbibliothek, Göttingen; Harvard showing Nuremberg: Valentin Neuber, 1567 (on loan from University of Toronto); Yale, Music Library/M2138/B115/1545b (facsimile of 1545 edition).

4.15

The booke of Common praier noted.

[London]: Richard Grafton, 1550.
STC (2d ed.) 16441.

Soon after the publication of the Prayer Book of Edward VI in 1549, Archbishop Cranmer commissioned John Merbecke (†ca. 1585) to produce an edition of the services with music based on the Sarum Breviary. Merbecke, who was the master of choristers of St. George's Chapel in Windsor, had narrowly escaped the stake in 1544 when condemned for his writings against the Catholic Church. His *Booke of Common praier noted* is the first choral book of the Anglican Church. Although designed for the Chapel Royal, it quickly became the model for choirs and congregations throughout England. Printed on a four-line stave, the plainsong services open with the Lord's Prayer for Matins. Merbecke provides only one setting for the Psalms, which is printed with the first verse of Psalm 6; otherwise, he advises, "and so forth with the rest of the Psalmes, as they be appoynted."

The text for the Psalms would have come from Cranmer's Bible (Item 3.11a), which, in the case of the Psalms, differs little from Coverdale's 1535 translation. Indeed, when the King James Version was adopted for other portions of the scriptural readings in 1611, the Psalter texts were not changed because the choirs and the people were accustomed to chanting the older version. By then, however, polyphonic settings had replaced Merbecke's plain chant.

Reference: Stevenson 1949.

Exhibition: Bridwell, 17612; Harvard and Union/Columbia, Bridwell copy; Yale, Beinecke/Vpl/2.

4.16

Marot, Clément, and Théodore de Bèze.

Les Pseavmes mis en rime françois.

Lyons: Jean de Tournes for Antoine Vincent, 1563.

Calvin did not have Luther's musical genius, but he did share Luther's deep concern for church music. Most distinctively, he promoted the exclusive use of monophonic psalms for congregational singing. His energetic support of the efforts to produce a complete Psalter certainly paid off, as Calvinist Psalters became tremendously successful throughout Europe and in the New World. (The first book printed in America, the *Bay Psalm Book* of 1640, was essentially a Calvinist Psalter, intended to be sung to the melodies of the Ravenscroft Psalter of 1621.) Calvin did, however, endorse polyphonic psalms for singing at home. In fact, Claude Goudimel (ca. 1510–72) and Louis Bourgeois (ca. 1510–ca. 1561), the two greatest Calvinist composers of psalm melodies, published polyphonic settings during Calvin's lifetime. After Calvin's death, polyphonic Psalters came to be used in churches in Geneva and elsewhere.

The Strasbourg hymnal of 1539 was the first Psalter Calvin promoted. Produced during his "exile" in Strasbourg, it contained eighteen psalms. The first Geneva Psalter was published in 1542. It included poetic paraphrases by Clément Marot (ca. 1496–1544) and twenty-two new melodies by Bourgeois. With the collaboration of Théodore de Bèze (who wrote more paraphrases) and Bourgeois (whose musical collaboration continued until at least 1551) as well as other composers who can no longer be identified, the first complete Geneva Psalter was published in 1562. The publication of the complete Geneva Psalter was organized, on a grand scale, by Antoine Vincent. He engaged a total of forty-five printers, who produced, it has been estimated, between thirty thousand and fifty thousand copies in 1562 alone.

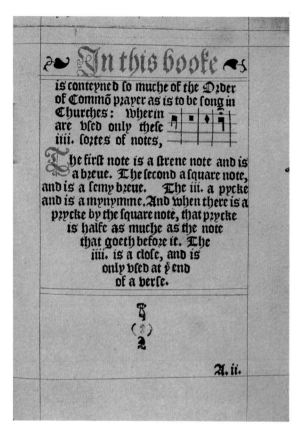

4.15, fol. A2ʳ

References: Bruinsma 1962, 666–74; Douen 1878–79; *Le Psautier de Genève* 1986.
Exhibition: Bridwell showing Paris: Pierre Des-Hayes, 1642 (10708); Harvard, Typ/515/63.210; *Union*/Columbia showing Geneva: Gabriel Cartier, 1607 (Cage/VN46/1607/M35); Yale showing Paris: Guillaume Thibout, 1547 (Beinecke/Hfb5/14y).

BIBLIOGRAPHY

Aland, Kurt. 1993. "Die Ausgabe der Vulgata des Neuen Testaments von Gutenberg bis zur Clementina." In *Philologia Sacra,* 2:654–69. Edited by Roger Gryson. Freiburg: Herder.

Allen, P. S., ed. 1906–58. *Opus Epistolarum Des. Erasmi Roterodami.* 12 vols. Oxford: Clarendon Press.

Allgeier, Arthur. 1943. "Exegetische Beiträge zur Geschichte des Griechischen." *Biblica* 24:261–88.

Altaner, Berthold. 1933. "Zur Kenntnis des Hebräischen im Mittelalter." *Byzantinische Zeitschrift* 21:288–308.

Alter, Robert, and Frank Kermode. 1987. *The Literary Guide to the Bible.* Cambridge: Belknap Press of Harvard University Press.

Amram, David Werner. 1909. *Makers of Hebrew Books in Italy.* Philadelphia: J. H. Greenstone.

Andresen, Andreas. [1864] 1973. *Jost Amman, 1539–1591: Graphiker und Buchillustrator der Renaissance.* Reprint, Amsterdam: G. W. Hissink.

Armand, Anna Marie. 1944. *Saint Bernard et la renouveau de l'iconographie au XIIe siècle.* Paris: Jouve.

Armstrong, Elizabeth. 1954. *Robert Estienne, Royal Printer.* Rev. ed. Abingdon, England: Sutton Courtenay.

Aspland, A. 1873. *The Four Evangelists.* Manchester: Holbein Society Reprints.

Astell, Ann W. 1990. *The Song of Songs in the Middle Ages.* Ithaca: Cornell University Press.

Aulotte, R. 1959. "Etudes sur l'influence de Plutarch au XVIe siècle." *Bibliothèque d'Humanisme et Renaissance* 21:609–13.

Babcock, Robert G., and Mark L. Sosower. 1994. *Learning from the Greeks.* New Haven: Beinecke Rare Book and Manuscript Library.

Backus, Irena Dorota. 1980. *The Reformed Roots of the English New Testament: The Influence of Theodore Beza on the English New Testament.* Pittsburgh: Pickwick Press.

Bainton, Roland H. 1950. *Here I Stand: A Life of Martin Luther.* Nashville: Abingdon Press.

———. 1960. *Hunted Heretic: The Life and Death of Michael Servetus.* Boston: Beacon Press.

———. 1969. *Erasmus of Christendom.* New York: Charles Scribner's Sons.

Bandiní, Marie Butí. 1941. *Donne d'Italia. Poetesse e Scrittrici.* Rome: Paolo Pellegatta.

Barker, Nicolas. 1992. *Aldus Manutius and the Development of Greek Script and Type in the Fifteenth Century.* 2d ed. New York: Fordham University Press.

Barnstone, Willis. 1993. *The Poetics of Translation: History, Theory, Practice.* New Haven: Yale University Press.

Baroni, Victor. 1986. *La Contre-Réforme devant la Bible: La question biblique avec un supplement du XVIIIe siècle à nos jours.* Geneva: Slatkin Reprints.

Bautz, Friedrich Wilhelm, and Traugott Bautz, eds. 1975– . *Biographisch-Bibliographisches Kirchenlexikon.* Herberg: Traugott Bautz.

Bedouelle, Guy, and Bernard Roussel, eds. 1989. *Le temp des réformes et la Bible.* Paris: Beauchesne.

Bentley, Jerry H. 1977. "Biblical Philology and Christian Humanism: Lorenzo Valla and Erasmus as Scholars of the Gospels." *Sixteenth Century Journal* 8(2):9–28.

———. 1983. *Humanists and Holy Writ: New Testament Scholarship in the Renaissance.* Princeton: Princeton University Press.

———. 1987. *Politics and Culture in Renaissance Naples.* Princeton: Princeton University Press.

Benzing, Josef. 1950. "Johann Albin zu Mainz als Reichsdrucker (1598–1620)." *Gutenberg-Jahrbuch* 1950:209–13.

———. 1956. *Ulrich von Hutten und seine Drucker.* Wiesbaden: Otto Harrassowitz.

———. 1982. *Die Buchdrucker des 16. und 17. Jahrhunderts im deutschen Sprachgebiet.* 2d ed. Wiesbaden: Otto Harrassowitz.

Bergin, Thomas G. 1965. *Dante.* New York: Orion Press.

Berkowitz, David Sandler. 1968. *In Remembrance of*

Creation: Evolution of Art and Scholarship in the Medieval and Renaissance Bible. Waltham, Mass.: Brandeis University Press.

Betz, Hans Dieter, ed. 1981. Gerhard Ebeling, James Barr, and Paul Ricoeur. *The Bible as a Document of the University.* Chico, Calif.: Scholars Press.

Beutenmüller, Otto. 1960. *Vorläufiges Verzeichnis der Melanchthon-Drucke des 16. Jahrhunderts.* Halle: Staatliches Melanchthonkommittee der DDR.

Bicknell, Edward J. 1947. *A Theological Introduction to the Thirty-nine Articles of the Church of England.* London: Longmans, 1961.

Bigliazzi, Luciana, Angela Dillon Bussi, and Giancarlo Savino. 1994. *Aldo Manuzio tipografo 1494–1515.* Florence: Biblioteca Medicea Laurenziana, Biblioteca Nazionale Centrale.

Bishop, Morris, ed. and trans. 1966. *Letters from Petrarch.* Bloomington: Indiana University Press.

Bizer, Ernst. 1958. *Fides ex auditu: Eine Untersuchung über die Entdeckung der Gerechtigkeit Gottes durch Martin Luther.* Neukirchen Kreis Moers: Verlag der Buchhandlung des Erziehungsvereins.

Blanke, Fritz, and Immanuel Leuschner. 1990. *Heinrich Bullinger: Vater der reformierten Kirche.* Zurich: Theologischer Verlag.

Blankenberg, Walter. 1962. "Luther, Martin." In *Musik in Geschichte und Gegenwart,* 8:1344–46. Edited by Friedrich Blume. 17 vols. Kassel: Bärenreiter Verlag, 1949–79.

Blau, Joseph Leon. 1944. *The Christian Interpretation of the Cabala in the Renaissance.* New York: Columbia University Press.

Bloch, Joshua. [1933] 1976. "Venetian Printers of Hebrew Books." Reprinted in *Hebrew Printing and Bibliography,* 65–88. Edited by Charles Berlin. New York: New York Public Library and KTAV Publishing House, 1976.

Bludau, August. 1902. *Die beiden ersten Erasmus-Ausgaben des Neuen Testaments und ihre Gegner.* Freiburg: Herder.

Bluhm, Heinz. 1984. *Luther Translator of Paul: Studies in Romans and Galatians.* New York: Peter Lang.

Bohatcová, Mirjam. 1992. "Die Kralitzer Bibel (1579–1594) — die Bibel der böhmischen Reformation." *Gutenberg-Jahrbuch* 67:238–53.

Bornkamm, Heinrich. 1969. *Luther and the Old Testament.* Translated by Eric W. Gritsch and Ruth C. Gritsch. Philadelphia: Fortress Press.

Bowersock, Glen W. 1993. *Hellenism in Late Antiquity.* Thomas Spencer Jerome Lectures. Ann Arbor: University of Michigan Press.

Brady, Thomas A., Jr., Heiko A. Oberman, and James D. Tracy, eds. 1994– . *Handbook of European History, 1400–1600: Late Middle Ages, Renaissance and Reformation.* Leiden: E. J. Brill.

Branner, Robert. 1977. *Manuscript Painting in Paris During the Reign of Saint Louis.* Berkeley: University of California Press.

Brod, Max. 1965. *Johannes Reuchlin und sein Kampf.* Stuttgart: Kohlhammer.

Brower, Reuben A., ed. 1959. *On Translation.* Cambridge: Harvard University Press.

Brown, Peter. 1967. *Augustine of Hippo: A Biography.* London: Faber and Faber.

Bruce, Frederick Fyvie. 1978. *History of the Bible in English.* 3d ed. New York: Oxford University Press.

Bruin, C. C. 1937. *De Statenbijbel en zijn voorgangers.* Leiden: A. W. Sijthoff.

Bruinsma, Henry A. 1962. "Calvinistische Musik." In *Musik in Geschichte und Gegenwart* 2:666–74. Edited by Friedrich Blume. 17 vols. Kassel: Bärenreiter Verlag, 1949–79.

Bruns, Gerald L. 1992. *Hermeneutics Ancient and Modern.* New Haven: Yale University Press.

Bunte, Wolfgang. 1994. *Rabbinische Traditionen bei Nikolaus von Lyra.* Frankfurt: Peter Lang.

Burckhardt, Jacob. [1929] 1958. *The Civilization of the Renaissance in Italy.* Translated by S. G. C. Middlemore. New York: Harper Torchbooks.

Burmeister, Karl Heinz. 1970. "Johannes Campensis und Sebastian Münster: Ihre Stellung in der Geschichte der hebräischen Sprachstudien." *Ephemerides Theologicae Lovanienses* 46:441–60.

Butterworth, Charles. 1941. *The Literary Lineage of the King James Bible, 1340–1611.* Philadelphia: University of Pennsylvania Press.

Cameron, Keith, Kathleen M. Hall, and Francis Higman, eds. 1967. Théodore de Bèze. *Abraham Sacrifiant.* Geneva: Droz.

Cammelli, Giuseppe. 1954. *Demetrio Calcondila.*

Florence: Felice le Monnier.

Carleton, James G. 1902. *The Part of Rheims in the Making of the English Bible.* Oxford: Clarendon Press.

Celenza, Christopher S. 1994. "Renaissance Humanism and the New Testament: Lorenzo Valla's Annotations to the Vulgate." *Journal of Medieval and Renaissance Studies* 24:33–52.

Chadwick, Henry. 1981. *Boethius: The Consolations of Music, Logic, Theology and Philosophy.* Oxford: Clarendon Press.

Chambers, Bettye Thomas. 1983. *Bibliography of French Bibles: Fifteenth- and Sixteenth-Century French-Language Editions of the Scriptures.* Geneva: Droz.

Chazelle, Celia M. 1992–93. "Images, Scripture, the Church, and the Libri Carolini." *Proceedings of the PMR Conference,* 16/17:53–76. Villanova, Pa.: Augustinian Historical Institute.

Chenu, M.-D. 1964. *Toward Understanding Saint Thomas.* Translated by A. M. Landry and D. Hughes. Chicago: Henry Regnery.

Christensen, Carl C. 1979. *Art and the Reformation in Germany.* Athens, Ohio, and Detroit: Ohio University Press and Wayne State University Press.

Coleman, Christopher Bush, ed. and trans. 1922. Lorenzo Valla. *On the Donation of Constantine.* New Haven: Yale University Press.

Copinger, W. A. 1897. *The Bible and Its Transmission.* London: Henry Sotheran.

Cranz, Ferdinand Edward. 1971. *A Bibliography of Aristotle Editions, 1501–1600.* Baden-Baden: Koerner.

Daniell, David, ed. 1989. *Tyndale's New Testament.* New Haven: Yale University Press.

———. 1992. *Tyndale's Old Testament: Being the Pentateuch of 1530, Joshua to 2 Chronicles of 1537, and Jonah.* New Haven: Yale University Press.

———. 1994. *William Tyndale: A Biography.* New Haven: Yale University Press.

De Hamel, Christopher. 1984. *Glossed Books of the Bible and the Origins of the Paris Booktrade.* Woodbridge, Suffolk: Boydell and Brewer.

De Jonge, H. J., ed. 1983. Erasmus. *Apologia.* In *Opera omnia,* 9/2. Amsterdam: North Holland Publishers, 1983. Introduction by H. J. de Jonge, 3–56.

Denifle, Heinrich. 1888. "Die Handschriften der Bibel-Correctorien des 13. Jahrhunderts." *Archiv für Literatur- und Kirchengeschichte des Mittelalters* 4:261–311, 471–601.

———. 1905. *Die abendländischen Schriftausleger bis Luther über Justitia Dei (Röm. 1,17) und Justificatio.* Mainz: F. Kirchheim.

Denzinger, Heinrich, and Adolf Schönmetzer, eds. 1963. *Enchiridion symbolorum definitionum et declarationum de rebus fidei et morum.* 32d ed. Freiburg: Herder.

Diestel, Ludwig. 1869. *Geschichte des Alten Testaments in der christlichen Kirche.* Jena: Mauke.

Dilthey, Wilhelm. 1964. *Weltanschauung und Analyse des Menschen seit Renaissance und Reformation.* 7th ed. Stuttgart: B. G. Teubner Verlagsgesellschaft.

Douen, O. 1878–79. *Clément Marot et le Psautier Huguenot.* 2 vols. Paris: Imprimerie nationale.

Dowley, Tim, ed. 1977. *Eerdmans' Handbook to the History of Christianity.* Grand Rapids: Wm. B. Eerdmans.

Drewniak, Franz [Leander]. 1934. *Die mariologische Deutung von Gen. 3:15 in der Väterzeit.* Breslau: R. Nischowsky.

Duke, Alastair. 1990. *Reformation and Revolt in the Low Countries.* London: Hambledon Press.

Durantel, J. 1919. *S. Thomas et le Pseudo-Denys.* Paris: Libraire Félix Alcan.

Ebeling, Gerhard. 1942. *Evangelische Evangelienauslegung: Eine Untersuchung zu Luthers Hermeneutik.* Munich: Albert Lemp.

Eichenberger, Walter, and Hennig Wendland. 1977. *Deutsche Bibeln vor Luther.* Hamburg: Friedrich Wittig.

Elert, Werner. 1962. *The Structure of Lutheranism.* Translated by Walter A. Hansen. Foreword by Jaroslav Pelikan. Saint Louis: Concordia Publishing House.

Elton, G. R., ed. 1962. *The New Cambridge Modern History,* vol. 2: *The Reformation, 1520–1559.* Cambridge: Cambridge University Press.

Engammare, Max. 1991. "Cinquante ans de révisions de la traduction biblique d'Olivétan: Les Bibles réformées genevoises en français au XVIᵉ siècle." *Bibliotheque d'Humanisme et Renaissance* 53(2):347–77.

Farner, Oskar. 1946. *Huldrych Zwingli: Seine Entwicklung zum Reformator 1506–1520.* Zurich: Zwingli-Verlag.

Feld, M. D. 1982. "Sweynehym and Pannartz, Cardinal Bessarion, Neoplatonism: Renaissance Humanism and Two Early Printers' Choice of Texts." *Harvard Library Bulletin* 30(3):282–335.

———. 1985. "A Theory of the Early Italian Printing Firm, I: Variants of Humanism." *Harvard Library Bulletin* 33(4):341–77.

Field, Frededrick, ed. 1875. *Origenis Hexaplorum quae supersunt.* 2 vols. Oxford: Clarendon Press.

Fletcher, Harris Francis. 1926. *Milton's Semitic Studies and Some Manifestations of Them in His Poetry.* Chicago: University of Chicago Press.

Fraenkel, Pierre. 1977. *De l'écriture à la disputé? Le cas de l'Académie de Genève sous Théodore de Bèze.* Lausanne: Revue de théologie et de philosophie.

Frankish, C. R., ed. [1550] 1969. Théodore de Bèze. *Abraham Sacrifiant.* New York: Johnson Reprint.

Franz, Gunther. 1988. "Die Schicksale der Trierer Gutenbergbibeln." *Gutenberg-Jahrbuch* 63:22–42.

Fristedt, Sven L. 1953–73. *Wycliffe Bible.* 3 parts. Stockholm Studies in English 4, 21, 28. Stockholm: Alquist and Wiksells.

Fueter, Eduard. 1911. *Geschichte der neueren Historiographie.* Munich: R. Oldenbourg.

Gaeta, Franco. 1955. *Lorenzo Valla: Filologia e storia nell'umanesimo italiano.* Naples: Istituto Italiano per gli Studi Storici.

Galden, Joseph A. 1975. *Typology and Seventeenth-Century Literature.* The Hague: Mouton.

Gameson, Richard, ed. 1994. *The Early Medieval Bible: Its Production, Decoration and Use.* Cambridge: Cambridge University Press.

Garside, Charles. 1966. *Zwingli and the Arts.* New Haven: Yale University Press.

Geanakoplos, Deno J. 1962. *Byzantium and the Renaissance: Greek Scholars in Venice.* Cambridge: Harvard University Press.

Gehman, Henry Snyder. 1938. "Milton's Use of Hebrew in the *De Doctrina Christiana.*" *Jewish Quarterly Review* N.S. 29:37–44.

Geiger, Ludwig. [1871] 1964. *Johann Reuchlin: Sein Leben und seine Werke.* Reprint, Nieuwkoop: B. de Graaf.

Geisendorf, Paul. F. 1949. *Théodore de Bèze.* Geneva: Labor et fides.

Geldner, Ferdinand. 1982. "Amerbach-Studien." *Archiv für Geschichte des Buchwesens* 23:684–88.

Gibson, Margaret T. 1993. *The Bible in the Latin West.* Notre Dame: University of Notre Dame Press.

Gistelinck, Frans, and Maurits Sabbe. 1994. *Early Sixteenth Century Printed Books 1501–1540 in the Library of the Leuven Faculty of Theology.* Louvain: Peeters.

Giustiniani, Vito R. 1979. "Plutarch und die humanistische Ethik." In *Ethik im Humanismus,* 45–62. Edited by Walter Rüegg and Dieter Wuttke. Boppard: Harald Boldt.

Glunz, Hans H. 1930. *Britannien und Bibeltext: Der Vulgatatext der Evangelien in seinem Verhältnis zur irisch-angelsächsischen Kultur des Frühmittelalters.* Leipzig: Bernhard Tauchnitz.

———. 1933. *History of the Vulgate in England from Alcuin to Roger Bacon: Being an Inquiry into the Text of Some English Manuscripts of the Vulgate Gospels.* Cambridge: Cambridge University Press.

Goshen-Gottstein, Moshe, ed. 1972. *Biblia Rabbinica: A Reprint of the 1525 Venice Edition.* 4 vols. Jerusalem: Makor.

Grafton, Anthony. 1981. "Epilogue: Boethius in the Renaissance." In *Boethius: His Life, Thought, and Influence,* 410–15. Edited by Margaret Gibson. Oxford: Blackwell.

Grafton, Anthony, ed. 1993. *Rome Reborn: The Vatican Library and Renaissance Culture.* Washington and New Haven: Library of Congress and Yale University Press.

Grane, Leif. 1975. *Modus loquendi theologicus: Luthers Kampf um die Erneuerung der Theologie (1515–1518).* Leiden: E. J. Brill.

Greenslade, Samuel L. 1963. *The Cambridge History of the Bible,* vol. 3: *The West from the Reformation to the Present Day.* Cambridge: Cambridge University Press.

Greive, Hermann. 1978. "Die hebräische Grammatik Johannes Reuchlins." *Zeitschrift für die alttestamentliche Wissenschaft* 90:395–409.

Guerra, Anna Morisi. 1990. "Santi Pagnini traducteur de la Bible." In *Théorie et pratique de l'exégèse,* 191–98. Edited by Irena Backus and Francis Higman. Geneva: Droz.

Guggisberg, Hans R. 1992. "Castellio auf dem Index (1551–1596)." *Archiv für Reformationsgeschichte* 83:112–29.

Hagen, Kenneth. 1990. "'De Exegetica Methodo': Niels Hemmingsen's *De Methodis* (1555)." In *The Bible in the Sixteenth Century*, 181–96. Edited by David C. Steinmetz. Durham: Duke University Press.

Hailperin, Herman. 1963. *Rashi and the Christian Scholars*. Pittsburgh: University of Pittsburgh Press.

Hall, Basil. 1995. "The Genevan Version of the English Bible: Its Aims and Achievements." In *The Bible, the Reformation and the Church: Essays in Honor of James Atkinson*, 124–49. Edited by W. P. Stephens. Sheffield, England: Sheffield Academic Press.

Hall, Edwin. 1991. *Sweynheym and Pannartz and the Origins of Printing in Italy: German Technology and Italian Humanism in Renaissance Rome*. McMinnville, Oreg.: Bird and Bull Press for Phillip J. Pirages.

Hallersleben, Barbara. 1984. "Thomas de Vio Cajetan." In *Katholische Theologen der Reformationszeit*, 1:11–25. Edited by Erwin Iserloh. Münster: Aschendorff.

Hampe, Theodor. 1907–50. "Amman, Jobst." In *Allgemeines Lexikon der bildenden Künste*, 1:410–13. Edited by Ulrich Thieme and Felix Becker. 37 vols. Leipzig: Seemann.

Hankins, James. 1990. *Plato in the Italian Renaissance*. Leiden: E. J. Brill.

Hargreaves, Henry. 1979. "Popularising Biblical Scholarship: The Role of the Wycliffite *Glossed Gospels*." In *The Bible and Medieval Culture*, 171–89. Edited by W. Lourdaux and D. Verhelst. Louvain: Leuven University Press.

Harlfinger, Dieter, ed. 1989. *Graecogermania: Griechischstudien deutscher Humanisten*. Weinheim: Acta Humaniora.

Harnack, Adolf von. 1905. [*Grundriß der*] Dogmengeschichte. Tübingen: J. C. B. Mohr (Paul Siebeck).

Harvard College Library. 1983. *Luther, 1483–1546: An Exhibition at the Houghton Library*. Cambridge: Harvard University Press.

Hauben, Paul J. 1967. *Three Spanish Heretics and the Reformation*. Geneva: Droz.

Headley, John M. 1963. *Luther's View of Church History*. New Haven: Yale University Press.

Hefele, Carl Joseph. [1851] 1968. *Der Cardinal Ximenes*. Reprint, Frankfurt: Minerva.

Hill, Christopher. 1993. *The English Bible and the Seventeenth-Century Revolution*. London: Penguin Press.

Hind, Arthur M. 1955. *Engraving in England in the Sixteenth and Seventeenth Centuries*. 3 vols. Cambridge: Cambridge University Press.

Holl, Karl. [1918] 1959. *The Cultural Significance of the Reformation*. Translated by Karl Hertz, Barbara Hertz, and John H. Lichtblau. Introduction by Wilhelm Pauck. New York: Meridian Books.

———. [1920] 1948. "Luthers Bedeutung für den Fortschritt der Auslegungskunst." *Gesammelte Aufsätze zur Kirchengeschichte*, 1, *Luther*, 544-82. 7th ed. Tübingen: J. C. B. Mohr (Paul Siebeck).

Idel, Moshe. 1988. *Kabbalah: New Perspectives*. New Haven: Yale University Press.

The Illustrated Bartsch. 1978– . General editors, Walter L. Strauss and John T. Spike. New York: Abaris Books.

Ing, Janet Thompson. 1988. *Johannes Gutenberg and His Bible*. New York: Typophiles.

Jacob, Walter. 1939. "Bemerkungen zu Ausgaben theologischer Texte vom XVI. bis zum XIX. Jahrhundert." *Zeitschrift für die neutestamentliche Wissenschaft und die Kunde der älteren Kirche* 38:191–96.

Jakubec, Jan. 1929–34. *Dějiny literatury české*. 2 vols. Prague: Nákladem Jana Laichtera.

James, William. [1902] 1990. *The Varieties of Religious Experience*. Introduction by Jaroslav Pelikan. New York: Vintage Books.

Jay, Pierre. 1982. "La datation des premières traductions de l'Ancient Testament sur l'hébreu par saint Jérôme." *Revue des études Augustiniennes* 28:208-12.

Jedin, Hubert. 1961. *History of the Council of Trent*, vol. 2: *The First Sessions at Trent, 1545–47*. Translated by Ernest Graf. London: Nelson.

Jeffrey, David, ed. 1992. *A Dictionary of Biblical Tradition in English Literature*. Grand Rapids: Wm. B. Eerdmans.

Jenny, Marcus. 1983a. *Luthers Gesangbuch*. In *Leben und Werk Martin Luthers von 1526 bis 1546: Festgabe zu seinem 500. Geburtstag*, 1:303–19. Edited by Helmar Junghans. 2 vols. Göttingen: Vandenhoeck und Ruprecht.

———. 1983b. *Luther, Zwingli, Calvin in ihren Liedern*. Zurich: Theologischer Verlag.

———. 1985. *Luthers Geistliche Lieder und Kirchengesänge. Vollständige Neuedition in Ergänzung zu Band 35 der Weimarer Ausgabe.* Cologne: Böhlau.

Jones, G. Lloyd. 1983. "Introduction." Johann Reuchlin. *On the Art of the Kabbalah.* Translated by Martin Goodman and Sarah Goodman. New York: Abaris Books.

Julian, John, ed. [1907] 1957. *A Dictionary of Hymnology.* Reprint edition in 2 vols. New York: Dover Publications.

Kavka, František, ed. 1964. *Stručné dějiny University Karlovy.* Prague: Universita Karlova.

Kelly, J. N. D. 1975. *Jerome: His Life, Times, and Controversies.* London: Gerald Duckworth.

Kinder, A. Gordon. 1975. *Cassiodora de Reina: Spanish Reformer of the Sixteenth Century.* London: Tamesis Books.

Klibansky, Raymond. 1939. *The Continuity of the Platonic Tradition During the Middle Ages: Outlines of a "Corpus platonicum medii aevi."* London: Warburg Institute.

Kneller, C. A. 1928. "Die Bibelbulle Sixtus V." *Zeitschrift für katholische Theologie* 52:202–24.

Koepplin, Dieter, and Tilman Falk. 1974–76. *Lukas Cranach: Gemälde, Zeichnungen, Druckgraphik.* 2 vols. Basel: Birkhäuser Verlag.

Köhler, Walther. 1917. *Wie Luther den Deutschen das Leben Jesu erzählt hat.* Leipzig: Verein für Reformationsgeschichte.

Kraeling, Emil. 1955. *The Old Testament since the Reformation.* New York: Harper and Brothers.

Kraus, H. J. 1969. *Geschichte der historisch-kritischen Erforschung des Alten Testaments.* 2d ed. Neukirchen: Neukirchener Verlag.

Krause, Carl. 1879. *Helius Eobanus Hessus.* 2 vols. Gotha: Friedrich Andreas Perthes.

Kristeller, Paul Oskar. 1961. *Renaissance Thought: The Classic, Scholastic, and Humanist Strains.* New York: Harper Torchbooks.

———. 1974–76. *Humanismus und Renaissance.* 2 vols. Munich: Wilhelm Fink.

Kukenheim, Louis. 1932. *Contributions à l'histoire de la grammaire italienne, espagnole et française à l'époque de la Renaissance.* Amsterdam: Noord-Hollandsche Uitgevers-Maatschappij.

———. 1951. *Contributions à l'histoire de la grammaire grecque, latine et hébraique à l'époque de la Renaissance.* Leiden: E. J. Brill.

Kurrelmeyer, William. 1904–15. *Die erste deutsche Bibel.* 10 vols. Stuttgart: Litterarischer Verein.

Kuttner, Stephen. 1979. "Die Reform der Kirche und das Trienter Konzil." In *Concilium Tridentinum,* 123–42. Edited by Remigius Baumer. Darmstadt: Wissenschaftliche Buchgesellschaft.

Lampe, Geoffrey W. H. 1969. *The Cambridge History of the Bible,* vol. 2: *The West from the Fathers to the Reformation.* Cambridge: Cambridge University Press.

Lawton, David A. 1990. *Faith, Text, and History: The Bible in English.* Charlottesville: University Press of Virginia.

Le Bachelet, Xavier-Marie. 1911. *Bellarmin et la Bible Sixto-Clementine: Etude et documents inédits.* Paris: Beauchesne.

Leclercq, Jean. 1962. *The Love of Learning and the Desire for God: A Study of Monastic Culture.* Translated by Catharine Misrahi. Mentor Omega edition. New York: New American Library.

Lerch, David. 1950. *Isaaks Opferung christlich gedeutet.* Tübingen: J. C. B. Mohr (Paul Siebeck).

Lowry, Martin. 1979. *The World of Aldus Manutius.* Ithaca: Cornell University Press.

Lubac, Henri de. 1959–64. *Exégèse médiévale: Les quatre sens de l'Ecriture.* 2 vols. in 4. Paris: Aubier.

Lyell, James Patrick Ronaldson. 1917. *Cardinal Ximenes.* London: Grafton.

Malin, William Gunn. 1881. *Catalogue of Books Relating to, or Illustrating the History of the Unitas Fratrum, or United Brethren.* Philadelphia: Collins.

Matěsíc, Josip, ed. 1993. *Matthias Flacius Illyricus: Leben und Werk.* Munich: Südosteuropa-Gesellschaft.

Mathiesen, Robert. 1985. *The Great Polyglot Bibles.* Providence: John Carter Brown Library.

Matter, E. Ann. 1990. *The Voice of My Beloved: The Song of Songs in Western Medieval Christianity.* Philadelphia: University of Pennsylvania Press.

McComish, William A. 1989. *The Epigones: A Study of the Theology of the Genevan Academy at the Time of the Synod of Dort, with Special Reference to Giovanni Diodati.* Allison Park, Pa.: Pickwick Publications.

McNeill, John Thomas. 1954. *The History and Character of Calvinism.* New York: Oxford University Press.

Meinhold, Peter. 1936. *Die Genesisvorlesung Luthers und ihre Herausgeber.* Stuttgart: W. Kohlhammer.

Melanchthon, Philipp. 1951–75. *Werke in Auswahl.* 6 vols. Edited by Robert Stupperich. Gütersloh: C. Bertelsmann.

———. 1993. *Loci Communes 1521.* Translated by Horst Georg Pöhlmann. Gütersloh: Gütersloher Verlagshaus.

Merkel, Helmut. 1971. *Die Widersprüche zwischen den Evangelien: Ihre polemische und apologetische Behandlung in der alten Kirche bis zu Augustin.* Tübingen: J. C. B. Mohr (Paul Siebeck).

Merrill, Eugene H. 1975. "Rashi, Nicholas de Lyra, and Christian Exegesis." *Westminster Theological Journal* 38:66–79.

Metzger, Bruce M. 1968. *The Text of the New Testament.* 2d ed. New York: Oxford University Press.

Metzger, Bruce M., Robert C. Dentan, and Walter Harrelson. 1991. *The Making of the New Revised Standard Version of the Bible.* Grand Rapids: Wm. B. Eerdmans.

Michel, Otto. 1972. *Paulus und seine Bibel.* Reprint, Darmstadt: Wissenschaftliche Buchgesellschaft.

Miller, Perry. 1961. *The New England Mind.* Beacon Paperback edition. Boston: Beacon Press.

Mirbt, Carl, ed. 1924. *Quellen zur Geschichte des Papsttums und des römischen Katholizismus.* 4th ed. Tübingen: J. C. B. Mohr (Paul Siebeck).

Mirković, Mijo. 1980. *Matija Vlačić Ilirik.* 2 vols. Pula: Rijeka.

Moldaenke, Günter. 1936. *Schriftverständnis und Schriftdeutung im Zeitalter der Reformation.* Stuttgart: W. Kohlhammer.

Morgan, Paul. 1990. "A King's Printer at Work: Two Documents of Robert Barker." *Bodleian Library Record* 13(5):370–74.

Mortimer, Ruth, comp. 1964. *Harvard Library Department of Printing and Graphic Arts: Catalogue of Books and Manuscripts.* Part 1: French Sixteenth Century Books. 2 vols. Cambridge: Belknap Press of Harvard University Press.

———. 1974. *Harvard Library Department of Printing and Graphic Arts: Catalogue of Books and Manuscripts.* Part 2: Italian Sixteenth Century Books. 2 vols. Cambridge: Belknap Press of Harvard University Press.

Mozley, James F. 1953. *Coverdale and His Bibles.* London: Lutterworth Press.

Murphy, Lawrence. 1983. "The Sixtine Bible of 1590." *American Book Collector* 4(6):11–20.

Needham, Paul. 1985. "The Paper Supply of the Gutenberg Bible." *Papers of the Bibliographical Society of America* 79:303–74.

Newman, Barclay M. 1981. "Translation and Interpretation: A Few Notes on the King James Version." *Bible Translator* 32(4):437–40.

Newman, John Henry, ed. 1841–45. Thomas Aquinas. *Catena aurea.* 3 parts. Oxford: John Henry Parker. Preface by John Henry Newman, 1:i–xiii.

Nixon, Leroy, ed. 1953. John Calvin. *The Gospel According to Isaiah: Seven Sermons on Isaiah 53 Concerning the Passion and Death of Christ.* Grand Rapids: Wm. B. Eerdmans.

Norton, F. J. 1958. *Italian Printers, 1501–1520.* London: Bowes and Bowes.

———. 1978. *A Descriptive Catalog of Printing in Spain and Portugal, 1501–1520.* Cambridge: Cambridge University Press.

Oberman, Heiko Augustinus. 1963. *The Harvest of Medieval Theology: Gabriel Biel and Late Medieval Nominalism.* Cambridge: Harvard University Press.

———. 1975. "'Tuus sum, salvum fac me.' Augustinréveil zwischen Renaissance und Reformation." In *Scientia augustiniana,* 348–94. Festschrift für Adolar Zumkeller. Edited by Cornelius Petrus Mayer and Willigis Eckermann. Würzburg: Augustinus Verlag.

———. 1977. *Werden und Wertung der Reformation: Vom Wegestreit zum Glaubenskampf.* Tübingen: J. C. B. Mohr (Paul Siebeck).

———. 1992. "The Discovery of Hebrew and Discrimination Against the Jews: The Veritas Hebraica as Double-Edged Sword in Renaissance and Reformation." In *Germania Illustrata: Essays on Early Modern Germany Presented to Gerald Strauss,* 19–34. Edited by Andrew C. Fix and Susan C. Karant-Nunn. Kirksville, Mo.: Sixteenth Century Essays and Studies.

———. 1994. *The Reformation: Roots and Ramifications.* Translated by Andrew Colin Gow. Grand Rapids: Wm. B. Eerdmans.

Oberman, Heiko Augustinus, and Frank A. James, III, eds. 1991. *Via Augustini: Augustine in the Later Middle Ages, Renaissance and Reformation.* Leiden: E. J. Brill.

Olin, John C. 1990. *Catholic Reform from Cardinal Ximenes to the Council of Trent, 1495–1563.* New York: Fordham University Press.

Olson, Oliver. 1990. "The *Clavis Scripturae sacrae* of Matthias Flacius Illyricus." In *Théorie et pratique de l'exégèse,* 167–75. Edited by Irena Backus and Francis Higman. Geneva: Droz.

O'Malley, John W. 1993. *The First Jesuits.* Cambridge: Harvard University Press.

Oppermann, Andreas. 1875. *Ernst Rietschel, the Sculptor: And the Lessons of His Life.* Translated by J. Sturge. London: Hodder and Stoughton.

Pani, Giancarlo. 1990. "Un centenaire rappeler: L'édition sixtine des Septante." In *Théorie et pratique de l'exégèse,* 413–28. Edited by Irena Bakus and Francis Higman. Geneva: Droz.

Panofsky, Erwin. 1955. *The Life and Art of Albrecht Dürer.* Princeton: Princeton University Press.

Parker, T. H. L. 1971. *Calvin's New Testament Commentaries.* London: S. C. M. Press.

Patch, Howard Rollin. 1935. *The Tradition of Boethius.* New York: Oxford University Press.

Pauck, Wilhelm. 1939. "Nationalism and European Christianity." In *Environmental Factors in Christian History,* 286–303. Edited by John T. McNeill, Matthew Spinka, and Harold R. Willoughby. Chicago: University of Chicago Press.

Pelikan, Jaroslav. 1946. "The Bible of Kralice." B.D. thesis, Concordia Theological Seminary, Saint Louis.

———. 1959. *Luther the Expositor.* Saint Louis: Concordia Publishing House.

———. 1971–89. *The Christian Tradition: A History of the Development of Doctrine.* 5 vols. Chicago: University of Chicago Press.

———. 1974. "The Doctrine of Filioque in Thomas Aquinas and Its Patristic Antecedents: An Analysis of *Summa Theologiae,* Part I, Question 36." *Saint Thomas Aquinas 1274/1974: Commemorative Studies,* 1:315–36. Edited by Armand A. Maurer. 2 vols. Toronto: Pontifical Institute of Mediaeval Studies.

———. 1986. *Bach Among the Theologians.* Philadelphia: Fortress Press.

———. 1990a. *Imago Dei: The Byzantine Apologia for Icons.* The Andrew W. Mellon Lectures for 1987 at the National Gallery of Art. Princeton and London: Princeton University Press and Yale University Press.

———. 1990b. "*Canonica Regula:* The Trinitarian Hermeneutics of Augustine." In *Proceedings of the PMR Conference,* 12/13 (1987–88): 17–30; *Collectanea Augustiniana,* I: *Augustine: "Second Founder of the Faith,"* 329–43. Edited by Joseph C. Schnaubelt and Frederick Van Fleteren. New York: Peter Lang.

———. 1993. *Christianity and Classical Culture: The Metamorphosis of Natural Theology in the Christian Encounter with Hellenism.* The Gifford Lectures at Aberdeen for 1992 and 1993. New Haven: Yale University Press.

Petzoldt, Martin, ed. 1985. *Bach als Ausleger der Bibel: Theologische und musikwissenschaftliche Studien zum Werk Johann Sebastian Bachs.* Göttingen: Vandenhoeck und Ruprecht.

Pierpont Morgan Library. 1947. *The Bible: Manuscript and Printed Bibles from the Fourth to the Nineteenth Century.* Illustrated Catalogue of an Exhibition December 1, 1947, to April 30, 1948. Foreword by Curt F. Bühler. New York: Pierpont Morgan Library.

Pitkin, Barbara. 1993. "David as Paradigm for Faith in Calvin's Psalm Exegesis." *Sixteenth Century Journal* 24(4):843–63.

Pope, Marvin H. 1977. *Song of Songs: A New Translation with Introduction and Commentary.* The Anchor Bible. Garden City: Doubleday.

Powicke, Maurice. 1961. *The Reformation in England.* Paperback edition. London: Oxford University Press.

Price, David. 1994. "Albrecht Dürer's Representations of Faith: The Church, Lay Devotion and Veneration in the *Apocalypse.*" *Zeitschrift für Kunstgeschichte* 57(4):688–96.

Proctor, Robert. [1900] 1966. *The Printing of Greek in the Fifteenth Century.* Reprint, Hildesheim: Georg Olms.

Le Psautier de Genève, 1562–1865. 1986. Geneva: Bibliothèque publique et universitaire.

Quasten, Johannes. 1983. *Music and Worship in Pagan and Christian Antiquity*. Translated by Boniface Ramsey. Washington: National Association of Pastoral Musicians.

Rabil, Albert. 1972. *Erasmus and the New Testament*. San Antonio: Trinity University Press.

Raeder, Siegfried. 1983. "Luther als Ausleger und Übersetzer der Heiligen Schrift." In *Leben und Werk Martin Luthers von 1526 bis 1546: Festgabe zu seinem 500. Geburtstag*, 1:253–78, 2:800–805. Edited by Helmar Junghans. 2 vols. Göttingen: Vandenhoeck und Ruprecht.

Reicke, Bo. 1966. "Erasmus und die neutestamentliche Textgeschichte." *Theologische Zeitschrift* 22:254–65.

Reinitzer, Heimo. 1983. *Biblia deutsch: Luthers Bibelübersetzung und ihre Tradition*. Wolfenbüttel: Herzog August Bibliothek.

———. 1987. "Oberdeutsche Bibeldrucke." *Die deutsche Literatur des Mittelalters: Verfasserlexikon* 6:1276–90.

Renouard, A. A. 1825. *Annales de l'imprimerie des Alde*. 2d ed. 3 vols. Paris: Antoine-Augustin Renouard.

———. [1843] 1972. *Annales de l'imprimerie des Estienne*. 2d ed. Reprint, New York: Burt Franklin.

Reu, J. Michael. 1934. *Luther's German Bible*. Columbus, Ohio: Lutheran Book Concern.

———. 1944. *Luther and the Scriptures*. Columbus, Ohio: Wartburg Press.

Reuss, Eduard, ed. 1897. *La Bible française de Calvin*. Paris: Librairie Fischbacher.

Rice, Eugene F., Jr. 1985. *Saint Jerome in the Renaissance*. Baltimore: Johns Hopkins University Press.

Richards, G. C. 1934. *A Concise Dictionary to the Vulgate New Testament*. London: Samuel Bagster and Sons.

Ronda, James P. 1982. "The Bible and Early American Indian Missions." In *The Bible and Social Reform*, 9–30. Edited by E. Sandeen. Philadelphia: Fortress Press.

Rosalia, Antonio de. 1957/58. "La vita de Costantino Lascaris." *Archivio storico siciliano* 3(9):21–70.

Rummel, Erika. 1985. *Erasmus as a Translator of the Classics*. Toronto: University of Toronto Press.

———. 1986. *Erasmus' Annotations on the New Testament*. Toronto: University of Toronto Press.

Ruppel, Aloys. 1937. *Peter Schöffer aus Gernsheim*. Mainz: Gutenberg-Gesellschaft.

———. 1967. *Johannes Gutenberg: Sein Leben und sein Werk*. 3d ed. Nieuwkoop: B. de Graaf.

Schellong, D. 1969. *Calvins Auslegung der synoptischen Evangelien*. Munich: Kaiser.

Schlingensiepen, Hermann. 1929. "Erasmus als Exeget." *Zeitschrift für Kirchengeschichte* 48(1):16–57.

Schmidt, Philipp. 1962. *Die Illustration der Lutherbibel 1522–1700*. Basel: Friedrich Reinhardt.

Schmitt, Charles B. 1979. "Aristotle's Ethics in the Sixteenth Century: Some Preliminary Considerations." In *Ethik im Humanismus*, 87–112. Edited by Walter Rüegg and Dieter Wuttke. Boppard: Harald Boldt.

———. 1983. *Aristotle and the Renaissance*. Cambridge: Harvard University Press.

Schmoller, Otto, and Alfred Schmoller. 1949. *Handkonkordanz zum griechischen Neuen Testament*. 8th ed. Stuttgart: Privilegierte Württembergische Bibelanstalt.

Schneider, Heinrich. 1954. *Der Text der Gutenbergbibel*. Bonn: Peter Hanstein.

Scholem, Gershom. 1987. "Die Erforschung der Kabbala von Reuchlin bis zur Gegenwart." In Scholem, *Judaica*, 3:247–63. Frankfurt: Suhrkamp.

Schorbach, Karl. 1932. *Der Strassburger Frühdrucker Johann Mentelin (1458–1478): Studien zu seinem Leben und Werke*. Mainz: Gutenberg-Gesellschaft.

Schottenloher, Karl. 1922. *Die liturgischen Druckwerke Erhard Ratdolts aus Augsburg*. Mainz: Gutenberg-Gesellschaft.

Schreiber, Fred. 1982. *The Estiennes: An Annotated Catalogue of Three Hundred Highlights of Their Various Presses*. New York: E. K. Schreiber.

Schubert, Hans von. 1921. *Geschichte der christlichen Kirche im Frühmittelalter*. Tübingen: J. C. B. Mohr (Paul Siebeck).

Schwarz, W. 1955. *Principles and Problems of Biblical Translation*. Cambridge: Cambridge University Press.

Schwiebert, Ernest G. 1950. *Luther and His Times*. Saint Louis: Concordia Publishing House.

Scribner, Robert W. 1981. *For the Sake of Simple Folk: Popular Propaganda for the German Reformation*. Cambridge: Cambridge University Press.

Seebaß, Gottfried. 1971. "Dürers Stellung in der reformatorischen Bewegung." In *Albrecht Dürers Umwelt. Festschrift zum 500. Geburtstag Albrecht Dürers am 21. Mai 1971*, 101–31. Nuremberg: Selbstverlag des Vereins für die Geschichte der Stadt Nürnberg.

Segert, Stanislav. 1994. "Masoretes and Translators — Karaites and Czech Brethren." *Religio: Revue pro religionistiku* 2:131–38.

Setz, Wolfgang, ed. 1976. Lorenzo Valla. *De falso credita et ementita Constantini donatione*. Weimar: Hermann Böhlaus Nachfolger.

Shaheen, Naseeb. 1984. "Misconceptions about the Geneva Bible." *Studies in Bibliography* 37:156–58.

Shapiro, Marianne. 1990. *"De vulgari eloquentia": Dante's Book of Exile*. Lincoln: University of Nebraska Press.

Sheppard, Leslie A. 1935. "The Printers of the Coverdale Bible." *Library* 16(3):280–89.

Shuger, Debora Kuller. 1994. *The Renaissance Bible: Scholarship, Sacrifice, and Subjectivity*. Berkeley: University of California Press.

Sicherl, Martin. 1962. "Neuentdeckte Handschriften von Marsilio Ficino." *Scriptorium* 16:50–61.

———. 1976. *Handschriftliche Vorlagen der Editio princeps des Aristoteles*. Mainz: Akademie der Wissenschaften und der Literatur.

Sims, James H. 1962. *The Bible in Milton's Epics*. Gainesville: University of Florida Press.

Skarsten, Trygve R. 1985. *Sixteenth Century Bibliography: The Scandinavian Reformation: A Bibliographic Guide*. Saint Louis: Center for Reformation Research.

Skehan, Patrick. 1952. "St. Jerome and the Canon of the Holy Scriptures." In *A Monument to St. Jerome*, 257–87. Edited by F. X. Murphy. New York: Sheed and Ward.

Smalley, Beryl. [1952] 1964. *The Study of the Bible in the Middle Ages*. Reprint, Notre Dame: University of Notre Dame Press.

Smolinsky, Heribert. 1984. "Hieronymus Emser (1478–1527)." In *Katholische Theologen der Reformationszeit*, 1:37–46. Edited by Erwin Iserloh. 5 vols. Münster: Aschendorff.

Soulié, Marguerite. 1989. "Le théâtre et la Bible au XVIᵉ siècle." In *Le temps des réformes et la Bible*, 635–58. Edited by Guy Bedouelle and Bernard Roussel. Paris: Beauchesne.

Spicq, C. 1944. *Esquisse d'une histoire de l'exégèse latine au moyen âge*. Paris: C. Vrin.

Spinka, Matthew. 1941. *John Hus and the Czech Reform*. Chicago: University of Chicago Press.

Spitz, Lewis W. 1963. *The Religious Renaissance of the German Humanists*. Cambridge: Harvard University Press.

Staedtke, Joachim. 1972. *Heinrich Bullinger Bibliographie*. 2 vols. Zurich: Theologischer Verlag.

Stegmüller, Friedrich. 1950–61. *Repertorium biblicum medii aevi*. 7 vols. Madrid: Instituto Francisco Suárez.

Steiner, George. 1992. *After Babel: Aspects of Language and Translation*. 2d ed. New York: Oxford University Press.

Steinlein, Hermann. 1912. *Luthers Doktorat: Zum 400 jährigen Jubiläum desselben (18. und 19. Oktober 1912)*. Leipzig: A. Deichert'sche Verlagsbuchhandlung.

Stevenson, Robert. 1949. "John Merbecke and the First English Prayerbook." *Anglican Theological Review* 31:142–52.

Stinger, Charles L. 1977. *Humanism and the Church Fathers: Ambrogio Traversari (1386–1439) and Christian Antiquity in the Italian Renaissance*. Albany: State University of New York Press.

Stolt, Birgit. 1983. "Luthers Übersetzungstheorie und Übersetzungspraxis." In *Leben und Werk Martin Luthers von 1526 bis 1546: Festgabe zu seinem 500. Geburtstag*, 1:241–52, 2:787–800. Edited by Helmar Junghans. 2 vols. Göttingen: Vandenhoeck und Ruprecht.

Stout, Harry S. 1982. "Word and Order in Colonial New England." In *The Bible in America: Essays in Cultural History*, 19–38. Edited by Nathan O. Hatch. New York: Oxford University Press.

Strachen, James. 1957. *Early Bible Illustrations*. Cambridge: Cambridge University Press.

Strand, Kenneth A. 1982. *Catholic German Bibles of the Reformation Era: The Versions of Emser, Dietenberger, Eck, and Others*. Ann Arbor, Mich.: Ann Arbor Publishers.

Street, J. S. 1983. *French Sacred Drama from Bèze to Corneille*. Cambridge: Cambridge University Press.

Swellengrebel, J. L. 1972. "A Portuguese Bible Translator in Java." *Bible Translator* 23(1):126–34.

Tarelli, C. C. 1943. "Erasmus' Manuscripts of the

Gospels." *Journal of Theological Studies* 44:155–62.

Tavard, George. 1959. *Holy Writ or Holy Church*. New York: Harper and Brothers.

Tooker, William W. 1897. "The Significance of John Eliot's Natick." *American Anthropologist* 10:281–87.

Toynbee, Paget. 1965. *Dante Alighieri: His Life and Works*. Edited by Charles S. Singleton. New York: Harper Torchbooks.

Unterlinden, Musée d'. 1991. *Le beau Martin*. Colmar: Musée d'Unterlinden.

Van der Coelen, Peter. 1994. "Illustration and Interpretation in Sixteenth-Century Picture Bibles: Gilles Corrozet's Biblical Picture Books." Précis of lecture at Institut d'Histoire de la Réformation, *Rapport d'Activité 1994*. Geneva: Droz.

Voulliéme, E. 1922. *Die deutschen Drucker des fünfzehnten Jahrhunderts*. Berlin: Reichsdruckerei.

Walsh, James E. 1991–94. *A Catalogue of the Fifteenth-Century Printed Books in the Harvard University Library*. 3 vols. Binghamton: Medieval and Renaissance Texts and Studies.

Wandel, Lee Palmer. 1995. *Voracious Idols and Violent Hands: Iconoclasm in Zurich, Strasbourg, and Basel*. Cambridge: Cambridge University Press.

Waszink, J. H. 1972. "Einige Betrachtungen über die Euripidesübersetzungen." *Antike und Abendland* 17(2):70–90.

Weigle, Luther A., ed. 1961. *The New Testament Octapla: Eight English Versions of the New Testament in the Tyndale–King James Tradition*. New York: Thomas Nelson and Sons.

Weinstein, Donald, and Valerie R. Hotchkiss, eds. 1994. *Girolamo Savonarola: Piety, Prophecy and Politics in Renaissance Florence*. Dallas: Bridwell Library.

Weisheipl, James A. 1974. *Friar Thomas D'Aquino: His Life, Thought, and Work*. New York: Doubleday.

Wengert, Timothy John. 1987. *Philip Melanchthon's "Annotationes in Johannem" in Relation to Its Predecessors*. Geneva: Droz.

Westcott, Brooks Foss. 1905. *A General View of the History of the English Bible*. 3d ed. London: Macmillan.

Wicks, Jared. 1983. *Cajetan und die Anfänge der Reformation*. Münster: Aschendorff.

Wilder, Amos Niven. 1964. *The Language of the Gospel: Early Christian Rhetoric*. New York: Harper and Row.

Williams, George Huntston. 1992. *The Radical Reformation*. 3d ed. Kirksville, Mo.: Sixteenth Century Essays and Studies.

Wilson, N. G. 1973. "Erasmus as Translator of Euripides: Supplementary Notes." *Antike und Abendland* 18:87–89.

Woody, Kennerly M. 1971. "A Note on the Greek Fonts of the Complutensian Polyglot." *Papers of the Bibliographic Society of America* 65:143–49.

Worth, Roland H., Jr. 1992. *Bible Translations: A History Through Source Documents*. Jefferson, N.C.: McFarland.

Wright, John. 1894. *Early Bibles of America*. New York: Thomas Whittaker.

Ziegler, Joseph. 1971. *Sylloge: Gesammelte Aufsätze zur Septuaginta*. Göttingen: Vandenhoeck und Ruprecht.

Zika, Charles. 1977. "Reuchlin and Erasmus: Humanism and Occult Philosophy." *Journal of Religious History* 9:223–46.

Zülch, W. K. 1907–50. "Merian, Matthäus." In *Allgemeines Lexikon der bildenden Künste*, 24:413–14. Edited by Ulrich Thieme and Felix Becker. 37 vols. Leipzig: Seemann.

Zweig, Stefan. 1951. *The Right to Heresy: Castellio Against Calvin*. Boston: Beacon Press.

INDEX OF BIBLICAL PASSAGES

Page numbers in italics refer to illustrations.

Genesis
1 — *130*
2:22 — 145
3:15 — 12
22:1–14 — 67
49:10 — 26

Exodus
3:14 — 18
15:1 — 70
15:21 — 70
20:2–17 — 51

Leviticus
11 — 51

Judges
16 — *142*

Ruth
3:15 — 149

1 Samuel
17 — 67, 71

1 Maccabees
6:16 — 32

Psalms
2:2 — 45
6 — 176
19:4 — 113
22 — 32
22:1 — 31, *110*
22:16 — 19, 20, 31

37:5 — 77
46 — 54, 74, 75, 77, *175*
46:3 — 75
68:15–16 — 43
104:4 — 19
110:3 — 19
111 — 32
118 — *171*

Song of Solomon
1 — *143*

Wisdom
13:5 — 35

Isaiah
7:14 — 19
29:13 — 27
40:8 — 62
53 — 31

Jeremiah
31 — *94*
31:10–34 — *92*
31:33 — 13

Daniel
3 — 69, *170*

Matthew
1 — *4, 140, 190*
1:23 — 19
1:46–48 — *64*
3:2 — 46
4:8–10 — 73

8:17 — 31
10 — 104
11:2–10 — 43
12:40 — 32
15:9 — 27
16 — *127*
16:18 — 28, 55
16:18–20 — 24, *117*
24:36 — 39
27:46 — 31

Mark
8 — *127*
15:34 — 31

Luke
1:46–55 — 74
1:68–79 — 74
2:29–32 — 74
4:5–8 — 73
6 — 33
9 — *127*
17:11–19 — 50, *133*
22:10 — 163
24:35 — 67

John
1 — *111*, 169
1:18 — 39
5:39 — 37
14:28 — 36
15:12 — 166
20:17 — 57, 150
21:6 — 47

Acts of the Apostles
8:26–35 — 31
17:34 — 8
20:28 — 39

Romans
3:28 — 44
4:3 — *172*
10:17 — 35
11:20 — 96
11:36 — 47
12:6 — 35, 37

1 Corinthians
12:3 — 36
14:35 — 48

2 Corinthians
3:15 — 43

Galatians
4:24 — 33

Ephesians
5:32 — 30

Colossians
2:9 — 38
3:16 — 76

2 Thessalonians
2:3–12 — 68

1 Timothy
3:16 — 39

Hebrews

1:7 — 19

8:10 — 13

1 Peter

2 — 48

2:21–25 — 31

3:15 — 38

1 John

5:1 — *102*

5:7 — 17, 39, 51, 61

5:7–8 — 102

Jude

3 — 35

Revelation

17 — 28, 68

INDEX OF NAMES

Page numbers in italics refer to illustrations.

Acciaiuoli, Maddalena Salvetti, 71, 173
Albin, Johann, 98
Alfred, King, 88
Allen, William, 147
Almeida, João Ferreira d', 157
Amerbach, Johann, 111, 116
Amman, Jost, 169, *169*
Andrews, Lancelot, 149
Anselm of Laon, 116
Anshelm, Thomas, 103, 105
Anslo, Reiner, 171
Antoninus of Florence, 99
Apiarius, Samuel, 159
Apostolis, Michael, 81
Argyropoulos, Joannes, 84
Aristotle, 9, 73, 84, *84*, 88
Ascensius, Badius, 82
Augustine, 7, 8, 11, 21, 25, 36, 38, 43, 46, 55, *87*, 88,
    118, 175
Aurispa, Giovanni, 85
Aurogallus, Matthias, 136
Autpertus, Ambrosius, 12

Bach, Johann Sebastian, 78
Baldung Grien, Hans, *22,* 120
Bapst, Valentin, 176
Barbirius, Nicolaus, 127
Barker, Robert, 149
Bebel, Johann, 106
Bede, 12
Bellarmine, Robert, 14, 98
Bembo, Pietro, 86
Bengel, Johann Albrecht, 23
Bernard of Clairvaux, 12–13, 34

Bèze, Théodore de, 30, 33, 37, 60, 75, 129, 146, 157,
    171–72, 177
Bishops' Bible, 35, 54–55, 144, *145,* 149
Blahoslav, Jan, 57, 151
Boel, Cornelius, 149
Boethius, 8, 9, 88
Boltz, Valentin, 168
Bomberg, Daniel, 27, 106
Bondenus, Joannes Maciochius, 86
Boulter, Robert, 173
Bourbon, Nicolas, 167
Bourgeois, Louis, 177
Bristow, Richard, 147
Brucioli, Antonio, 60
Bruni, Leonardo, 83, 84
Bry, Johann Theodor de, 98, 171
Bucanus, William, 36
Bucer, Martin, 126, 159
Buchanan, George, 171
Budé, Guillaume, 100
Bugenhagen, Johannes, 58, 108, 137, 153
Bullinger, Heinrich, 28, 68, 128
Burckhardt, Jakob, 5
Bussi, Giovanni Andrea de', 95, 118

Cajetan, Cardinal, 24, 126
Calcidius, 8
Calvin, John, 20, 23–27, 30–33, 36, 59–60, 66, 88,
    126–27, *127,* 129, 155, 159, 160, 177
Campano, Giovanni Antonio, 85
Caneo, G. A., 173
Carafa, Antonio, 108
Carlstadt, Andreas Rudolf Bodenstein von, 66, 161,
    166–67

Cartier, Gabriel, 177
Castellio, Sebastian, 34, 39, 45, 160
Cawood, John, 115
Cervicornus, Eucharius, 144, 171
Chalcondyles, Demetrios, 81, 83
Charles V, Emperor, 59, 61–62
Chaucer, Geoffrey, 88
Chelidonius, Benedictus, 163, 165
Chovët, Pietro, 156
Christian II, King, 58
Christian III, King, 49, 58, 153, 153
Chrysoloras, Manuel, 83, 86
Cicero, 10, 88, 126
Clement VIII, Pope, 14, 98
Colonna, Marco Antonio, 98
Columbus, Christopher, 113
Complutensian Polyglot, 20, 96, 100, 109–10, 110–11, 113, 146
Corrozet, Gilles, 34, 167
Corteau, Thomas, 127
Coverdale, Miles, 40, 46, 53–54, 143, 144, 146, 149, 176
Cranach, Lucas, the Elder, 68, 132, 134, 135–37, 136, 139, 139, 161, 162, 168, 168
Cranmer, Thomas, 54, 115, 144–45, 145, 147, 176
Crastonus, Joannes, 86
Cratander, Andreas, 99
Creutzer, V., 124
Croce, Ricoldo Pennini de Monte, 57
Crom, Matthew, 143
Cromwell, Thomas, 144

Damilas, Demetrios, 81
Danckertz, Dancker, 170–71
Dante Alighieri, 13, 15, 41, 42, 71, 88
Day, John, 128
Daye, John, 156
Decembrio, Uberto, 83
Demetrios of Phaleron, 95
Didymus the Blind, 8
Dietz, Ludwig, 59, 137, 153
Diodati, Giovanni, 60, 75–76, 156

Dionysius the Areopagite, 8
Döring, Christian, 135, 136, 161
Ducas, Demetrios, 109
Dunster, Henry, 156
Dürer, Albrecht, 67, 135, 163, 164–66, 165–67

Eck, Johann, 27–28
Edward VI, King, 115, 155, 160, 176
Eliot, John, 45, 61, 156, 157
Elizabeth I, Queen, 88, 146, 147
Emser, Hieronymus, 52, 68, 139
Episcopius, Nikolaus, 106
Erasmus, Desiderius, 5–6, 16, 20, 39, 45, 51, 52, 59, 82, 88, 100–102, 111, 124, 126, 127, 129, 143, 154
Erigena, John Scotus, 8
Erythropilus, Johannes Justus, 129
Estienne, Henri, 30, 129, 171
Estienne, Robert, 13, 16–17, 39, 96, 102–3, 126, 127, 129, 146
Euripides, 82, 82

Faber, Johann, 139
Faber Stapulensis, Jacobus. See Lefèvre d'Etaples, Jacques
Fabricius, Peter, 169
Felix of Prato, 106
Feyerabend, Siegmund, 169
Ficino, Marsilio, 6, 83
Filelfo, Francesco, 82
Fischer, Jacob, 99
Flacius Illyricus, Matthias, 29, 30, 35, 36, 75, 129
Fogny, John, 55, 147
Foxe, John, 144
Francis I, King, 36, 96, 103
Frederick, Elector of Saxony, 120
Frederick I, King, 58
Frellon, Jean, 67, 167
Froben, Johann, 16, 82, 100, 106, 108, 182–83
Fust, Johann, 13, 91, 93

Garamond, Claude, 103
Gastius, Matthias, 126

Geneva Bible, 35, 54, 143, 146, 147

George, Duke of Saxony, 139

Gerhardt, Paul, 77–78

Gerson, Jean, 88

Gilby, Anthony, 146

Giunta, Filippo, heirs of, 82

Giunta, Jacopo, 126

Giustiniano, Agostino, 113

Goes, Damião de, 61

Goezius, Christian, 129

Gottlieb, Johann Ludwig, 69, 170

Goudimel, Claude, 177

Graf, Urs, 100

Grafton, Richard, 143, 176

Great Bible, 35, 54, 144, *145*, 146, 147

Green, Samuel, 156

Gregory XIII, Pope, 108

Gregory of Nazianzus, 38

Griffo, Francesco, 84

Grimm, Sigmund, 124

Grunenberg, Johann. *See* Rhau-Grunenberg, Johann

Grüninger, Johann, 88, 99

Guarin, Thomas, 62, 159

Gutenberg, Johannes, 13, 90, 91, 93

Hall, Rouland, 146

Han, Ulrich, 10

Handel, George Frideric, 70–71

Harding, John, 149

Haßler, Hans Leo, 77–78

Henricipetri, Sebastian, 105, 129

Henry VII, King, 37, 53–54

Henry VIII, King, 144

Herwagen, Johannes, 125

Hessus, Eobanus, 74, 171

Holbein, Hans, 67, 144, 167, *167*

Holsteyn, Peter, 170

Höltzel, Hieronymus, 163, 165

Homer, 7, 8, 10, *80*, 81

Hus, Jan, 6, 56, 57, 67, 151

Hutten, Ulrich von, 15, 99

Irenaeus of Lyons, 12

Isingrin, Michael, 106

Isocrates, 52

Jacob ben Chayyim, 106

Jacob ben Jehiel Loans, 103

James I, King, 55, 149

Jenson, Nicolas, 10, 85, 88

Jerome, 8, 11, 12, 17, 20, 26, 91, 95, 96, 110, 111, 143, 151, *152*

Johnson, Marmaduke, 156

Jonas, Justus, 137

Juda, Leo, 146

Jugge, Richard, 54, 115, 144

Kempffer, Erasmus, 170

Ken, Thomas, 76

Kierkegaard, Søren, 33

Kimchi, David, 103

Kimchi, Moses, 103

King James Version, 34, 35, 42, 55, 70, 146, *148*, 149, 176

Knobloch, Johannes, 123

Knox, John, 146

Koberger, Anton, 67, 116, 120, 163

Koelhoff, Johann, the Younger, 91

Kralice Bible, 42, 57, 151

Langton, Stephen, 90

Lascaris, Constantinos, 9, 46, 81, 84, 86, *86*

Lefèvre d'Etaples, Jacques, 60, 155

Lemberger, Georg, 68, 139

Leo I, Pope, 12

Leo X, Pope, 18, 37, 53–54, 81, 105

Lettersnyder, C. H., 59, 154

Libri, Bartolommeo di, 81

Liesveldt, Jacob van, 154

Lightfoot, John, 113

Lively, Edward, 149

Locatellus, Bonetus, 118, 120

London Polyglot, 113

Lotter, Melchior, the Younger, 50, 51, 123, 124, 133, 135, 136, 139
Lotter, Michael, 123
Lufft, Hans, 52, 137
Luther, Martin, 1, 3, 5–7, 18, 21, *22,* 26–29, 31, 32, 37, 38, 42–53, 56–58, 62, 66–68, 70, 76–77, 88, 99, 102, 106, 108, 118, 120–26, 129, 131–37, *132–34, 138,* 139, 143, 144, 146, 151, 153, 154, 159, 161, 171–72, 174–77, *175*
Lützelburger, Hans, 167

Manutius, Aldus, 9, 82, 84, 86, 111
Manutius, Paulus, 114–15
Marot, Clément, 60, 75, 177
Martin, Gregory, 147, *147*
Mary I, Queen, 128, 144, 146
Mather, Cotton, 156
Matthew, Thomas. *See* Rogers, John
Matthew's Bible, 143–44
Medici, Cosimo de', 83
Medici, Ferdinando de', 151
Medici, Giovanni de'. *See* Leo X, Pope
Medici, Piero de', 81
Melanchthon, Philipp, 3, 7, 9, 23, 36, 44, 124–25, *124–25,* 128, 129, 135–37, 171
Mendelssohn-Bartholdy, Felix, 78
Mentelin, Johann, 49–50, 88, 116, 120, 131, 163
Merbecke, John, 176
Merian, Matthäus, 69, 170–71
Milton, John, 72–74, 77, 173–74, *174*
Montaigne, Michel de, 85
More, Thomas, 88, 143
Münster, Sebastian, 18, 106, 108, 146
Mylius, Crato, 171

Nerli, Bernardo, 81
Nicholas of Cusa, 15, 99
Nicholas of Hereford, 141
Nicholas of Lyra, 26, 27, 31, 118, *119,* 126, 136
Nicholson, James, 144

Oecolampadius, Johannes, 159
Olivétan, Pierre-Robert, 60, 146, 155, *155*

Opitz, Martin, 176
Oporinus, Johann, 160
Origen of Alexandria, 19–20, 26
Otmar, Silvan, 121

Pagnini, Santi, 18, 39, 108, 144, 146, 159
Pannartz, Arnold, 88, 95, 118, 120
Parasole, Leonardo, 151
Parcus, Jacob, 160
Parker, Matthew, 115, 144, 146
Parker, Peter, 173
Paul III, Pope, 114
Pecock, Reginald, 15
Pedersen, Christiern, 153
Pellikan, Konrad, 18, 106, 113
Pelt, Johan, 154
Petreius, Johann, 132
Petri, Heinrich, 106
Pfefferkorn, Johannes, 104
Philo Judaeus, 10
Pico della Mirandola, Giovanni, 6, 81, 105
Pius IV, Pope, 114
Pius V, Pope, 108
Pius XII, Pope, 98
Plato, 7–8, 83, *83,* 88
Plutarch, 10, 85, *85*
Poliziano, Angelo, 83
Pollicarius, Johannes, 68, 168
Porro, Pietro Paolo, 20, 111
Purvey, John, 141

Quentell, Heinrich, 89, 163

Rabelais, François, 85
Raimondi, Giovanni Battista, 151
Rebhun, Paul, 172
Regnault, Pierre, 167
Reims-Douai Bible (Douai Version), 35, 55, 147, *147*
Reina, Cassiodoro de, 44, 62, 159
Reuchlin, Johannes, 18, 81, 100, 103–6, *104–5,* 136
Rhau, Georg, 133, 168
Rhau-Grunenberg, Johann, 28–29, 120

Rheims Bible. *See* Reims-Douai Bible

Rogers, John, 53, 143

Rörer, Georg, 52

Rottmaier, Georg, 132

Rouille, Guillaume, 115; heirs of, 99

Rusch, Adolf, 85, 116

Sachs, Hans, 85, 135

Salomo ben Isaac, 26

Schöffer, Peter, 13, 93

Schongauer, Martin, 163

Schonwetter, Johann Theobald, 99

Scotus, Octavianus, 118, 120

Septuagint, 11, 12, 18–20, 45, 95, 108–11, *109*, 172

Servetus, Michael, 18, 39, 159, 160

Shakespeare, William, 85, 146

Silber, Marcello, 126

Simons, Menno, 59

Sixtus V, Pope, 14, 19, 98, 108

Solín, Zacharias, 151

Solis, Virgil, 169

Soter, Johannes, 144

Spalatin, Georg, 124

Spengler, Lazarus, 132

Starkey, John, 173

Steelsius, Joannes, 167

Stephanus. *See* Estienne, Robert

Stöckel, Wolfgang, 52, 68, 139

Strabo, Walafrid, 116

Stuchs, Johann, 125

Sturm, Johannes, 84

Sweynheym, Conrad, 88, 95, 118, 120

Sylvester I, Pope, 15, 199

Tausen, Hans, 58

Tempesta, Antonio, 151

Teofilo, Massimo, 60

Thibout, Guillaume, 177

Thomas Aquinas, 8–9, 25, 118, 126

Tournes, Jean de, 177

Trechsel, Melchior and Gaspar, 167

Tyndale, William, 35, 42, 44, 52–53, *142,* 143, 144, 146, 149

Uberti, Lucantonio degli, 151

Ussher, James, 32, 113

Valera, Cyprian de, 62, 159

Valla, Lorenzo, 6, 15, 16, 30, 45, 99, *99*

Vergecio, Angelo, 103

Vincent, Antoine, 83, 177

Vio, Tommaso de. *See* Cajetan, Cardinal

Vlačić-Ilirik, Matija. *See* Flacius Illyricus, Matthias

Vries, João de, 61, 157

Vulgate Bible, 11–21, 24, 35, 39, 46, 90–98, 100, 102, 108, 110, 111, 113, 126, 127, 129, 131, 139, 141, 144, 147, 154, 172

Walker, Matthias, 173

Walter, Johann, 176

Walton, Brian, 113, *113*

Warham, William, 82

Watts, Isaac, 76

Wenssler, Michael, 118

Westphal, Joachim, 31

Whitchurch, Edward, 143, 144

Whittingham, William, 146

Whytchurche, Edward. *See* Whitchurch, Edward

William of Moerbeke, 9

Wingle, Pierre de, 155

Wirsung, Marx, 124

Wolfram von Eschenbach, 131

Wycliffe, John, 57, 141, *141*

Ximénez de Cisneros, Francisco, 20, 61, 100, 109–10

Zannetti, Francisco, 19, 108

Zell, Ulrich, 91

Žerotina, Jan ze, 151

Zetzner, Lazarus, heirs of, 171

Zuñiga, Diego López de, 109

Zwingli, Huldrych, 7, 66, 74, 128